TIMELESS

TIMELESS

Ancient Psalms for the Church Today

Volume Three: Sing to God a New Song • Psalms 90–150

R. MARK SHIPP
GENERAL EDITOR

Abilene Christian University Press

TIMELESS

Ancient Psalms for the Church Today
Volume Three: Sing to God a New Song • Psalms 90–150

ACU PRESS

ISBN 978-1-68426-282-3

Printed in the United States of America

Cataloging-in-Publication Data is on file at the Library of Congress, Washington, DC.

Cover design by Bruce Gore
Interior text design by Sandy Armstrong, Strong Design
Music Typography by The Paperless Hymnal®, LLC, Austin, TX.

For information contact:
Abilene Christian University Press
ACU Box 29138
Abilene, Texas 79699

1-877-816-4455
www.acupressbooks.com

23 24 25 26 27 28 29 // 7 6 5 4 3 2 1

This volume is dedicated to two musicians and poets who used their lives and their talents for the cause of Christ:

Glover H. Shipp

and

Randy Daw

Glover H. Shipp
1927–2016

Randy Daw
1954–2019

Timeless Committee Members

Timeless Review Committee

Cynthia Agnell
Michele Broadway
Julianne Brown
Kelly Cavender
Wanda Childress
M. L. Daniels
†Randy Daw
Debbie Dorman
Jack Dorman
Tammy Driskell
Marva Hughes
Michelle Latson
Bradley H. Merrell
Dan Merrell
Laura Merrell
Gary Pendergrass
Jack R. Reese
†Glover H. Shipp
Jerry Shipp
R. Mark Shipp
Michael E. Showalter
Clyde Slimp
Ruth Ann Somervell
Becky Stewart
James Tackett
Libby Weed
Judy Witcher
Mel Witcher
Melinda Worley

Timeless Editorial Committee

Cynthia Agnell, Associate Editor
D. J. Bulls, Associate Editor, music
†Randy Daw, Associate Editor
Jack R. Reese, Editorial Assistant, responsive readings
R. Mark Shipp, General Editor
Jerry Shipp, Editorial Assistant, commentaries, metrical index
Michael E. Showalter, Editorial Assistant, commentaries
Ruth Ann Somervell, Associate Editor, music
Becky Stewart, Editorial Assistant, commentaries
Libby Weed, Editorial Assistant, commentaries

Timeless Lyric Sub-Committee

Cynthia Agnell
Matthew Bassford
Kelly Cavender
†Randy Daw
Jack R. Reese
†Glover H. Shipp
Jerry Shipp
R. Mark Shipp
Michael E. Showalter

Timeless Music Sub-Committee

D. J. Bulls
M. L. Daniels
†Randy Daw
Michael E. Showalter
Ruth Ann Somervell
James Tackett
Mel Witcher

Table of Contents

Introduction and Acknowledgments

The Timeless project began as an outgrowth of a "Metrical Psalter review committee," formed by Dr. David Worley prior to 2004 as an attempt to recover psalm singing within our churches. It has been eighteen years since *Timeless* was first conceived in St. Petersburg, Russia, with the translation of some fine Russian hymns by Konstantin Zhigulin. Upon return to the US, several close friends and associates, including Mel Witcher, Judy Witcher, Becky Stewart, Michele Broadway, Dan Merrell, Brad Merrell, Dr. M. L. Daniels, and James Tackett began meeting at my house to determine how to go about making a new metrical psalter, including new translations and commentaries on the Psalms and new musical settings based on those translations. In the course of time, many others were added to this "review committee," including Randy Daw, D. J. Bulls, Cynthia Agnell, Deb and Jack Dorman, Ruth Ann Somervell, Dr. Jack Reese, Jerry Shipp, Mike Showalter, Dr. Glover Shipp, Marva Hughes, Kelly Cavender, Julianne Brown, Norman and Katelyn Horn, Gary Pendergrass, Tammy Driskell, Michelle Latson, Clyde Slimp, Wanda Childress, Dr. Libby Weed, and Melinda Worley.

Timeless has had many supporters over the years who have helped this project in many tangible and intangible ways. Preeminent among these was Dr. David Worley, who encouraged the project and provided counsel over the years. The faculty and administration of Austin Graduate School of Theology also gave us a great deal of encouragement, among whom are Mr. Dave Arthur, Dr. Todd Hall, Dr. Stephen Lawson, Dr. Allan McNicol, Dr. Jeffrey Peterson, Dr. Stan Reid, Dr. Keith Stanglin, Dr. Michael Weed, and Dr. Woody Woodrow. Of particular note is the sage counsel provided by Mr. Rayford Walker, elder *extraordinaire* at Brentwood Oaks Church of Christ. The list of financial contributors to the project is too long to include here, but their contributions have been critical to the development of the *Timeless* products.

The majority of musical settings for the Psalter were composed by members of the various *Timeless* committees, although we branched out from this base early on, soliciting settings from many Christian traditions in many different locations. By 2016 we had two volumes of "Psalter/Commentaries," and this third volume represents the culmination of almost twenty years of labor. Since 2011 we have produced nine recording projects of our songs with the Timeless Vocal Tapestry group from Orlando, Florida. Over 200 of these songs are now available on the www.TimelessPsalter.com website, plus PDFs and Powerpoint slides of the songs. We have a dozen slide presentations of our songs on our "Timeless Ancient Psalms for the Church" YouTube page, as well as a Facebook page.

The long duration of this project has seen many changes to the various committees and committee members. Some have moved away, while others are now deceased. Among these latter are Michael Morgan, extraordinary hymn lyricist, church musician, and collector of biblical manuscripts and metrical psalters. We want to especially highlight Mr. Randy Daw, my first associate editor, without whom this project could not have been completed. Also, my father, Dr. Glover Shipp, was one of the staunchest supporters of the project. He passed away in 2016, after ensuring that he had ample lyrical offerings for Psalms 90–150, this final volume! This volume is lovingly dedicated to these two warriors and artists for Christ.

R. Mark Shipp
Austin, Texas, Friday, March 8, 2022

How to Use this Volume

For the most part, using the three volumes of *Timeless* is intuitive. The following is a basic orientation to the layout, organization, and signs that have been used in all three volumes.

§ *Commentary contents and organization*: Each psalm entry begins with a new *translation* of a psalm, followed by brief *translation notes*, if any. Extra spacing between some of the verses indicates where a new section (or strophe) of the psalm begins, based upon information provided by the commentator. Translation notes are provided for words transliterated from the Hebrew, places where the meaning of the Hebrew is unclear, or where significant differences in ancient translations, such as in the Greek Septuagint, exist. Occasionally, words are provided by the translator as reading helps which do not exist in the Hebrew. These words are in italics.

Following the translation is a section on the *structure and poetics* of the psalm. This section normally includes a structural outline of the psalm and any important literary features found in the psalm.

The *theology and application* section highlights the theological flow of the psalm and important terms that occur, as well as giving the reader insights into how each may be appropriated by communities of faith today.

At the end of each psalm entry is a brief section called "*For Those Who Sing Psalm ____.*" This is sometimes a summary of some of the important features found in the previous commentary, and sometimes gives specific comments on how to use the psalm in worship. In every case, it bridges the gap between the reading and studying of the psalm and its use in worship.

§ *Responsive readings signs*: To the left of each psalm verse is either an asterisk (*) or a dagger (†, obelus). The dagger reserves a specific verse or set of verses for the leader to read, while the asterisk marks those for the congregation to read in response.

§ *Musical settings of the Psalms*: Each psalm commentary is followed by at least two new musical settings based upon each psalm translation. The lyrics are in almost every case "metrical psalms," or versified and rhyming versions of the entire psalm, laid out sequentially. The degree of difficulty of each musical setting is indicated in the top left corner of each song by a system of quills: one quill (easy for most congregations), to two and three quills (harder, but doable by many congregations), to four quills (difficult for most congregations), to five quills (for choral use only).

Psalm 90

Translation

A prayer of Moses, the man of God.

†1 Lord, you have been our dwelling place from generation to generation.
†2 Before the mountains were born, before the earth and the cosmos came to birth, from eternity to eternity you are God.

†3 You turn humans back to dust. You say, "Turn back, you mortals,"
†4 for a thousand years in your eyes are like yesterday when it has passed or as a watch at night.
†5 You cut their life short with the sleep[a] of death, like grass that sprouts up in the morning.
†6 In the morning it flourishes and sprouts up; in the evening it droops and withers,

*7 for we are consumed by your anger; we are terrified by your wrath.
*8 You have set our guilt before you, our secrets in the light of your face,
*9 for all our days pass under your anger; our years pass away like a sigh.
*10 The days of our life are seventy years, or eighty if we are strong, but their span is toil and trouble; they are quickly cut off and removed.
*11 Who really knows the intensity of your anger? Your wrath is as strong as the fear that you are due.
*12 So teach us to count our days, that we might have a wise heart.

†13 Turn back, O Lord! How long? Have compassion on your servants.
†14 Satisfy us in the morning with your loyalty, then we will celebrate and be glad all of our days.
*15 Make us glad as many days as you have afflicted us and as many years as we have seen trouble.
*16 Let your work be seen by your servants and your majesty by your children.
*17 Let the favor of the Lord our God be on us; establish for us the deeds of our hands; establish the deeds of our hands.

[a] The Hebrew is difficult, literally best rendered "you sweep sleep." The translation is an attempt to make the meaning intelligible.

Structure and Poetry

The opening of the psalm makes us think it might be a wisdom psalm, reflecting on the fragility of life and including a request for a "wise heart" (v. 12). But the appeal at the end, beginning with the request that God "turn back," along with the plaintive question "How long?" reveals that the psalm is a lament sung to God in the midst of trouble.

The psalm is associated with Moses in the title, referred to simply as "the man of God." The title would have us believe that this psalm is one of the oldest in the collection. The lament opens by stating that God has been his people's "dwelling place" from the beginning of time (vv. 1–2). This assertion of confidence then gives way to a statement about the fragility of human life (vv. 3–6). We are like grass that sprouts up quickly in the morning, only to wither and die in the evening. To God, for whom the passing of a thousand years is like yesterday to us, our lives are incredibly brief. God is the one who makes us that way ("you turn humans back to dust," v. 3).

But why are we so short-lived? The psalmist says that it is because of God's anger against our sin (vv. 7–12). Whether or not the story of the fall is in the mind of the psalmist, one can think of God's anger toward Adam and Eve's sin resulting in their removal from the Tree of Life (Gen. 3). Life is short and full of pain. One might expect that the psalmist would ask for a long life, but, no, instead the psalmist asks for a "wise heart" in order to make the most of the time that we do have ("to count the days"). In the final stanza (vv. 13–17), the composer now addresses the suffering of the community by pleading with God to relent. They have suffered enough, and now it is time for them to find joy in life. He specifically asks God to bring their work to fruition ("establish the deeds of our hands").

Theology and Application

The psalm is a healthy reminder that our lives are short and often painful. Like the psalmist, we need a "wise heart" to navigate and appreciate our brief lives. We too, like the psalmist, should acknowledge the role of sin—our own and the sins of others—in bringing suffering into our lives. Even though not all suffering is the result of our personal sin, human rebellion against God has so disrupted God's harmonious creation that it is impossible for us to escape the pain of life. We can and should call on God to alleviate our suffering, bring us joy, and establish the work of our hands. After all, God is our "dwelling place" (v. 1). We can find our rest in him in the midst of a turbulent world.

For Those Who Sing Psalm 90

Life is hard. Our lives are short and then we die. Our human lives contrast with God, who is eternal and has been the "dwelling place" of his people from the very beginning, and he will be to the end of time. With the psalmist we call on God to help us make the most of our brief and fragile lives. We call on him to alleviate our suffering and bring us joy. We call on him to establish the work of our hands. In his classic hymn, "O God, Our Help in Ages Past," John Wesley captured Psalm 90's pathos of our brief lives along with our ultimate trust in God's abiding presence. Reading the psalm in the light of the New Testament reminds us that our short and difficult lives are not the end of the story. Because of Jesus's death and resurrection, we can have comfort in the midst of our suffering and hope for life eternal in the presence of God.

Tremper Longman

O Lord, You Are a Dwelling Place

Psalm 90

Mark Shipp

Michael E. Showalter

O Lord, You Are a Dwelling Place

How Long, O Lord, These Weary Years?

Psalm 90

John A. Ogren | John A. Ogren

Psalm 91

Translation

†1 He who dwells in the shelter of the Most High abides in the shadow of the Almighty.
*2 I will say to the Lord, "My refuge and my stronghold, my God in whom I trust!"

†3 He rescues you from the fowler's snare and from the destructive plague.
†4 With his pinions he covers you, and under his wings you find refuge. His faithfulness will be a shield and buckler.
†5 You will not be afraid of the terror of the night, the arrows that fly during the day,
†6 the plague that stalks in darkness, or the scourge that lays waste at noon.
†7 A thousand may fall at your side, and ten thousand at your right hand, but nothing will touch you.
†8 You will only look with your eyes and see retribution on the wicked.

*9 For you have made the Lord your refuge,[a] the Almighty your dwelling place.
†10 No harm will come on you; no plague will come near your tent,
†11 for he will order his angels on your behalf to protect you on all your paths.
†12 They will lift you up with their hands lest you strike your foot on a rock.
†13 You will tread over lion cub and viper; you will trample young lion and serpent.

*14 "For I will save the one who loves me; I will exalt him because he knows my name.
*15 He who calls to me I will answer. I will be with him in distress. I will rescue him and honor him.
*16 I will satisfy him with length of days and show him my victory."

[a] Heb., "For you are my refuge, O Lord."

Structure and Poetry

Psalm 91 is a psalm of confidence, comforting those who are in the midst of war. Images of protection and comfort abound throughout the poem.

In the opening stanza (vv. 1–2), the worship leader reminds those listening that those who seek the presence of God will enjoy his protection ("shade"/"shadow"). In turn, they affirm that God is indeed their defense ("refuge"/"stronghold").

In the second stanza (vv. 3–8), we learn that plague and arrows threaten the people of God. Arrows are a metonymy for all weapons of war, and plague was a special problem in ancient war camps. But God takes care of his people, who are likely the army. The "fowler's snare" (v. 3) was an image of great danger, but God rescues his people from that threat. The fowler hunted birds for food, but God was like a mother bird that protects her chicks under her wings. God was faithful and, using military images, was like a "shield" and "buckler" (a small shield) for his people in the midst of conflict. Thus, while the enemy will suffer large casualties, God's people will stand strong. The enemy is wicked, and God will bring victory against them as a matter of justice (v. 8).

The third stanza (vv. 9–13) returns to an emphasis on God's protection ("refuge"/"dwelling place") in the midst of conflict. The worship leader comforts his hearers by informing them that God has commissioned his angels to protect them, so no harm will come to them. The enemy is dangerous like a lion and a serpent, but thanks to God and his angels, God's people will overcome and even dominate them.

The final stanza (vv. 14–16) contains a divine oracle affirming God's intent to answer those who pray for his help. God will rescue and provide victory for his praying people.

Theology and Application

Many psalms find their original setting in the context of warfare. Some call on God to "rise up" and fight for his people (Ps. 7), while many celebrate God's victory over an attacking enemy (Pss. 24, 98). Psalm 91 is an example of a psalm that reminds God's people of his presence and help in the midst of war. God is a warrior (Exod. 15:3), and he fights to protect his obedient people.

In the Old Testament, Israel does not have *carte blanche* to wage war against anyone that they choose to fight. No, God must show them that it is his will that they fight (see Josh. 5:13–15; 1 Sam. 23:1–6), since God uses warfare to bring his justice to bear on sinful people. We also have a number of examples of God using war against disobedient Israel, most notably the Babylonian defeat of Jerusalem (2 Kings 25; Lam. 2). At the end of the Old Testament period, when Israel lived under the oppressive hand of the Babylonians and then the Persians, God's prophets looked forward to a time when God, the warrior, would return to free them (Dan. 7; Zech. 14).

The message of the New Testament is that this expectation is met in a surprising way. Jesus is the divine warrior who takes the battle to Satan and the demonic powers. These enemies cannot be fought with sword and spear. Indeed, they cannot be defeated by killing, but by Jesus's death on the cross (Col. 2:13–15). While it is true that this victory is not completed until the second coming (Rev. 19:11–21) when Jesus will return to defeat all evil, spiritual and human, Christians today live in a time of spiritual warfare ("we aren't fighting against human enemies but against rulers, authorities, forces of cosmic darkness, and spiritual powers of evil in the heavens," Eph. 6:12 CEB).

Psalm 91 maintains its importance to Christians today. Like ancient Israel, we are engaged in warfare and against a more powerful enemy. Thus, the message of God's protection is relevant to God's people as we engage a dangerous world.

For Those Who Sing Psalm 91

Life is full of conflicts. Christians in China face significant restrictions on their religious life and many in the Middle East confront situations that are life-threatening. Those of us who live in the West enjoy considerable freedom in the exercise of our faith. We all, however, live in a fallen world and face many struggles on a daily basis. On the basis of our experience, we might easily grow afraid. The worship leader of Psalm 91, addressing God's people in the midst of battle, reminds us of God's protective presence and concern for our safety. God will take care of us no matter what. That does not mean we won't struggle or even die, but the Christian knows that Jesus has defeated death on the cross and has secured our eternal life by means of his resurrection. We can find comfort in our awareness that Jesus, our warrior, has won the battle for us.

Tremper Longman

God Is My Shelter

Psalm 91

Mark Shipp — Michael E. Showalter

Those Who Dwell with God Most High

Psalm 91

M. W. Bassford

Byron Rogers

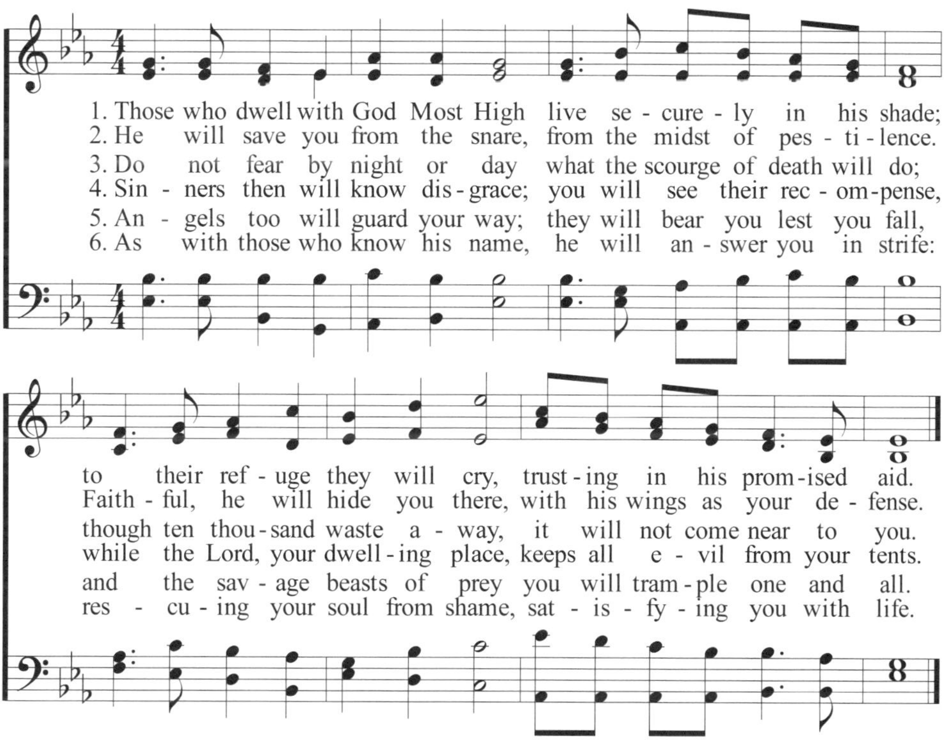

Psalm 92

Translation

A psalm. A song for the Sabbath day.

†1 It is good to give thanks to the Lord and to make music to your name, Most High.
*2 It is good to proclaim your loyal love in the morning and your faithfulness at night
*3 on the ten-string lyre and on the harp, to the melody of the lyre.

†4 For you, O Lord, have made me glad by your work. I sing for joy at the deeds of your hands.
*5 How great are your deeds, O Lord; your thoughts are exceedingly deep.
†6 A stupid person does not know; a fool does not understand this:
†7 Though the wicked sprout like grass and all evildoers prosper, they will be destroyed forever.

*8 But you, O Lord, are forever on high.
*9 For, indeed, your enemies, O Lord, for indeed your enemies will perish. All evildoers will be scattered.
†10 But you have raised my horn like that of a wild ox. You have poured fine oil on me.
†11 My eyes have looked in triumph[a] on my enemies; my ears have heard the doom[b] of the evil ones who rise up against me.

*12 The righteous bloom like a palm tree; they grow like a cedar in Lebanon.
*13 They are planted in the house of the Lord; in the courts of our God they bloom.
*14 They even bear fruit in old age; they are full of sap and green.
*15 They proclaim, "The Lord is virtuous; he is my rock, in whom there is no fault."

[a] "In triumph" is implied from the context. Hebrew has "my eyes have looked on my enemies."

[b] "The doom" is implied from the context. Hebrew has "my ears have heard the evil ones who rise up against me."

Structure and Poetry

Psalm 92 "gives thanks" (v. 1) to the Lord, though it is not until late in the psalm (v. 11) that we hear that the reason for thanks is that God has not allowed the psalmist's enemies to defeat him. This thanksgiving psalm also thanks God for making the righteous flourish like a cedar or a palm tree (v. 12).

In the opening stanza (vv. 1–3), the psalm proclaims that it is good, because it is fitting, to thank God for his faithfulness and loyal love, qualities that are associated with the covenant that God has with his people. This thanksgiving was to be sung accompanied by instrumental music, probably in the context of the sanctuary (note the title that connects it to the Sabbath).

The second stanza (vv. 4–7) identifies the rationale for praise in God's mighty deeds and profound thoughts. While these deeds are not specified, verses 6–7 suggest that God had demolished the wicked who had temporarily been successful. The book of Proverbs does acknowledge that the wicked can flourish, but claims that their prosperity will not last forever (Prov. 11:8; 21:6; 22:16; also Ps. 73:3–6, 12). Only "stupid" people don't understand this truth.

The third stanza (vv. 8–11) takes the principles of the previous stanza and applies them to the present situation. God has defeated and scattered the wicked enemy. The result was that God exalted (lifting up his horn like a proud bull) and refreshed (pouring oil on his head to moisten his dry skin) the psalmist.

While the wicked were earlier compared to grass (Ps. 90:5–6) which springs up but soon withers, now in the final stanza (vv. 12–15) the worship leader describes the righteous like a magnificent tree, both a palm and a cedar. The palm tree grows in a well-watered oasis and bears fruit, representing life and fertility. The cedar is a stately tree. Interestingly, cedar was used in the construction of the temple (1 Kings 5) and the palm in its symbolic iconography (1 Kings 6:29, 32, 35; 7:36). The psalmist speaks about the righteous as trees planted in the house of the Lord, that is, in God's abiding presence. He ends by citing the righteous who bear witness to God's perfect virtue.

Theology and Application

Life is unfair. Bad people sometimes, maybe even often, succeed, while people who try to do the right thing suffer. The psalmist apparently struggled at the hands of the wicked. He was righteous. To be righteous does not mean being sinless, but it does mean having a relationship with God and trying to obey him and, when failing to do so, acknowledging failure and turning back to God (repentance). This psalm reminds God's people that such injustice does not last forever. God will see that the wicked are punished, while the righteous will grow and bear fruit like stately, well-watered trees. They will enjoy the intimate presence of God. When blessings come to the righteous, they respond with enthusiastic song-filled worship.

For Those Who Sing Psalm 92

The psalmist celebrates God's reversal of his fortunes. God had delivered him from wicked enemies and given him a flourishing life. Christians who sing Psalm 92 understand that such a reversal does not always take place in this life. Some, maybe many, end their lives in misery, not in triumph. However, as Jesus taught, death is not the end of the story, but "My Father's house has room to spare. . . . I will return and take you to be with me so that where I am you will be too" (John 14:2–3 CEB). As the psalmist envisions, we can rest assured that we will be planted and will bloom in the "house of the Lord" (v. 13).

Tremper Longman

It Is Good To Give Thanks to the Lord!

Psalm 92

Randy Daw (1954–2019) | Randy Daw (1954–2019)

It Is Good to Give Thanks

Psalm 92

Mark Shipp | Jack R. Reese

It Is Good to Give Thanks

Psalm 93

Translation

†1 The Lord reigns! He is robed in majesty; the Lord is robed. He is girded with strength. The world is firmly established; it will not be shaken.
†2 Your throne is established from the distant past; you are from eternity.

*3 The rivers have lifted up, O Lord; the rivers have lifted up their voice. The rivers have lifted up their roaring waves.
*4 Greater than the sound of the many waters, more majestic than the breakers of the sea, the Lord on high is majestic!

*5 Your decrees stand firm; holiness ornaments your house, O Lord, for length of days.

Structure and Poetry

"The Lord reigns!" Thus begins the first of a series of psalms that celebrate God as king (see also Pss. 95–99). God is king, not just of Israel, but of the entire cosmos.

After proclaiming God's reign, the psalmist in the opening stanza (vv. 1–2) depicts this king as robed not in purple finery but with strength and majesty. God's kingship is not newly established, rather it has always been and will always be. For this reason, the world is stable. Of course, the psalmist was aware of earthquakes and warfare, but such things do not undermine the fact that the creation is not in complete flux. It carries on a kind of rhythmic stability promised by God in connection with his covenant with creation: "As long as the earth endures, seedtime and harvest, cold and heat, summer and winter, day and night will never cease" (Gen. 8:22 NIV).

The second stanza (vv. 3–4) makes clear that there are, indeed, serious threats to that stability. In the ancient Near East, the waters often represent the forces of chaos that threaten the creation. We can see this in the Mesopotamian myth of creation (*Enuma Elish*) where the creator god Marduk subdues Tiamat (the Sea) or in Canaanite thought where Baʿal fights Yām (Sea). Though the waters rage, God controls them.

Kings control their realms through decrees, and so, according to the climactic third stanza (v. 5), the divine king issues decrees that maintain his cosmic kingdom. These laws, including the Ten Commandments, express God's will for how his human subjects should live in a way that pleases the king and is good for the enjoyment of his subjects. God's house (the sanctuary) is made holy by his presence.

Theology and Application

How reassuring it is to know that God is in control in spite of the chaos. As we look at the turmoil in the world, even in our own lives, we wonder whether everything will simply unwind. We feel threatened by what the psalmist calls the "mighty waters." Will they overwhelm the creation and return it to its pre-creation "formless and empty" state (Gen. 1:2) as the flood waters did at the time of Noah? According to our psalmist, the answer is no, thanks to God who subdues the waters of chaos and controls our world and our lives through his decrees. Even in the midst of struggle, we can put our confidence in God.

For Those Who Sing Psalm 93

The Lord is king of the cosmos; he is king of our lives. As we sing Psalm 93, we are reminded of these calming truths in the midst of our struggles. His decrees maintain our lives in a healthy order. As New Testament singers of Psalm 93, we can think of Jesus as our Messiah, or anointed king, who has come to establish God's kingdom. He demonstrates that he is more powerful than the waters as he stills the waves and walks on the water (Matt. 8:23–27; Mark 6:45–56; John 6:16–24). He indeed is God who controls and calms the chaos of life.

Tremper Longman

Jehovah Reigns in Majesty

Psalm 93

Mark Shipp

Mark Shipp
arr. Mark Shipp and Randy Daw

The Lord in ho - ly splen - dor reigns; in right - eous judg - ment
they thun - der might - y as the
makes de - crees.
seas.
Je - ho - vah reigns in maj - es - ty, en -
wrapped in splen - dor, clothed in might. Es - tab - lished is his
rit.
un - i - verse, se - cure - ly fixed his throne of light.

The Lord in His Majesty Reigns

Psalm 93

Marva L. Hughes | Marva L. Hughes

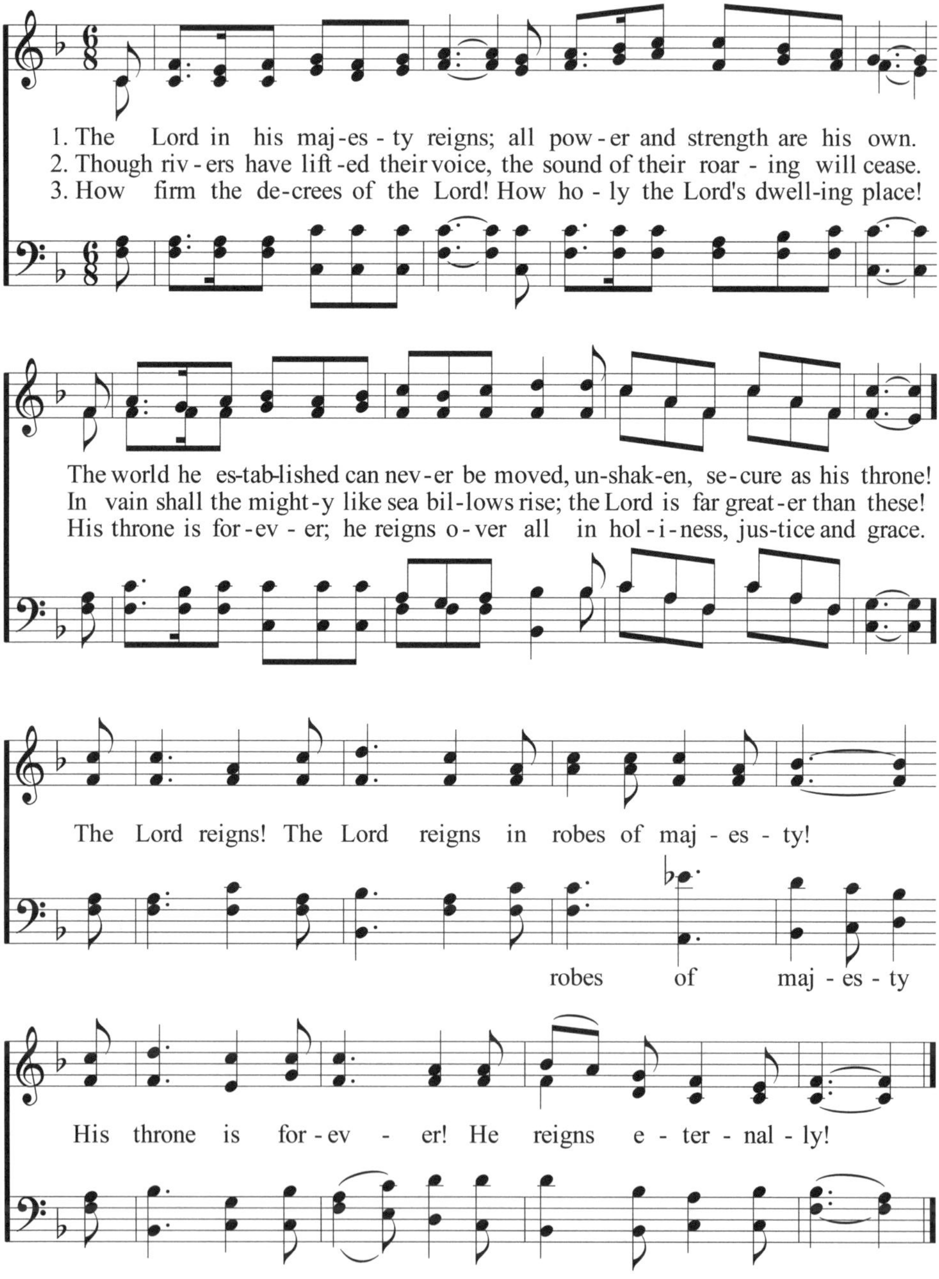

PSALM 94

Translation

†1 O God of vengeance, O LORD! O God of vengeance, shine forth!
*2 Rise up, O judge of the earth! Bring retribution on the proud!
*3 How long, O LORD, will the wicked, how long will the wicked rejoice?

†4 They gush; they speak with arrogance. All these evildoers boast.
†5 They crush your people, O LORD; they afflict your inheritance.
†6 They kill widows and immigrants; they murder orphans.
*7 They claim, "The LORD does not see; the God of Jacob does not understand."

†8 Try to understand, you stupid people. You fools, when will you become wise?
†9 Does the one who plants the ear not hear? Does the one who forms the eye not see?
†10 Does the one who disciplines the nations not punish? Is the one who teaches humanity not knowledgeable?
†11 The LORD knows the thoughts of humans, that they are without substance.

*12 Blessed is the person whom you discipline, O LORD, whom you teach from your Torah!
*13 He will provide calm during troubling days, until a pit is dug for the wicked.
*14 For the LORD does not abandon his people; he does not forsake his inheritance.
*15 Justice will return for the righteous, and all the virtuous will follow it.

†16 Who will rise up for me among the wicked? Who will take a stand for me against evildoers?
*17 Unless the LORD were my help, I would soon dwell in silence.
†18 When I said, "My foot is slipping," your loyal love, O LORD, steadied me.
*19 When my anxiety is overwhelming, your comfort cheers me up.

†20 Can a corrupt throne be allied with you, one that brings trouble by statute?
†21 They band together against the righteous and condemn the innocent to death.
*22 The LORD has become a fortress to me. My God is my rock and my refuge.
*23 He turns their iniquity back on them. He annihilates them in their evil; the LORD our God annihilates them.

Structure and Poetry

The psalmist leads the congregation in a lament, bemoaning the attacks of the wicked on the righteous people of God. At the beginning of the poem, he calls on God to rise up to confront the threat, and at the end, he closes on a note of confidence.

In the first stanza (vv. 1–3), the worship leader calls on God to come and deal with the wicked who are making God's people suffer. The urgent request that he would "shine forth" is the hope that he would make his resplendent and glorious presence manifest among them. God is the "judge of the earth" and, as such, will bring justice (vengeance) against the wicked foe. However, he has not yet come, and thus the psalmist plaintively asks, "How long?"—a question that expresses the idea that it has already been too long.

We come to understand the reason for the psalmist's pleas as the second stanza (vv. 4–7) describes the depredations of the enemy. They are proud and murderous. They afflict the vulnerable (orphans, widows, and immigrants).[1] The enemy harms God's people, here described as his "inheritance," and they don't think God will do anything about it.

However, as expressed in the third stanza (vv. 8–11), the psalmist knows better. The wicked are foolish to think that God will not act as judge and bring vengeance. They are ignorant to believe that God is unaware of the travails of his people. In the fourth stanza (vv. 12–15), the psalmist expresses awareness that their present troubles are a result of the discipline of God and thus are really a blessing. In spite of these present troubles, he knows that God is in control and will have the victory when he executes justice for his people.

In the fifth stanza (vv. 16–19), the psalmist asks who will rise up for him to help him in the conflict. He confesses that only the Lord can help him, and the Lord responds. Only God can save him from anxiety, suffering, and death. The final stanza (vv. 20–23) may reveal the origin of the trouble, a corrupt throne, many examples of which can be found in the book of Kings. But in spite of such a powerful enemy, the psalmist can find comfort in the protection and power of God.

Theology and Application

Life is warfare. For us that war may not be a physical conflict as the psalmist and the righteous may have experienced when the psalm was first composed, but we do battle against spiritual powers and authorities (Eph. 6:10–20) that often manifest themselves in the conflicts and hostilities that we experience in our daily

[1]For God as the protector of these fragile people, see Ps. 146:7a, 9ab.

lives. The psalmist exhorts us to call on God to help us in the midst of the fray and also to find confidence in his protection and power.

For Those Who Sing Psalm 94

The psalmist appeals to God to ask for help against forces that attack his people, most notably the vulnerable. He asks "how long" before God comes, but ultimately the psalmist comes to a place of trust and confidence. Above, we have likened the physical battles that gave rise to the original setting of the psalm to the spiritual battles that we fight today. The book of Revelation pictures God's people who have been slain "because of the word of God and the testimony they had maintained," also crying out, "How long?" (Rev. 6:9–11 NIV). In response, they are each given a white robe and told to wait a little longer before Jesus, the judge of the earth, will come and bring justice to the world. Isaac Watts (1674–1748) wrote two hymns based on this psalm. The first, "O God to Whom Revenge Belongs," calls on God to bring justice to bear on the wicked. The second, "Who Will Arise and Plead My Right," expresses the wish that God will defend his people from the machinations of evil people.

Tremper Longman

My Refuge, Firm and Strong

Psalm 94

Ray McClendon

James W. Tackett

My Refuge, Firm and Strong

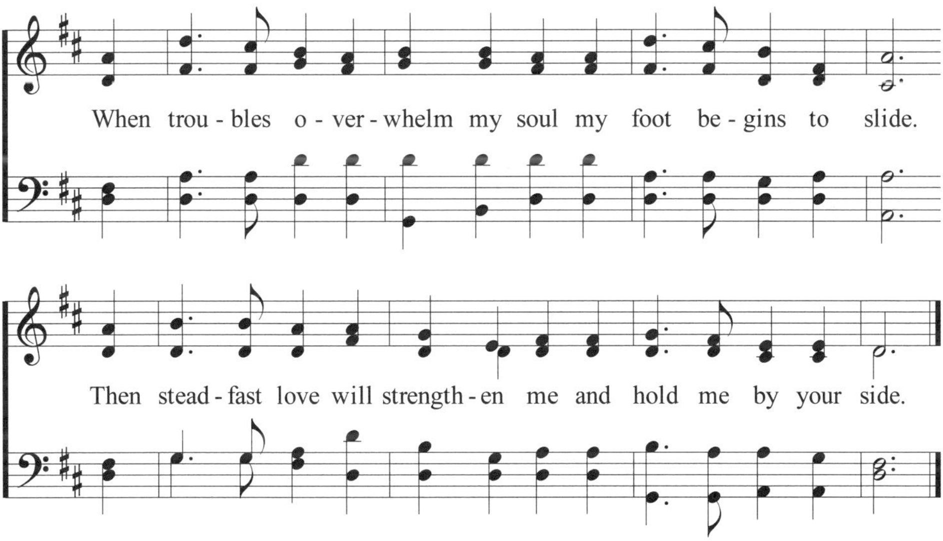

Shine Forth, O God of Vengeance

Psalm 94

M. W. Bassford — Michael E. Showalter and Ruth Ann Somervell

Psalm 95

Translation

†1 Come, let us shout for joy to the Lord; let us shout to the rock of our salvation!
†2 Let us approach his presence with thanksgiving; with songs let us shout to him!
*3 For the Lord is a great God, and a great king over all gods.
*4 In his hands are the depths of the earth, and the mountain peaks are his.
*5 The sea is his since he made it, and his hands formed the dry land.

†6 Come let us bow down and kneel; let us bend the knee before the Lord our maker.
*7 For he is our God, and we are the people of his pasture, the flock of his hand.

* Today hear his voice!
†8 "Do not harden your hearts like at Meribah, like the day at Massah in the wilderness.
†9 There your fathers tested me; there they tried me even though they saw my work.
*10 I was disgusted with that generation for forty years, and I said, "They are a people with straying hearts; they do not know my ways."
*11 So I swore in my anger: "They will not enter my resting place!"

Structure and Poetry

Psalm 95 is a hymn celebrating God as king of the cosmos that he created (see also Pss. 93, 96–99) and as shepherd of his people. In the first stanza (vv. 1–5), the worship leader calls on the congregation to worship God with song. He protects them ("rock of my salvation"), and he is in a place to do so since he is greater than all the other gods, indeed their king. Psalm 95 is an example of a text that uses the term "god" (*'ĕlōhîm*) to refer to all spiritual powers. God is the creator of everything, even the "gods." Elsewhere in Scripture, these created gods are called angels or demons. The one, true God is the one who controls the earth because he formed every part of it (both the "depths" and the "peaks" as well as the "sea" and the "dry land").

While the first stanza celebrates God as king and creator, the second (vv. 6–7b) calls on Israel to extol him as shepherd of his people. As a shepherd guides, protects, and provides sustenance for the sheep, so God acts toward his people.

The third and final stanza (vv. 7c–11) issues a warning. The psalmist tells the congregation to pay urgent attention to the divine oracle that concludes the psalm. God calls them to obey his instructions and not rebel by grumbling. He reminds them of their forefathers in the wilderness, who rebelled against God after experiencing the crossing of the sea and receiving the law. God specifically cites the events, described in Exodus 17:1–7 and Numbers 20:1–13, at Meribah ("Quarreling") and Massah ("Testing"). The grumbling in the wilderness led to God's judgment that eventually meant that all of the generation that had been rescued from Egypt would die in the wilderness. The present generation reading the psalm needs to learn that lesson and obey God.

Theology and Application

God is the creator, our king, and our shepherd. He made us and he rules over us. He protects, guides, and provides for us. We must worship him and obey him, avoiding the sin of the wilderness generation which rebelled and thus died before reaching the land of promise.

The author of Hebrews cites this psalm (specifically vv. 7–11; Heb. 3:7–19) and applies it to the Christian life. Christians live a life analogous to the wilderness generation, which had been freed from Egyptian bondage and was heading toward Canaan, the land of promise. Christians have been freed from sin and death by Christ's death and resurrection and are heading toward heaven. The Christian life, therefore, is in a period of wandering in the wilderness. The author of Hebrews thus uses Psalm 95 to warn Christians to continue to obey on threat of perishing in the wilderness and never entering heaven.

For Those Who Sing Psalm 95

Worship the Lord who is our creator, king, and shepherd. Respond with obedience, unlike the wilderness generation at Meribah and Massah. And remember that Jesus Christ modeled what it means to be the obedient son of God, as opposed to the disobedient wilderness generation, during his three temptations in the wilderness (Matt. 4:1–11). In the light of this psalm, we should remember that Jesus resisted the temptation to "test" God (*Massah*). Many hymns through the ages, from "O Come, Let Us Sing to the Lord" (Scottish Psalter, 1650) to "Worship and Bow Down" (John Michael Talbot, 2011), have captured Psalm 95's exuberant call to worship and to obey God.

Tremper Longman

Come, O Come

Psalm 95

Debbie Dorman

Debbie Dorman & Ruth Ann Somervell

Sing for Joy to the Lord

Psalm 95

Glover Shipp (1927–2016) D. J. Bulls

Sing for Joy to the Lord

Psalm 96

Translation

†1 Sing a new song to the Lord. Sing to the Lord, all the earth.
†2 Sing to the Lord. Bless his name. Proclaim his deliverance day after day.
†3 Recount his glory among the nations and his wonders among all the peoples—
*4 for the Lord is great and most deserving of praise, inspiring more awe than all gods,
*5 because all the peoples' gods are worthless, but the Lord made the skies.
*6 Splendor and majesty are before him. Strength and glory are in his sanctuary.[a]

†7 Credit the Lord, you families of peoples—credit the Lord with glory and strength.
†8 Credit the Lord with the glory due his name. Bring an offering and enter his courts.[b]
†9 Worship the Lord in holy splendor. Tremble before him, all the earth.
†10 Say among the nations:[c]
* "The Lord reigns! The world is firmly ordered and will never be shaken. He will judge the peoples fairly."[d]

†11 May the skies rejoice and the earth be glad. May the sea and everything in it roar.
†12 May the field and everything in it celebrate. Then the forest and all its trees will shout joyfully
†13 before the Lord,
* for he is coming—for he is coming[e] to judge the earth. He will judge the world righteously and the peoples accurately.

[a] The composite poem in 1 Chronicles 16:23–33 includes most of Psalm 96, with some revised wording that obscures overt references to the temple in Jerusalem. For example, 1 Chronicles 16:27 reads "place" instead of "sanctuary." Narratively, 1 Chronicles 16 is set during David's lifetime, before the temple was built.

[b] 1 Chronicles 16:29 reads "before him" instead of "enter his courts."

[c] 1 Chronicles 16:30b–31 corresponds to Psalm 96:10b, 11a, 10a. The reason for this rearrangement remains unclear.

[d] Psalm 96:10c and 13b have no counterpart in 1 Chronicles 16.

[e] 1 Chronicles 16:33 reads "he is coming" only once. Skipping one iteration of a repeated phrase and copying the same phrase twice are both well-attested scribal mistakes, so this difference could be just a copyist's error in one text or the other. Or perhaps the Chronicler intentionally eliminated the repetition for aesthetic reasons.

Structure and Poetry

Along with Psalms 47 and 93, Psalms 96–99 form a category that scholars call "enthronement psalms." Some include Psalms 94–95 as well. These psalms share a common focus on God's superintendence of the entire world, expressed through the metaphor of God as the cosmic high king. They also exhibit a prominent alternation between calls to praise and praise as such.

Psalm 96 unfolds in three strophes, each consisting of a call to praise God followed by a summary of the praise to be offered. One easily imagines a kind of responsive chant between Levitical singers (issuing the calls to praise) and the congregation assembled for worship (answering with the statements of praise). Three thematic elements—humanity, nature, and justice—are arranged in pairs to form a kind of ring:

Verses 1–6:	All humanity is called to praise God for creating the natural world.
Verses 7–10:	All humanity is called to praise God for establishing a just human world.
Verses 11–13:	The natural world is called to praise God for (imminently or eschatologically) reestablishing a just human world.

Theology and Application

In most English translations, verse 1 opens with a call to "sing a new song," but the psalm does not ask worshipers to come up with impromptu original compositions. Indeed, verses 4 and 10 prescribe the exact words, or at least sentiments, that worshipers should use to praise God. Rather, Psalm 96:1 enjoins worshipers to take up ancient themes afresh. The phrase "new song" is in this sense more comparable to the phrase "new moon" than "new car."

For some scholars, the pairing of "deliverance" and "wonders" in verses 2–3 evokes thoughts of Israel's deliverance from Egypt, heralded by the ten plagues, called "wonders" in the book of Exodus. This leads to the suggestion that the first strophe (vv. 1–6) is more narrowly addressed to Israel than verse 1 might imply. However, the specific "wonder" invoked in verse 5 is the creation of the skies. In ancient Israel, as in other ancient Near Eastern cultures, divine creative activity was often described as the sequel to the creator's victory over the forces of "chaos." Just such a scenario is implied in Psalm 29, which verses 7–8 apparently quote (with modifications), and in Psalm 93:1–4, another "enthronement psalm." Creation theology rather than Israel's historical traditions seems to ground verses 1–6.

The creation theme continues in the second strophe (vv 7–10), though the focus shifts from the physical world to the social world. While still addressed to all humanity, this strophe clearly invites worship in the temple in Jerusalem and strongly implies that the psalm was composed to accompany public worship services that included a ritual offering. Thematically, this strophe turns to the social world. For the psalmist, the moral foundations of a just society were created by God no less than the physical skies above. The claim in verse 10 that the world "will never be shaken" is not a statement of geophysics, still less of astrophysics, but refers to the bedrock principle of divine justice.

In the third strophe (vv. 11–13), creation becomes the active agent of praise. Skies and seas, forests and fields praise God—not with literal speech, of course (as Ps. 19:3 explicitly acknowledges), but by continuously and reliably fulfilling their allotted roles. The psalmist draws a subtle but potent parallel, implying that nature's consistent obedience to God's original creative commands testifies that God will someday—either soon, or in the ultimate consummation of all things—reestablish equitable justice in the human sphere. This hope may comfort and sustain those in whose present circumstances equitable justice may not be evident, for example, those trying to live faithfully to God while scattered among "the nations."

For Those Who Sing Psalm 96

In every generation, we find ourselves suspended between God's primordial infusion of justice into our world and God's eschatological restoration of that justice. Many, if not all, believers live in times when God's justice is not fully evident "among the nations." When we sing Psalm 96, we affirm—even in the face of contrary experience—that God's justice will, sooner or later, win the day.

Christopher Heard

Sing to the Lord a New Song

Psalm 96

Gary Pendergrass | Gary Pendergrass

va - tion pro - claim as we sing to the Lord a new song.
Optional Ending
Sing to the Lord splen - dor and maj - es - ty go out be - fore him,
Sing to the Lord a new song, sing a new
Sing to the Lord splen - dor and maj - es - ty go out be - fore him,
give him the glo - ry and hon - or all due him,
song, sing a new
give him the glo - ry and hon - or all due him,
rit.
fields and the for - est re - joice as we sing a new song.
song, as we sing a new song.
fields and the for - est re - joice as we sing a new song.

Sing a New Song of Glory

Psalm 96

Jack R. Reese | Jack R. Reese

For additional effect, the composer suggests ignoring the ritard, repeating back to the DS Sign, singing the last section of the song again one step higher, and observing the ritard at the end.

Psalm 97

Translation

†1 The LORD reigns! May the earth celebrate and many coastlands rejoice.
*2 Thick, dark clouds surround him. Righteousness and justice are his
throne's foundation.
†3 Fire goes before him and scorches his foes on every side.
*4 His lightning bolts light up the world. The earth sees this and trembles.
*5 Mountains melt like wax before the LORD—before the whole earth's master.
*6 The skies declare his righteousness, and all peoples behold his glory.

†7 Those who serve statues, who direct praise toward idols, will be ashamed; all
gods bow down[a] to the LORD.
*8 Zion hears this and rejoices, and the villages of Judah[b] celebrate because of
your just decrees, LORD,
*9 for you, LORD, are high above the whole earth and very high above all gods!

†10 You who love the LORD, hate evil![c] He preserves the lives of those loyal to
him and delivers them from the power of wicked folk.
*11 Light falls[d] on the righteous and joy on those with upright hearts.
*12 Rejoice in the LORD, you righteous ones, and offer praise[e] to commemorate
his holiness.[f]

[a] Some English translations, including KJV and NIV, render this verb as an imperative. The translation here concurs with NRSV, CEB, and other translations in reading the verb as indicative. For this verb, the two forms are identical.

[b] Literally "daughters," used here as a metaphor for smaller towns dependent on Zion (Jerusalem). Compare Joshua 17:11.

[c] The translation given here follows the standard Hebrew text. Some speculate that an ancient scribe made two very small spelling errors, like writing *y* instead of *yy* and *v* instead of *y*. If so, the original sense would have been "The Lord loves those who hate evil" (as in the NRSV).

[d] The manuscript tradition is split between "light is scattered [like seed] for the righteous" (the majority reading) and "light dawns for the righteous." In Hebrew, "is scattered" and "dawns" sound very much alike. Modern translators and commentators have reached no consensus on the preferable reading.

[e] Modern translations commonly read "give thanks," and indeed the verb here does mean "to thank" in post-biblical Hebrew, including modern Hebrew. In biblical Hebrew, however, the form used here implies positive testimony about someone else, hence "praise." A related form implies negative testimony about oneself, or confession.

[f] Literally "to the memorial of his holiness." Modern translations commonly read "his holy name," which is defensible but requires readers to take "name" in the sense of "reputation" in order to get the point.

Structure and Poetry

Psalm 97 has three distinct strophes:

Verses 1–6:	God's presence is manifested in a theophany reminiscent of Sinai.
Verses 7–9:	Witnesses associated with Zion react to the theophany.
Verses 10–12:	The psalmist exhorts other worshipers.

The psalm's thought progresses in overlapping movements. The first strophe turns toward the skies, specifically recalling God's appearance to the Israelites at Mt. Sinai. The second and third strophes turn toward the earth and toward Mt. Zion. But the second and third strophes exhibit their own movement, from worship to ethics. The psalm's structure thus seems to echo the structure of Exodus 19–20, from theophany to the ten commandments ("just decrees"), which themselves move from worship to ethics.

Theology and Application

Psalm 97 is very much a "sister psalm" to Psalm 96, emphasizing like it the theme of God's universal reign manifested in justice and righteousness. Opening with a jubilant acclamation of God's kingship and a summons to praise, the psalmist describes a theophany, that is, a visible and audible manifestation of God's presence. In this case, frightful disturbances in the sky (vv. 2 and 4) and on the ground (vv. 3 and 5) announce and testify to God's presence. This type of imagery is common in Old Testament theophany descriptions—especially when deliverance from enemies is in view—and in Canaanite epic poetry featuring Ba'al. God's appearance to the Israelites at Sinai (Exod. 19:16–20) may be the most famous and pertinent example, but see also Judges 5:4–5; Psalm 18:7–15; Habakkuk 3; and, for a fascinating variation on the theme, 1 Kings 19:11–18. The combination of meteorological and seismic phenomena reminds worshipers, without using this exact terminology, that Israel and Judah acclaim the Lord as the maker of both heaven and earth.

The second strophe describes two different responses to the divine theophany, wrapping one response around the other to create a concentric structure. In such a structure, the main point is usually at the center, with the outer rings supporting that point. Here the outer frame, verses 7 and 9, reveals the cosmic response: all the gods of the nations acknowledge the LORD's superiority. The full flower of monotheism—the metaphysical claim that one and only one god actually exists—had not yet blossomed at the time Psalm 97 was composed. This psalmist accepts that the gods worshiped among the nations exist, but depicts them as subservient to the LORD God of Israel. This outer frame sets a cosmic context and motivation for the more central point, that Zion (Jerusalem) and the villages of Judah acclaim God as the dispenser of earthly justice.

Verses 10–12 develop the idea behind verse 8 more fully, urging worshipers to embody God's divine justice in their own lives. Unlike some modern countries, ancient Israel and Judah did not separate the creation, adjudication, and enforcement of laws. Rather, all these were royal duties and prerogatives. This psalm holds God up as the ultimate example of a king giving, adjudicating, and enforcing just laws throughout his dominions—which in God's case means the entire cosmos.

For Those Who Sing Psalm 97

Psalm 97:9 supplies half of the words for the popular worship song "I Exalt Thee," set to music by Pete Sanchez in the 1970s and often sung using "we" instead of "I." For our psalmist, God's exaltation is already an accomplished fact. When we "exalt" God in praise, we are really acknowledging the exalted status that the Lord already occupies. To fully manifest God's exaltation above all gods, however, worshipers must promote divine justice—envisioned here not chiefly as punishment for the wicked, but as deliverance for the innocent. God uses his exaltation to bless the lowly.

Christopher Heard

God Reigns

Psalm 97

Michael Morgan (1948–2022)

D. J. Bulls

The Lord Reigns

Psalm 97

Jerry Shipp

Ruth Ann Somervell

The mountains melt like sealing wax; with trembling all the earth replies.
for light will dawn upon the just and joy on those with upright hearts.
The heavens show his righteousness; let earth his holiness proclaim.
Rejoice in God, you righteous ones, and praise, you saints,
his holy name, and praise, you saints, his holy name.
Broadly
The Lord reigns! The Lord reigns!

Psalm 98

Translation

A psalm.

†1 Sing a new song to the Lord,
* for he has done wonders. His right hand and his holy arm have brought him victory.[a]
*2 The Lord has made his victory known. In the nations' sight he has revealed his righteousness.
*3 He has remembered his loyalty and faithfulness to the house of Israel. All the ends of the earth have seen our God's deliverance.

†4 Shout to the Lord, all the earth. Break out in joyful song! Sing praise!
†5 Sing praise to the Lord accompanied by a lyre—accompanied by a lyre and the sound of singing.
†6 Accompanied by trumpets and the blast of a horn, shout before the king, the Lord.

†7 May the sea and its inhabitants roar; likewise the land, and those who live on it.
†8 May the rivers clap their hands, and the mountains shout together with joy
†9 before the Lord,
* for he is coming to judge the earth. He will judge the world righteously and the peoples fairly.

[a] NIV and some other translations read "salvation" instead of "victory" here and in verse 2. Lexically, both translations lie within the scope of the basic verb used, but grammatically, the preposition that follows it makes "victory" more likely. Theologically, the Lord does not need deliverance, but might have reasons to exhibit victory.

Structure and Poetry

The three-part structure of Psalm 98 somewhat resembles Psalm 96. The psalm as a whole constitutes a call to praise, with the specific emphasis and even the grammar shifting as one moves from strophe to strophe.

Verses 1–3: Called to praise, worshipers briefly narrate God's deliverance of Israel.
Temporal focus: the past

Agentival focus: Israel
Grammatical focus: indicative, "God did this"

Verses 4–6: Called to praise, worshipers play lyres and blow trumpets and horns.
Temporal focus: the present
Agentival focus: all humanity
Grammatical focus: imperative, "do this"

Verses 7–9: Called to praise, nature announces God's imminent or eschatological judgment of the world.
Temporal focus: the future
Agentival focus: all creation
Grammatical focus: wishful, "may they do this"

Theology and Application

Psalm 98 opens with a brief invitation for worshipers to summarize God's great acts of deliverance on Israel's behalf. Preeminent among these would be the Exodus from Egypt, and some of the vocabulary in verses 1–3 recalls the vocabulary of Exodus 15:1–18. These verses are by no means limited to an Exodus allusion, but worshipers steeped in Israel's traditions would find it hard not to think of the Exodus while reciting these words.

The shift from indicative back to imperative in verse 4 marks the beginning of a new strophe, and the references to musical instruments in verses 5–6 recommend taking verses 4–6 as separate from the nature-oriented verses that follow. Since psalms generally lack "stage direction," there is no overt notice of worshipers implementing the musical instructions. Since the calls to praise in verses 1 and 7–8 are answered by indicative statements of praise, however, it seems reasonable to infer that worshipers—one should probably think of Levitical musicians, as described for example in Chronicles—answered with appropriate performances when this psalm was actually used in Israelite worship.

Another grammatical shift, as from "do this" to "I wish you would do this," ushers in the third strophe. In tone, topic, structure, and even precise word choice, this strophe very strongly resembles the third strophe of Psalm 96. Since the mountains cannot literally shout the words quoted in verse 9, we should imagine worshipers giving audible voice to nature's nonverbal praise.

Like Psalm 96, Psalm 98 suspends worshipers between a foundational past and a distant future, and by so doing puts their present in context. In Psalm 96, that foundational past was the creation of the world. In Psalm 98, the foundation event seems rather to be some historical deliverance that the psalmists or (more likely) their ancestors experienced, perhaps the Exodus. Whatever specific event was in mind, the psalmists use concrete experiences of prior deliverance to ground their hopes of future salvation.

For Those Who Sing Psalm 98

On what basis might anyone cling to a hopeful vision for the future? This psalm asserts that we can base confidence in God's future judgment because of his track record of deliverance in the past. The Exodus serves to anchor that record for this particular psalm, as for so many Old Testament passages. But that need not be the only anchor. Scripture, church history, and personal experience may suggest other anchors—preeminently for Christians, the life, crucifixion, resurrection, and ascension of Jesus Christ.

Christians today may tend to assimilate thoughts of God's "judgment" to an eschatological "judgment day" when God will reward the righteous and punish the wicked. Certainly the dynamic of this psalm—past deliverance grounding present worship in anticipation of future divine action—applies to those eschatological expectations. But we need not *limit* God's judgment to the end of time. The psalmist would have expected God's judgment to manifest itself in this world, evidenced not merely in some reward-and-punishment exchange, but in a broader movement of Israel, all humanity, and all creation toward righteousness and equity.

Christopher Heard

O Sing a New Song

Psalm 98

Laura Kate Collum

Ruth Ann Somervell

Sing to God a New Song

Psalm 98

Gary Pendergrass

Gary Pendergrass

Sing to God a New Song

Psalm 99

Translation

†1 The Lord reigns—the peoples tremble! He sits *enthroned* on the cherubim—
the earth quakes!
*2 The Lord is great in Zion, and he is exalted above all the peoples.
†3 May they praise your great and awe-inspiring name, *saying*, "He is holy!"
*4 Mighty king who loves justice,[a] you have established uprightness; you have
made justice and righteousness in Jacob.
*5 Exalt the Lord our God and bow down at his footstool. He is holy!

†6 Moses and Aaron were among his priests, and Samuel was among those who
called on his name. They called out to the Lord and he answered them.
†7 God would speak in a pillar of cloud. They obeyed his decrees and the rules
that he gave them.
*8 O Lord, our God, you answered them. You were a forgiving God to them,
but also one who punished their misdeeds.
*9 Exalt the Lord our God and bow down at his holy mountain, for the Lord
our God is holy.

[a] This reading alters one Hebrew vowel sound slightly, with CEB and NRSV. A strict reading yields "a king's strength loves justice" (very odd word choice) or "a king is mighty; he loves justice" (grammatically awkward).

Structure and Poetry

The structure of Psalm 99 is complex. Attention naturally gravitates toward the threefold acclamation of God's holiness in verses 3, 5, and 9. In verses 5 and 9, that acclamation responds to a direct call to praise ("exalt," imperative); in verse 3, however, it is preceded by an indirect wish that praise occur ("may they praise," subjunctive). The primary division, therefore, seems to be into two strophes:

Verses 1–5: The Lord reigns as the just king on Mt. Zion.
Verses 6–9: The Lord reigns as the just lawgiver on Mt. Sinai.

Theology and Application

Psalm 99 draws together God's two holy mountains, Zion and Sinai, although the latter is not invoked by name. Psalms 96–98 celebrate God as the ultimate righteous judge of all the earth, but still limit themselves primarily to royal metaphors. In ancient Israel and Judah, as in the ancient Near East generally, the king was the ultimate legal human authority, both as legislator and court of final appeal. Those who asked Samuel for a king wanted "a king to judge us" (1 Sam. 8:5–6), Absalom gathered support by painting David as deficient in jurisprudence (2 Sam. 15:1–4), and Solomon boosted his approval rating by clever rulings from the bench (1 Kings 3:16–28). Isaiah makes the link clear and powerful: "The Lord is our judge; the Lord is our lawgiver; the Lord is our king; he will save us" (Isa. 33:22 esv).

Yet Psalm 99 links God's justice to the Mosaic Torah in a way unmatched by any other "enthronement psalm." The thrice-repeated exclamation of the Lord's holiness (vv. 3, 5, 9) undoubtedly reminds many readers of Isaiah's prophetic call, but it hearkens also to the Torah, perhaps especially the "Holiness Code" in Leviticus 17–26, which grounds justice in God's holiness (Lev. 19:1–2, 11–18, 33–37). God's "footstool" in verse 3 is undoubtedly the ark of the covenant (compare 1 Chron. 28:2; Ps. 132:7), an object with powerful connections to both Moses, who commissioned its construction, and David, who installed it in Jerusalem. With the ark functioning literarily as a kind of hinge between the two strophes, the psalm then calls out nonroyal lawgivers by name—Moses, Aaron, Samuel—and reminds readers that long before Israel had any kings, Moses mediated God's justice in the wilderness. Verse 8 may allude specifically to the "creedal" summary of God's mercy and judgment in Exodus 34:6–7.

Our poet closes the loop by inviting worshipers to God's "holy mountain," a phrase that oscillates between Sinai, tied to priestly lawgiving, and Zion, tied to royal jurisprudence. The psalm does not call on worshipers to choose between Sinai and Zion; each is God's holy mountain, in its own way. But pairing these mountains provides a counterpoint to any royal pretensions to godlike importance in matters of justice. The union of God as king, God as lawgiver, and God as judge in Isaiah 33:22 might tempt earthly kings to exaggerate their role as disbursers of God's justice in their societies. Psalm 99 reminds these monarchs that God has other servants, other channels for lawgiving, that limit royal authority.

For Those Who Sing Psalm 99

Like other "enthronement psalms," Psalm 99 celebrates God's role as cosmic judge. But Psalm 99 also draws attention to the human mediators of God's justice. The marriage of Mosaic and Davidic traditions in Psalm 99 goes deeper than "separation of powers" or "checks and balances," although both of these phrases may help modern worshipers conceive of the relationship between priestly and royal justice. The sense here, though, is more of two institutions unified in pursuit of God's justice, but not collapsed together. Whether justice is mediated by civic or religious leaders, though, our psalmist is sure of one thing: the ultimate ground of justice is found in the Lord.

Christopher Heard

Above the Earth He Sits Enthroned

Psalm 99

Mark Shipp

Michael E. Showalter

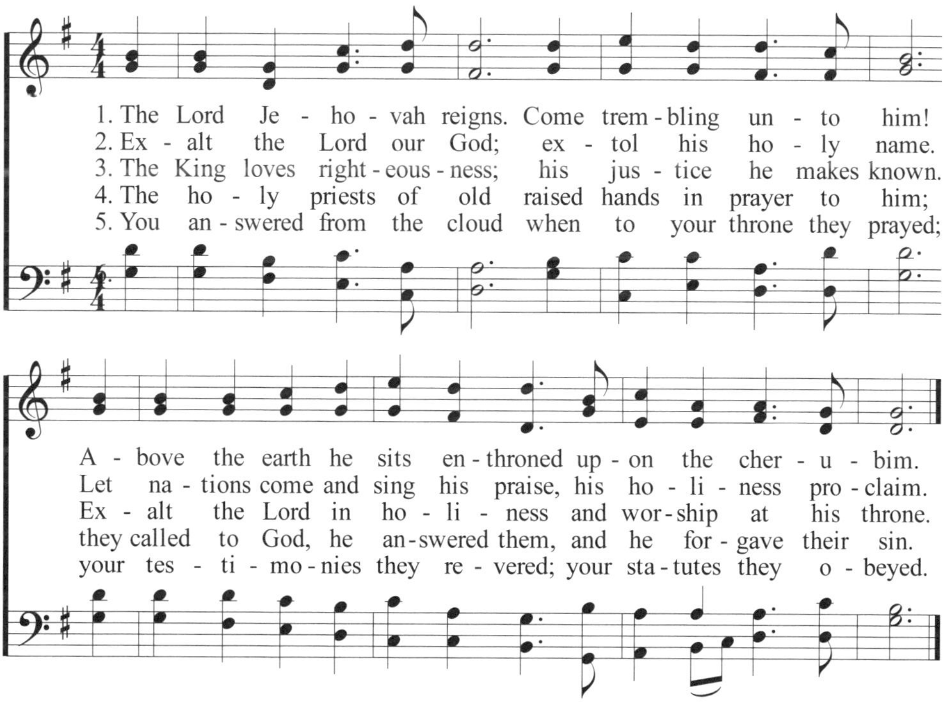

The Lord Jehovah Reigns

Psalm 99

Ray McClendon

M. L. Daniels

Psalm 100

Translation

A psalm of thanksgiving.

†1 Shout to the LORD, all the earth.

†2 Worship the LORD joyfully. Come before him with joyful shouts.

†3 Acknowledge that the LORD is God.

* He made us, and we are his.[a] We are his people and the sheep of his pasture.

†4 Enter his gates with thanksgiving and his courts with praise. Praise him; bless his name.

*5 The LORD is good! His loyalty lasts forever, and he is trustworthy generation after generation.[b]

[a] The Hebrew text reads "and not we," that is, "we did not make ourselves." A longstanding Jewish tradition substitutes almost identical sounds meaning "we are his." This translation follows that tradition, which results in tighter parallelism with the second part of the verse.

[b] Compare 2 Chronicles 5:13; 7:3; Psalm 118:1–4; and above all Psalm 136, where almost identical phrases serve as choral antiphons or congregational responses.

Structure and Poetry

Despite its brevity, Psalm 100 exhibits a distinct two-part structure, in which calls to praise, perhaps extended by a priest or other worship leader, are answered by praise itself, presumably from the congregants:

Verses 1–3:	A call to praise evokes an affirmation that the LORD is God.
Verses 4–5:	A call to praise evokes an affirmation that the LORD is good.

Theology and Application

The central affirmation of Psalm 100 is straightforward: God made and sustains his worshipers, for which they should be grateful. The psalm was almost certainly used as an "entrance liturgy" in temple worship, a song used to welcome worshipers and invite them in. If so, then the "thanksgiving" enjoined in verse 4 may be more than a mere attitude. Indeed, the word translated "thanksgiving" is also the name of a worship ritual during which one offered both sacrifices and testimony (see Lev. 7; Jon. 2:9; Pss. 50:14, 23; 107:22; 116:17).

In that connection, it is significant that God's goodness is not merely asserted as a general quality, but is grounded in specific actions. But the final line, emphasizing God's eternal loyalty and trustworthiness, grounds the worshipers' present thanksgiving in Israel's grand story. Verse 3 underscores this point by emphasizing group identity—"we are his sheep," not "I am his sheep." "Forever" and "generation after generation" look both forward and backward. The past and future of the worshiping community are in God's gracious hands.

For Those Who Sing Psalm 100

This simple, beautiful, artful psalm reminds us today—as it did ancient worshipers—that we depend on God for our very existence. Presumably, we like being alive, and therefore should respond with thanks. It is too easy, though, to simply dash off a quick prayer of "God, thank you for my life." This psalm would have us proclaim our thanksgivings, testifying in public worship to God's concrete acts of goodness in our lives and, even more than in our individual lives, in the corporate experience of the worshiping community stretching back into the deepest past. By our thanksgivings we also anticipate that God's goodness will continue into the farthest conceivable future. Many other psalms provide concrete examples of adapting this general principle to particular circumstances (e.g., Ps. 22:22–31 and Ps. 107).

Christopher Heard

Shout for Joy to the Lord

Psalm 100

Glover Shipp (1927–2016) Debbie Dorman

Shout to the Lord, All the Earth

Psalm 100

Jack R. Reese

Jack R. Reese

Make a Joyful Noise

Psalm 100

M. L. Daniels

M. L. Daniels

Psalm 101

Translation

A psalm of David.

†1 Let me sing concerning loyalty and justice! To you, O Lord, let me make music!
*2 Let me contemplate the way of integrity; when will it come to me? I will walk in the integrity of my heart in the midst of my house.
†3 I will not set a worthless matter before my eyes. To do transgressions I abhor; it will not cling to me.
*4 Turn a perverse heart away from me! I do not know evil.

†5 The one who slanders his neighbor in secret, I will silence him. The high-minded and arrogant I will not endure.
*6 My favor is upon the faithful of the land, so that they may dwell beside me. The one who walks in the way of integrity, he will minister to me.
†7 The one who practices deceit will not dwell in the midst of my house; the one who speaks falsehoods will not be established before my eyes.
*8 Every morning I will silence all the wicked of the land, to cut off from the city of the Lord all those who practice iniquity.

Structure and Poetry

This psalm is dedicated to David. It appears to be divided into two parts: verses 1–4, where the psalmist challenges himself to praise the Lord and turn from evil, and verses 5–8, where the psalmist states what he will do to the wicked in his daily life. The psalm is either a royal psalm that David is purported to have sung and demonstrates his pledge to uphold justice, which would fit the talk of silencing enemies (vv. 5 and 8), or else it is a type of wisdom psalm meant to instruct in general. The psalmist deliberately distances himself from the wicked. A great divide is depicted where the righteous act one way and the wicked act another. This is similar to the teaching of the two ways found in the wisdom literature: the way of wisdom and folly. The psalmist becomes God's zealous advocate in the second half, similar to Phinehas in Numbers 25:7–8, who impales an Israelite who is having relations with a Moabite woman.

Several words in the psalm are repeated, which serves to bind the psalm together. The word for "integrity" is in verses 2 and 6; "eyes" in verses 3, 5–7; "heart" in verses 2, 4–5; "dwell" in verses 6–7; "way" in verses 2 and 6; "house" is in verses 2 and 7; "midst" in verses 2 and 7; "land" in verses 6 and 8; and "annihilate" in verses 5 and 8.

Theology and Application

As Christians, we too should take the side of the righteous and pious over against the wicked and impious. However, the vengeance promised in the latter half of the psalm cannot be applicable for Christians. As Paul states, "Vengeance is mine, I will repay, says the Lord" (Rom. 12:19 NRSV), which cites Deuteronomy 32:35. We must also not forget that in the Old Testament "righteousness" and "piety" meant primarily being concerned about justice and attempting to bring it to those who were oppressed. In other words, from an Old Testament perspective, righteousness was not an individualistic virtue but had serious social implications. Christians should always be the ones on the side of the poor and oppressed and not simply sustainers or condoners of the wealthy and powerful and the status quo.

For Those Who Sing Psalm 101

Christians who sing this psalm should be proud to take the side of those most vulnerable in our society and against their oppressors. The way of integrity and justice will win in the end. We should sing this psalm viewing ourselves as change agents who want to bring a bit of the kingdom of heaven to earth. This psalm resonates with the early-twentieth-century hymn by Methodist missionary Frank Mason North, "Where Cross the Crowded Ways of Life," which had New York City as its backdrop. The title alludes to Matthew 22:9 ("Go ye therefore into the parting of the highways"). It is famous as a "social gospel" hymn.

Mark Sneed

Come to Me, Lord

Psalm 101

Jerry Shipp | Ruth Ann Somervell

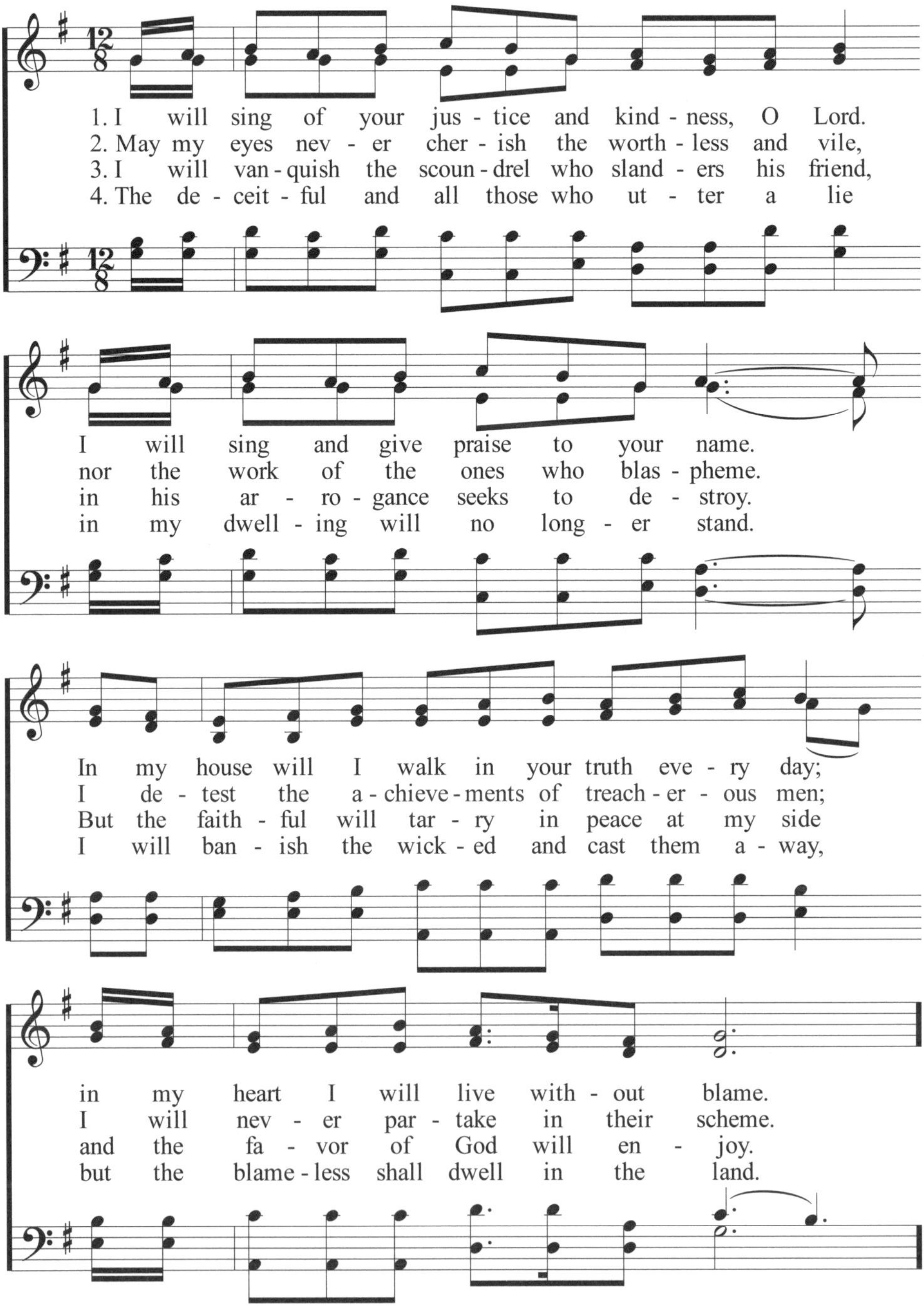

Come to Me, Lord

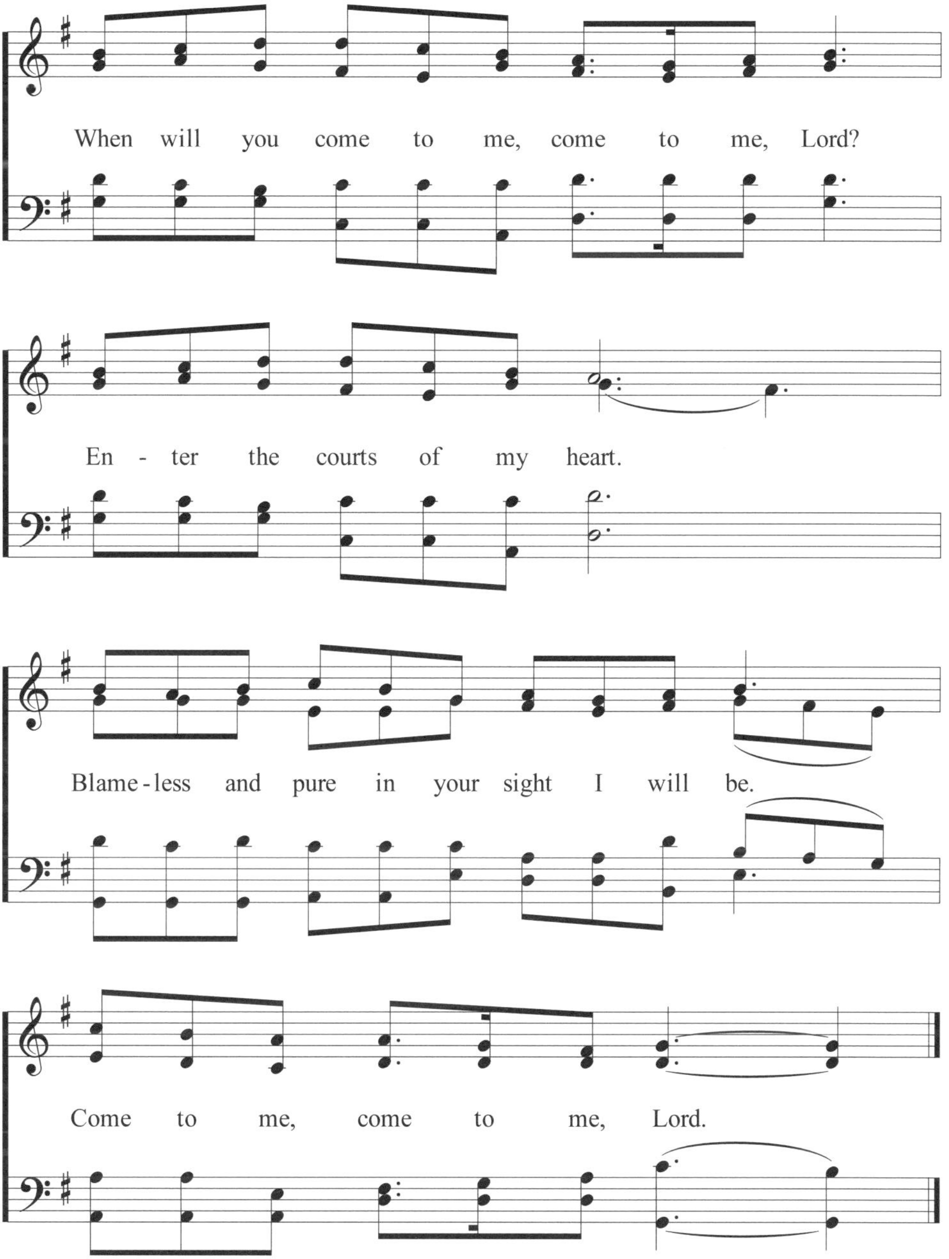

Praise for a Righteous God

Psalm 101

Tim L. Berman | D. J. Bulls

PSALM 102

Translation

A prayer for the oppressed when he is weak; let him[a] pour out his complaint before the LORD.

†1 O LORD, hear my prayer; let my cry come to you!

*2 Do not hide your face from me in the day of my distress. Extend to me your ear. When I call, answer me quickly!

†3 For my days perish in smoke, and my bones are burned as in a hearth.
†4 My heart is beaten like grass and dries up, for I have forgotten to eat my food.
†5 From the sound of my groaning my skeleton clings to my flesh.
†6 I resemble a bird of the wilderness; I am an owl of the ruins.
†7 I keep watch and am like a bird alone upon the roof.
†8 All day my enemies reproach me; those who mock me curse me,
†9 for I eat dust for food, and I mix my drink with tears
†10 on account of your indignation and wrath, for you lifted me up and cast me out.
†11 My days are like an evening shadow, and I am dried up like grass.

*12 But you, O LORD, will remain forever, and your remembrance from generation to generation!
*13 You will arise and have compassion on Zion, for it is time to be gracious to her, for the appointed time has come,
*14 for your servants find pleasure in her stones, and they have compassion concerning her soil.[b]
*15 And the nations will fear the name of the LORD and all the kings of the earth, your glory,
*16 for the LORD rebuilt Zion, and he appeared in his glory.

†17 He turned to the prayer of the destitute and did not despise their prayer.
†18 Let this be written for a coming generation, so that a people to be created will praise the LORD.

*19 For the LORD looked down from his holy heights; from the heavens he looked upon the earth
*20 to hear the crying of a prisoner, to free those doomed to die,

*21 in order to declare the name of the LORD in Zion, his praise in Jerusalem,
*22 when the peoples are gathered together, and the kingdoms serve the LORD.

†23 He has weakened my strength in the way. He has shortened my days.
†24 I say, "Do not take me away in the midst of my days, during the eternity of your years."

*25 Formerly you established the earth and the heavens, the work of your hands.
*26 They perish but you remain, but all of them become like worn-out clothing.
Like the clothing, you change them, and they pass away,
*27 but you are the same, and your years are never completed.
*28 The children of your servants will dwell, and their seed will be established before you!

[a] The pronoun is masculine but refers to any Israelite.
[b] The Hebrew word could mean "rubble."

Structure and Poetry

The superscription properly identifies this psalm as a lament. It is also an orphan psalm because it is not ascribed or dedicated to anyone. The lament vacillates between an individual (vv. 1–12, 23–24) and group orientation (vv. 13–22). This probably means the "I" is meant to personify Israel as a nation. This type of psalm involves an individual or group that attempts to motivate God to act on his or their behalf because of some crisis, like enemies, disease, or other calamities. The psalm employs a theme found in the wisdom literature that contrasts the impotence and ephemeral nature of humans over against the substantiality and eternality of God (vv. 11–12, 24–27; cf. Eccles. 1:4; 3:19–21; 9:1–6; 12:1–7 and Ps. 49). Its lament structure is the following:

Invocation: v. 1
Petition for help: v. 2
Complaint: vv. 3–11
Affirmation of confidence: vv. 12–16
Petition for help: vv. 17–18
Affirmation of Confidence: vv. 19–22
Complaint: v. 23
Petition for help: v. 24
Conclusion: vv. 25–28

The psalmist is attempting to persuade God to act on Israel's behalf. The petitions, complaints, and affirmations of confidence employ an interesting strategy to motivate God. The first petition (v. 2) implies that the Lord has forsaken the psalmist and has not reacted quickly enough. This is intended to spur the Lord on so that he might act. The first complaint (vv. 3–11) attempts to motivate the

Lord to have compassion for the complainant, describing how sorry his condition has become and how alienated he feels. The first affirmation (vv. 12–16) appeals to God's honor when it speaks of his eternality and the people's memory of him. Also, in verse 15 the increasing of God's prestige will be the effect of his action on behalf of his people—definitely motivation! In the second petition (vv. 17–18) appeal is made to future generations who will praise God for his intervention and also the recording of the event, again certainly motivation for God to act. In the second affirmation (vv. 19–22) again appeal is made to the increase of God's prestige via praise from the people. In verses 23–24, the psalmist appeals to God's sympathy by asking him not to end his life prematurely. In the conclusion (vv. 25–28), the psalmist contrasts the fleeting nature of humanity with God's eternality and power, again, appealing to his compassion for a weaker party.

Theology and Application

This psalm assumes that God is a rational being who also has emotions and concerns. It assumes that there is no shame in attempting to persuade God to act on one's behalf. The psalm assumes a covenantal relationship that is bilateral, with obligations for both parties. It also reveals the close relationship that Israel felt it had with God. Christians share the same relationship with God and should be as bold as this psalmist in expressing their fears, doubts, and crises, whether as individuals or the church as a whole. We shouldn't be afraid to approach God in our darkest hours and ask for his healing and salvation. Neither should we fear attempting to persuade him to act on our behalf—that's part of the relationship.

For Those Who Sing Psalm 102

This psalm is appropriate for a Christian who finds herself in dire straits and needs God's intervention. Though few of our songs in the hymnals are true laments, this is the dominant type of psalm in the Psalter. It's okay to let God know how we feel and what we need. The psalm resonates with the modern hymns, "Precious Lord, Take My Hand" and "Does Jesus Care." Also, consider "Count Your Many Blessings" and "Peace Be Still," which treat Jesus's calming of the sea (e.g., Matt. 8:23–27) as a metaphor for calming life's distresses.

Mark Sneed

Allow My Prayer to Come before You

Psalm 102

M. W. Bassford | Debbie Dorman

Allow My Prayer to Come before You

You, O Lord, Will Live Forever

Psalm 102

Marva L. Hughes

Marva L. Hughes

You, O Lord, Will Live Forever

Psalm 103

Translation

Of David.

†1 Bless the LORD, my soul! All my innermost being, bless his holy name!

*2 Bless the LORD, my soul, and do not forget all his deeds—
†3 the one who forgives all your sins, who heals all your diseases,
†4 who redeems your life from destruction and crowns you with loyalty and compassion,
†5 who satisfies your craving with goodness,[a] so that your soul is renewed like a young eagle.
†6 The LORD, who brings righteousness and justice for all the oppressed,
†7 who made known his ways to Moses, his deeds to the children of Israel—
*8 the LORD is compassionate and gracious, patient and abundantly loyal!
*9 He will not judge forever, and he will not keep his wrath[b] forever.
*10 He does not act toward us according to our sins, and he does not treat us according to our iniquities.
*11 For as high as the heavens are over the earth, so his loyalty increases upon those who fear him.
*12 As far as sunrise to sunset, so far he removes our sins from us.

†13 Like the compassion of a father for his children, the LORD is compassionate to all who fear him,
†14 for he knows our form, remembering that we are dust.
*15 A human's days are like the grass; he will blossom like a flower of the field.
†16 For the wind passes over it and it is no more, and no one will recognize again where it was,
*17 but the loyalty of the LORD is everlasting and forever upon those who fear him. His justice is for posterity,
*18 for those who keep his covenant, for those who remember to do his commands.
*19 The LORD establishes his throne in the heavens, and his kingdom rules over everything.

*20 Bless the LORD, all his angels, those mighty in strength who do his words, who heed the sound of his word!
*21 Bless the LORD, all his host, his ministers who do his pleasure!

*22 Let all his works bless the LORD among all the places of his dominion.

* Let my soul bless the LORD!

[a] "Craving" from the LXX (Greek Septuagint) instead of the Hebrew Masoretic text's "ornaments."
[b] According to the LXX.

Structure and Poetry

This psalm is properly a hymn. Hymns praise God for who he is in general, i.e., his nature and character, and do not represent the giving of thanks for specific acts of salvation that have been petitioned, as is true for psalms of thanksgiving. This psalm begins and ends with a call for the psalmist's "soul" to bless the Lord (vv. 1–2a, 5, 22b). Verses 2b–12 praise God for his merciful and just nature. Verses 13–19 praise him for his fatherly concern for those who fear him. Verses 20–22a are a call to praise for the entire cosmos, not just the psalmist. The word "soul" in Hebrew is difficult to translate into English. Basically, it means the psalmist himself as a person. It is awkward for us moderns to hear the psalmist refer to himself as a "soul" in the third person. But this is common in the psalms. "Soul" does not denote the New Testament sense of a spirit or ghost. This psalm resembles the previous one in its contrast between God's substantiality and eternality and humanity's ephemeral nature and powerlessness (vv. 14–17; cf. 102:11–12, 24–27).

The psalm especially emphasizes God's continual forgiveness of sins and his mercy and grace. It also stresses God's paternal role (v. 13). The conclusion in verses 20–22 is a final call for humans, nature, the heavenly host, and even the world to praise the Lord. This psalm uses several striking metaphors to depict various phenomena and people: young eagles = sinners redeemed by God (v. 5); distance = the degree of God's mercy and forgiveness (vv. 11–12); father = God (v. 13); grass/flowers = human ephemeral nature (v. 15); wind = death (v. 16).

Theology and Application

This hymn praises God for his mercy and grace, especially in his forgiveness of sins. It is consoling to know that however badly we Christians might mess things up, as long as we are truly penitent and faithful, God will extend his grace. This psalm resonates well with Paul's view of grace and salvation. The psalm also makes the important distinction between mortals and the immortal. So does Paul, who holds to what is called a pessimistic anthropology, the notion that humans are largely incapable of accomplishing much on their own. Though as Christians we continue to emulate God, we are not gods and never shall be. The emphasis on God's "loyalty" refers to his faithfulness to his people, such as a patron to his clients, as long as they remain strictly loyal to him (monotheism) and honor him, especially with praise.

For Those Who Sing Psalm 103

Christians who sing this psalm should take confidence in God's gracious nature, especially in the sacrifice of his Son. We should also acknowledge the difference between us and God, a difference that should help us realize how dependent we are on him. Of course, "Amazing Grace," "There Is Power in the Blood," or "On the Cross" come to mind. The emphasis on keeping the covenant resonates also with "Trust and Obey."

Mark Sneed

Let My Soul Bless the Lord

Psalm 103

Glover Shipp (1927–2016) — Ruth Ann Somervell

Bless the Lord, O My Soul

Psalm 103

Mark Shipp

Konstantin Zhigulin
adapted by Randy Daw

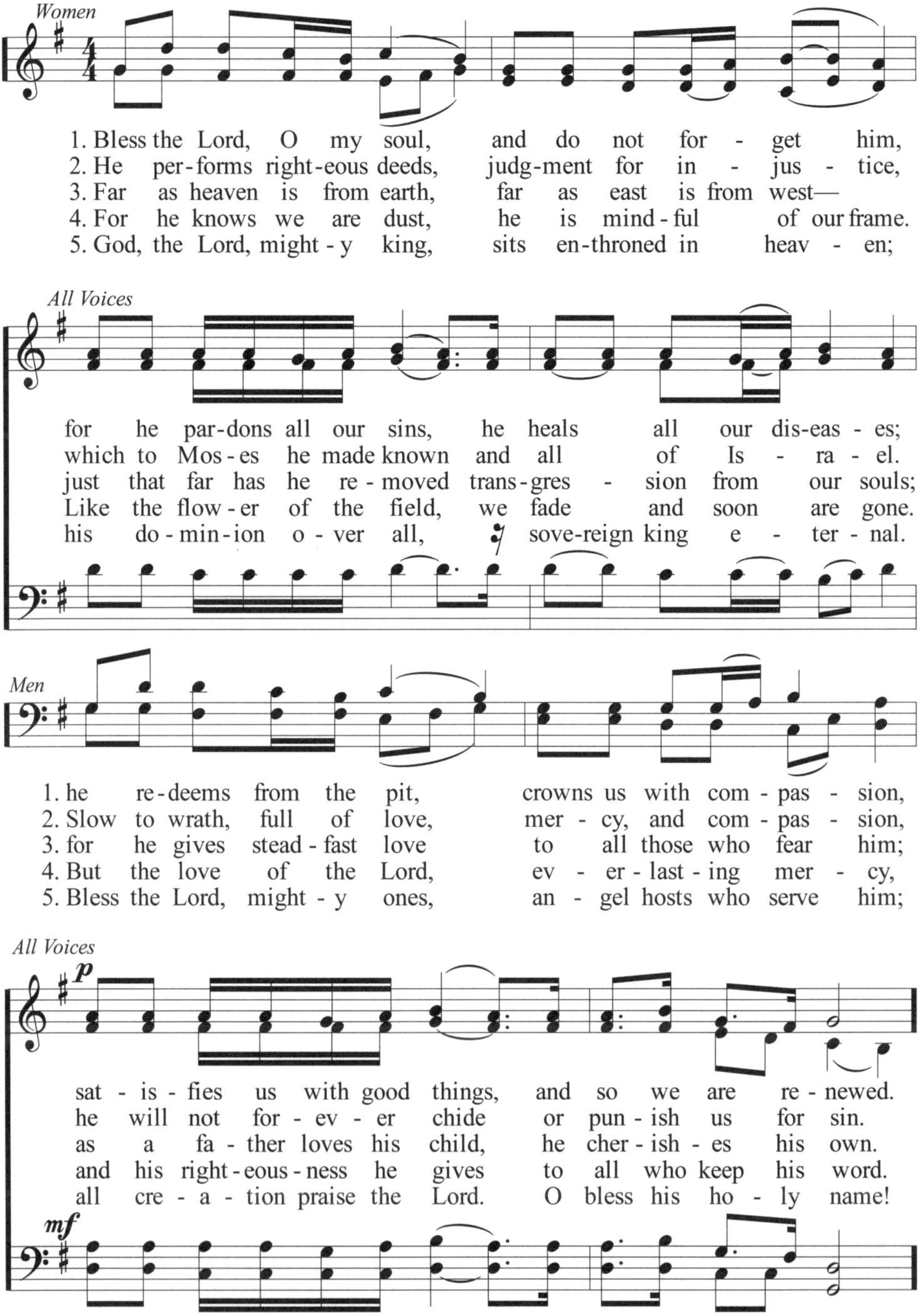

Bless the Lord, O My Soul

PSALM 104

Translation

†1 Bless the LORD, O my soul!

* O LORD, my God, you are exceedingly great; you clothe yourself in majesty and honor—

*2 who wraps himself up with light like a cloak, who stretches out the heavens like a curtain,

*3 who constructs his upper rooms with beams on the waters, who sets the clouds as his chariot, who walks about upon the wings of the wind,

*4 who makes the winds his servants, a blazing fire, his ministers.

†5 He has established the earth upon its foundations; it will not ever totter.

†6 He covers the deep like clothing; the waters stand upon the mountains.

*7 They flee from your rebuke; they hurry away from the sound of your thunder.

*8 The mountains will ascend, and the valleys will descend to the place that you will establish for them.

†9 You set a boundary that they cannot pass over; they cannot return to cover the earth.

*10 You are the one who sends out springs in the wadis, who causes them to flow between the mountains.

†11 They water every living creature of the field; the donkeys quench their thirst.

†12 The birds of the air dwell by them; they sing among the foliage.

*13 You are the one who irrigates the mountains from your heights; the earth is satisfied by the fruit of your works.

*14 You are the one who causes grass to sprout for the beasts and herbage for the toil of humanity, in order to bring forth food from the earth.

*15 And wine makes merry the heart of humanity, oil makes faces shine, and food sustains the heart of humanity.

†16 The trees of the LORD are watered, the cedars of Lebanon which he has planted,

†17 where birds nest; the heron builds in its tops.[a]

†18 The high hills are for the goats; cliffs are a refuge for the badgers.

*19 He made the moon for the seasons; the sun knows its setting.

*20 You establish darkness, and it becomes night; in it all the living creatures of the forest creep.
†21 The young lions roar for prey in order to seek their food from God.
†22 The sun rises, and they are gathered; they lie down in their lairs.
†23 A human goes forth to his work and to his labor until evening.

*24 How many are your works, O LORD! All of them you do with wisdom; the earth is filled with your accomplishments.
†25 There is the sea, great and wide; there are innumerable creeping things, living creatures, small and great.
†26 Ships travel there, and you created Leviathan[b] to play in it.

*27 All of them hope in you, so that you give them food in its time.
†28 When you give it to them, they gather it up; when your hand opens, they are well satisfied.
†29 When you conceal your face, then they are terrified; when you remove their spirit, they die, and they return to their dust.
*30 When you send out your spirit, they are created, and you renew the face of the earth.

*31 Let the prestige[c] of the LORD continue forever! Let the LORD rejoice in his works—
*32 who gazes at the earth, and it trembles; he touches the mountains, and they smoke.
*33 Let me sing to the LORD; in my lifetime let me sing praises to my God forever!
*34 Let my talk be pleasing to him; I will rejoice in the LORD.
*35 Let sinners be destroyed from the earth and the wicked be no more.
* Bless the LORD, O my soul! Praise the LORD!

[a] The LXX (Greek Septuagint) reading.

[b] See the commentary below for the identification of Leviathan.

[c] Usually translated as "glory," "prestige" captures more the fact that God's status is elevated within the cosmos due to his creative power.

Structure and Poetry

This beautiful psalm is what is called a creation hymn in that it praises God for the creation and maintenance of the cosmos. It begins and ends, similarly to the previous psalm, with a call for the psalmist's "soul" to bless the Lord (vv. 1, 35). It is properly an orphan psalm since it has no superscription. This psalm is all about God's glory and honor in his creative power and benevolent acts in sustaining the universe. The psalm especially resonates with the first creation account (Gen. 1:1–2:4a). Verses 1b–10 describe God's greatness in creating the inanimate cosmos and restraining the deep (the watery chaos). God's providence of providing water to the animate world—beasts, birds, and humans—is treated in verses 11–18. Verses 19–23 return to the inanimate world: the celestial bodies and the times and seasons. The animate world returns with the sea creatures (vv. 24–26). Creaturely dependence is treated in verses 27–30. A call to praise finishes the body of the psalm (vv. 31–35a). The psalm is not a scientific description of the way God created the world, but is rather a poetic encomium that praises God's power and benevolence and the beauty and wonder of his creation. Poetry is the perfect medium for this, in contrast to narrative, because it can touch the emotions more deeply, befitting the spectacle of the creation. The conclusion (vv. 31–35) switches gears by invoking God's wrath on sinners (v. 35). The psalm also links with the previous one with its reference to "ministers" (v. 4; cf. 103:21).

The psalm is intriguing for its allusions to various ancient Near Eastern themes and its particular understanding of nature. It is typically compared with the "Hymn to the Aten," the Egyptian sun god in the form of the solar disc. In this hymn, the writer praises Aten for his creation of the cosmos and care for the animals and humans. There are also Canaanite parallels. The reference to God's clouds as chariots (v. 3) is similar to an epithet of Baʿal: "Hail, Baʿal the Conqueror! Hail, Rider on the Clouds!"[2] Verse 4 is interesting for Christians because it is cited in Hebrews 1:7: "He makes his angels winds and his servants flames of fire" (NRSV). The author of Hebrews cites the Septuagint here (Greek translation of the Hebrew Bible), which reverses the role of the elements and servants. The author of Hebrews shows that Jesus is superior to angels, beings the psalm does not necessarily denote. In verse 21, there is a description of lions roaring for their prey. They appear to be roaring to God to provide them prey, as if in prayer. Verse 26 refers to Leviathan, a term used in poetic texts that usually refers to a sea monster (symbolizing evil and chaos) that the Lord defeats or controls (Pss. 74:13–14; 89:10; Isa. 51:9–10; Job 26:12–13; 41:1–34). It is, thus, a negative image. Similarly, the Babylonian god Marduk defeats the sea dragon Tiamat, and Baʿal defeats the sea monster Lothan (the Canaanite equivalent of "Leviathan"). In this psalm, Leviathan appears to be simply one of God's creatures—though a powerful one—who frolics in the water, so the image is more benign.

Theology and Application

Christians often think of God's primary purpose in their life as the forgiveness of their sins. But this psalm emphasizes God's greater purposes, such as the creation and maintenance of the universe. Our God is great! This psalm also displays God's concern for the animal world. God's purposes are much broader and larger than our own, often narcissistic, perspectives! This psalm resonates with the divine speeches in Job (chaps. 38–41), which emphasize that the cosmos

[2] Michael D. Coogan and Mark S. Smith, eds. and trans., *Stories from Ancient Canaan*, 2nd ed. (Louisville: Westminster John Knox Press, 2012), 99.

and its workings are not anthropocentric (centered on humans) but theocentric (centered on God). God is savior, but he is also creator!

For Those Who Sing Psalm 104

The Christian who sings this psalm should take great pride in our God who has created a remarkable and complexly beautiful world. Our responsibility is to praise and honor him with our words and deeds. What an awesome God we serve! This psalm resonates with the hymns, "Beyond the Azure Blue" and "How Great Thou Art." It is interesting that at Prince Philip's funeral (April 17, 2021), the choir sang Psalm 104, which the Duke of Edinburgh requested should be set to music by William Lovelady. Originally composed as a cantata in three movements, it was first sung in honor of the duke's seventy-fifth birthday.

Mark Sneed

Come Bless the Lord Always, My Soul

Psalm 104

Mel Witcher

Mel Witcher

Awe - some in might, you come rid - ing the clouds
Wa - ters of cha - os dis - persed at your voice;
Gath - er - ing food from the earth you have made,
When the sun ris - es, the crea - tures with - draw,
Each one is fed when you o - pen your hand;
Let all my words be a bless - ing to you;
on wings of the winds you con - trol,
they fled from the storm you con - trol.
we thrive by the gifts you con - trol.
in rhy - thms of life you con - trol.
their life and their death you con - trol.
my cha - os sub - mit to con - trol.
light - ning, your en - voy, your ser - vants, the storms.
Moun - tains broke through, then the val - leys e - merged.
You have pro - vid - ed us glad - ness and joy.
Peo - ple a - rise and go out to their work.
Earth is re - newed when you send forth your breath.
Let me sing prais - es as long as I live!
Come bless the Lord, al - ways my soul!

All Creation Hopes in You

Psalm 104

Gary Pendergrass

Gary Pendergrass

All Creation Hopes in You

Psalm 105

Translation

†1 Praise the Lord! Call on him. Make known his deeds among the people.
*2 Sing to him; praise him! Meditate upon all his wonders.
†3 Praise his holy name! Let the heart of those who seek the Lord rejoice.
*4 Seek the Lord and his might; seek his face continually.

†5 Remember his wonders which he has done, his signs and the decrees of his mouth,
†6 O seed of Abraham, his servant, children of Jacob, his chosen ones.
*7 He is the Lord our God. His acts of justice are in all the earth.
*8 He has remembered his covenant forever, the word he commanded to a thousand generations—
*9 the one he made with Abraham, and his oath to Isaac,
*10 and he established it for Jacob as a statute, for Israel as an eternal covenant.
*11 Saying, "To you I will give the land of Canaan as a territory of your inheritance."
†12 When they were a few people, little and strangers in it,
†13 and roamed about from nation to nation, from one kingdom to another people,
†14 he allowed no one to oppress them, and he reproved kings concerning them:
†15 "Do not touch my anointed! And do not treat my prophets badly!"

†16 When he summoned a famine upon the land, he shattered every food supply.
†17 He sent out before them a man, Joseph, who was sold as a slave.
†18 They bound his feet with fetters; iron came upon his neck
†19 until the time when his word came about, the word of the Lord tested him.
†20 The king sent forth and released him, and a ruler of peoples loosed him.
†21 A lord set him over his house, a ruler over all his possessions,
†22 to bind his princes, that he might teach his elders wisdom.
†23 Then Israel came to Egypt, and Jacob sojourned in the land of Ham.

*24 Then he made his people very fertile, and he made them more numerous than their enemies.
*25 He turned their heart to hate his people and to behave deceptively with his servants.

*26 He sent out his servant Moses, Aaron whom he had chosen.
*27 They performed his signs among them and wonders in the land of Ham.
*28 He sent darkness, and it became dark; did they not rebel against his words?
*29 He turned their waters to blood, and he slew their fish.
*30 Frogs swarmed their land and the chambers of their kings.
*31 He spoke and flies came, gnats among all their borders.
*32 He brought their rain showers as hail, flaming fire into their land.
*33 He smote their vine and their fig, and he shattered the trees of
their territory.
*34 He spoke and locusts came and grasshoppers without number,
*35 and they consumed all of the grass of their land and ate the fruit of
their ground.
*36 He smote all of the firstborn in their land, the first fruit of their manly vigor,
*37 and he brought them out with silver and gold and there was none among his
tribes who stumbled.
*38 Egypt rejoiced when they departed, for dread of them fell upon them.

†39 A cloud stretched out as a covering and a fire to lighten the night.
†40 They asked and he brought quail, and he satisfied them with food
from heaven.
†41 He opened a rock and water flowed out; it ran in the desert like a river,
*42 for he remembered his holy word with Abraham his servant.
*43 He brought out his people with rejoicing and his chosen ones
with exultation,
*44 and he gave to them the lands of the nations, and they possessed the produce of the toil of the peoples,
*45 in order that they might keep his statutes and observe his laws.

* Praise the LORD!

Structure and Poetry

This very long but beautiful psalm is what can be called a historical hymn, as opposed to a creation hymn. Instead of focusing on God's creation and sustenance of the universe like the previous psalm, this psalm praises God for his acts of salvation that begin with Abraham and end when the Israelites conquer the land of Canaan. The placing of these two psalms together demonstrates that the Israelites did not strictly separate creative acts from redemptive ones. Both sides of God's nature and character were important for the Israelites, and they praised him for both kinds of activities. For Israel, the Lord was both creator of the world and savior of his people. Again, this psalm is technically an orphan psalm since it has no superscription. The psalm begins and ends with a call to praise the Lord (vv. 1, 45b). There is a call to praise and seek the Lord in verses 1–4, then the rest of the psalm (vv. 5–45a) involves the praising of God's redemptive acts. Verses 5–15 treat the patriarchs, verses 16–23 Joseph, verses 24–38 Moses and the plagues, verses 39–45 the giving of the Law and the wilderness wandering. This psalm demonstrates that history or narrative can be recounted in poetic form, which again means that poetry can do some things better than prose. Interestingly, the crossing of the Red Sea is depicted both in poetry and prose (Exod. 14–15); similarly, the story of the Israelite defeat of the Canaanites is found in Judges 4–5. And Proverbs 7 is a story about an adulterous woman told in poetic form.

This psalm contains a couple of interesting features. One, the notion of divine determinism is found in verse 25, where the Lord is depicted as hardening the Pharaoh's heart (cf. Exod. 9:12) and orchestrating the Egyptians' deception of his own people. The problem of hardening the heart is a modern concern. The Israelites apparently did not see any real conflict between God determining someone's behavior and allowing individuals to choose freely what they will do. Second, when one counts the plagues listed in the psalm, there are only 7, not the 10 found in Exodus (chaps. 7–11). This is probably evidence that the story of the plagues was told in more than one version. It can also be explained as due to the poetic form of the psalm, because poetry does not usually emphasize historical accuracy. Poetry aims more for emotive effect.

Theology and Application

This hymn emphasizes God as savior rather than as creator, particularly his salvific acts for his people Israel. As Christians, this history of his people's deliverance from Egypt and occupation of the promised land is also our history. The Exodus becomes reconfigured in Christianity from the redemption from literal slavery to deliverance from the slavery of sin. The Lord's Supper is also a reconfiguration of the Passover meal. Now our Lamb does much more than protect from the death angel; he has conquered death for good and for both Jew and Gentile! The hymn also points to the fact that we don't serve a Deistic god, but one who is intricately connected to history and still today intervenes in our lives.

For Those Who Sing Psalm 105

Christians who sing this psalm should take pride in their Israelite heritage and appreciate their own inclusion into the people of God made possible by God's Son. Singing this song should also reinforce for us the reality of God as the god of history, and that he intervenes in our lives even today. The God of the patriarchs and Moses still cares for us today as much as he cared for Israel back then.

Mark Sneed

Praise Him, Hallelujah!

Based on Psalm 105

Michael Morgan (1948–2022), adapted from *Psalms For All Seasons* — Randy Daw (1954–2019)

God Has Kept His Covenant

Psalm 105

Mark Shipp

Debbie Dorman

God Has Kept His Covenant

Psalm 106

Translation

†1 Praise the Lord!

† Praise the Lord because he is good; his steadfast love endures forever.
*2 Who declares the mighty works of the Lord or makes known all of
his praises?
*3 Blessed are those who promote justice, those who do righteousness all
the time.

†4 Remember me, O Lord, when you show favor on your people; look upon[a]
me when you deliver them,
†5 so that I may look upon the prosperity of your chosen ones, so that I may
rejoice with the rejoicing of your nation, so that I may offer praise with your
heritage.[b]
*6 We and our ancestors have sinned—we committed iniquity; we have
acted wickedly.
†7 When our ancestors were in Egypt, they did not consider your wonder-
ful works. They did not remember your many acts of steadfast love; they
rebelled by the sea, by the Red Sea.
*8 Yet he saved them for the sake of his name, in order to make known his
mighty power.
†9 He rebuked the Red Sea and it became dry, and he led them through the
deeps as though it were a desert.
†10 And he delivered them from the hand of the foe, and he redeemed them
from the hand of the enemy.
†11 The waters covered their foes; not even one of the enemies remained.
*12 Then they believed his promises, and they sang his praises.

†13 But they quickly forgot his acts of deliverance and did not wait for his plan.
†14 In the wilderness they desperately craved for meat,[c] and they tested God in
the desert.
*15 So he gave them what they asked and sent a disease[d] among them.

†16 Those in the camp were jealous of Moses and Aaron, the holy one of
the Lord.
†17 The earth opened and swallowed up Dathan and covered over the company
of Abiram.

†18 Fire burned their group; the flame burned up the wicked ones.
†19 They made a calf at Horeb, and they worshiped a cast image.
*20 They exchanged their Glory[e] for the image of a bull that eats grass.
*21 They forgot God, their savior, the one who had done great things in Egypt,
*22 wonderful works in the land of Ham, awe-inspiring things by the Red Sea.
†23 So he said that he would destroy them, had not Moses, his chosen one, stood in the breach before him in order to turn away God's wrath from destroying them.

†24 Then they despised the pleasant land; they did not believe in his promise.
†25 They murmured in their tents; they did not obey the voice of the Lord.
*26 He raised up his hand and swore to them, that he would make them fall in the wilderness
*27 and cause their descendants to fall to the nations, scattering them among the lands.

†28 Then they yoked themselves to the Ba'al of Peor and ate sacrifices to the dead.
†29 They angered *the Lord* with their actions, and a plague broke out on them.
†30 Then Phineas stood up and intervened, and the plague ceased,
*31 and this was credited to him as righteousness from generation to generation forever.
†32 By the waters of Meribah they angered God, and trouble came upon Moses because of them.
†33 They made his spirit bitter, and caused him to speak rashly.

*34 They did not destroy the peoples as the Lord had instructed them,
*35 but they intermingled with the nations and learned their ways.
†36 They served their idols, which became a snare for them.
†37 They sacrificed their sons and their daughters to demons.
†38 They poured out innocent blood, the blood of their sons and daughters, which they sacrificed to the idols of Canaan; the land was polluted with blood.
†39 They became unclean because of their activities, and they played the harlot by their deeds.

†40 The anger of the Lord burned against his people, and he despised his heritage.[f]
†41 And then he gave them into the hands of the nations, so that those who hated them ruled over them.
†42 Their enemies oppressed them and they were subdued under their power.[g]
†43 He delivered them many times, but they remained rebellious and were brought down by their iniquity.
*44 Yet he looked upon their distress when he heard their cry,
*45 and he remembered his covenant with them, and he relented because of his abundant steadfast love.

*46 He caused them to be pitied by all those who held them captive.

*47 Save us, O LORD our God, and gather us from the nations so that we may praise your holy name, so that we may glory in your praise.[h]

*48 Blessed be the LORD, the God of Israel, from everlasting to everlasting. And let all people say, "Amen!"

* Praise the LORD!

[a] The term can mean "to see or look upon," but in this instance, the verb functions idiomatically, meaning to look upon in the sense of remembering.

[b] I.e., God's people.

[c] The word "meat" does not appear in the Hebrew text, but the psalmist is no doubt referring to the incident in Numbers 11.

[d] Lit., "he sent leanness among them."

[e] In this instance, the word "glory" likely functions as a metonym for YHWH. A similar usage appears in Jeremiah 2:11, "Has a nation changed its gods even though there are no gods? But my people have exchanged *their glory* for something that does not profit" (translation and emphasis mine). To make the metonym in Psalm 106:20 and Jeremiah 2:11 clear, the NIV renders the term "glorious God."

[f] As in verse 5, "heritage" refers to the people of God.

[g] Lit., "they subjected them under their hand."

[h] The people will glory in the "praise-worthy" acts of God.

Structure and Poetry

Although Psalm 106 is typically classified as one of the "historical psalms" in the Psalter (cf. 78; 105), this psalm contains elements of thanksgiving and praise, confession and penitence. The very structure of the psalm itself follows the general contours of Israel's history, but the chief emphasis falls on Israel's rebellious ways (as suggested below). The "body" of the psalm provides a theological rendering of Israel's history, yet on either side of the historical recital is the call to praise God (vv. 1b–5, 47–48b). Even further, the exclamation "Hallelujah" ("praise the Lord") stands as the first and last word in the psalm, perhaps suggesting that the proper posture for such remembering is a spirit of praise.

The psalm follows a very clear structure:

Hallelujah	v. 1a
Call to praise God	vv. 1b–5
Israel's sin in Egypt	vv. 6–12
Israel's sin on the way to Mt. Horeb	vv. 13–23
Israel's sin en route to the promised land	vv. 24–33
Israel's sin upon entrance into the promised land	vv. 34–46
Plea for deliverance and call to praise God	vv. 47–48b
Hallelujah	v. 48c

Theology and Application

Psalm 106 is the final psalm in Book 4 of the Psalter (Pss. 90–106). This section of the Psalter is well known for the psalms that explicitly announce the kingship of God (Pss. 93, 95–99). Israel's God is king of the cosmos (see Ps. 97) but also Israel's covenant partner. The final two psalms in Book 4 (Pss. 105–106) provide a recitation of Israel's history with a decidedly theological assessment of that covenantal relationship. Psalm 105 celebrates Israel's deliverance out of Egypt, focusing entirely on God's faithfulness to his people and the covenant that binds them together. Like Psalm 105, Psalm 106 provides a historical recital but this recitation moves in a markedly different direction. In each of the five stanzas, the psalmist recounts key episodes in Israel's historical narrative, beginning with Israel's deliverance out of Egypt and culminating with their arrival in the land. Yet this psalm does more than simply track Israel's travel. The psalmist gives considerable attention to the obstinate and rebellious spirit of God's people as they made their way to the promised land. The ancestors were rebuked for a myriad of rebellious acts: failing to remember the works of God in Egypt (v. 7); failing to trust in the plans of God (v. 13); exchanging their worship of the living God with the worship of a metal idol (vv. 19–20); yoking themselves to the Ba'al of Peor (v. 28); rebelling against the Spirit of God (v. 33); and sacrificing their sons and daughters to false gods (v. 37). This shocking and scandalous list demonstrates Israel's utter faith*less*ness to God and the covenant that binds them together. Whereas Psalm 105 goes to great lengths to highlight God's faith*full*ness, Psalm 106 goes to similar lengths to expose Israel's faith*less*ness. Yet what proves striking in Psalm 106 is not simply Israel's rebellion, but God's response. In each stanza the community confesses the failures of the ancestors, but it also acknowledges the faithfulness of God (vv. 8, 23, 30, 43–45). God responds to Israel's rebellion with faithfulness. Any attempt by Israel to abrogate the covenant is overridden by the inexplicable mercy expressed in God's faithfulness. It is because of God's faithfulness that the congregation can once more call out to God, "Save us" (v. 47), and it is because of God's faithfulness that the people conclude that God is deserving of praise forever and ever (v. 48).

For Those Who Sing Psalm 106

This psalm recalls Israel's past, a past that is dotted by episodes of rebellion and sinfulness. In many ways, this psalm invites us to remember our own brokenness and waywardness. And like our spiritual ancestors who sang this psalm, we too are invited to recall the ways in which God's faithfulness met us in our faith*less*ness. We would do well to remember both, because it is only in remembering both that a true spirit of praise will pour forth from our lips. And in such moments, our voices will join the psalmist in declaring, "Hallelujah, praise the Lord."

W. Dennis Tucker Jr.

O Praise the Lord for He Is Good

Psalm 106

Jerry Shipp

Rachel McInturff
harm. Randy Daw, arr. Ruth Ann Somervell

Restore Us, That We May Rejoice

Psalm 106

M. W. Bassford | C. E. Couchman

Restore Us, That We May Rejoice

Psalm 107

Translation

†1 Give thanks to the Lord, for he is good; his steadfast love endures forever.
*2 Let the redeemed of the Lord say so, those he has redeemed from the power of the foe,
*3 and from the lands he gathered them, from the east and from the west, from the north and from the sea.[a]

†4 They wandered through the desert wastelands; they did not find a city in which to dwell.
†5 Hungry and thirsty, they fainted in exhaustion.
*6 They cried out to the Lord in their trouble; he delivered them from their affliction,
*7 and he led them on a straight road so that they might find a city to dwell in.
*8 Let them give thanks to the Lord for his steadfast love and for his wonderful works for his people,[b]
*9 for he has satisfied those who are thirsty, and he has filled the hungry with good things.

†10 They sat in darkness and gloom, prisoners in affliction and iron shackles,
†11 because they had rebelled against the words of God, and they spurned the counsel of the Most High.
†12 He humbled their hearts with hard labor; they stumbled, and there was no one to help.
*13 They cried out to the Lord in their trouble; he delivered them from their affliction.
*14 He brought them out of darkness and gloom and tore off their shackles.
*15 Let them give thanks to the Lord for his steadfast love and for his wonderful works for his people,[c]
*16 for he shattered the doors of bronze and cut through the bars of iron.

†17 They were fools because of their sinful ways, and because of their iniquities they suffered affliction.
†18 They loathed any type of food and drew near[d] to the gates of death.
*19 They cried out to the Lord in their trouble; he delivered them from their affliction.
*20 He sent his word and healed them and delivered them from their pit.[e]

*[21] Let them give thanks to the LORD for his steadfast love and for his wonderful works for his people.[f]
*[22] Let them offer sacrifices of thanksgiving and with loud voice tell of his works.

†[23] They went down to the sea in ships to do business on the mighty waters.
†[24] They saw the acts of the LORD and his wondrous works in the deep.
†[25] He spoke and caused a stormy wind to rise up, which lifted up the waves of the sea.
†[26] They went up to the heavens, they went down to the depths; their courage[g] melted away in their calamitous circumstance.
†[27] They swayed and staggered like a drunken person, and all their wisdom was confused.
*[28] They cried out to the LORD in their trouble; he brought them out of their affliction.
*[29] He caused the storm to be calm,[h] and the waves of the sea were silenced.
*[30] Then they rejoiced because the waters were silent, and he led them to the safe harbor they desired.
*[31] Let them give thanks to the LORD for his steadfast love and for his wonderful works for his people.[i]
*[32] Let them extol him in the congregation of the people, and let them praise him in the assembly of the elders.

†[33] He turns rivers into a desert, springs of water into thirsty ground,
†[34] a fruitful land into a salty wasteland, because of the evil of its inhabitants.
†[35] He turns a desert into pools of water, a parched land into springs of water,
†[36] and there he allowed the hungry to dwell, and they established a city to live in.
*[37] They sowed fields and planted vineyards, which produced a harvest of fruit.
*[38] And he blessed them and they multiplied greatly; he does not let their cattle decrease.

†[39] When they were diminished and brought low because of oppression, calamity, and anguish,
†[40] he poured contempt upon princes and made them wander in a wasteland[j] with no path,
*[41] but he raised up the poor out of affliction and made their families like flocks.
*[42] The upright will see it and be glad, and every wicked person will shut his mouth.
*[43] Whoever is wise, let him give heed to these things, and let them consider the steadfast love of the LORD.

[a] The Hebrew reads *yām*, "sea," which admittedly sounds out of place given the three other directional points mentioned. As a remedy, the critical apparatus in the Biblia Hebraica Stuttgartensia (Hebrew text) proposes *ûmîyāmîn*, "from the south," and nearly all English translations follow this suggestion. That said, no Hebrew manuscript attests to this emendation, and the LXX, the Syriac Peshitta, and the Latin Vulgate all retain the Hebrew *yām* ("sea"). The Aramaic Psalms Targum

expands the verse to read "the southern sea," in an attempt to remain consistent with the Hebrew text while also providing an explanatory note. The term may function as a double entendre of sorts in this psalm. The reference to the sea may be driven by the contents of the third stanza (vv. 23–32) and the threat associated with the sea. On a more figurative level, the term appears throughout the Psalter and much of the Old Testament, functioning often as a metaphor for chaos (e.g., Pss. 33:7; 65:7; 74:13). The reference to the "north" (*ṣāpôn*) might also be understood as a double entendre. Clearly the term can mean a specific direction, but the north (*ṣāpôn*) is also associated with the disruptive forces of chaos. To limit the interpretation of verse 3c to a geographic understanding alone fails to capture the full range of meanings possible. The people are to give thanks to the Lord because he has gathered them from the lands but also from places that have unleashed chaos into the lives of God's people.

[b] Although the Hebrew reads "sons of man," the focus is not on humanity in general, but on God's people. God's deliverance of them should manifest itself in thanksgiving.

[c] See note b.

[d] The Hebrew verb "draw near" (*nāga'*) can also mean "to touch" perhaps creating a spatial image of the psalmist's proximity to death.

[e] The Biblia Hebraica Stuttgartensia suggests that the Hebrew term *miššəḥîtôtām*, "from their pits," be divided into *miššḥat ḥayyātām*, "their life from the pit." Because pit is synonymous with death and the threat to life, the two translations are functionally equivalent.

[f] See note b.

[g] The Hebrew word is *nefeš*, which can mean "soul," "life," or "being," but in this instance, the notion of "courage" appears preferable.

[h] Lit., "he raised the storm to stillness." This verse reverses the imagery found in verse 25 where God raises up the stormy wind.

[i] See note b.

[j] The word for "wasteland" (*tohû*) is the same word that appears in Genesis 1:2 describing the chaotic, uncreated condition of the earth. It is to this kind of existence that the princes are assigned.

Structure and Poetry

The structure of the psalm includes an introduction (vv. 1–3), followed by four sections of uneven length (vv. 4–32), but with two common refrains. In each perilous situation described, once the people realized they have no hope, the psalmist recounts: "Then they cried to the Lord in their trouble, and he delivered them from their distress" (vv. 6, 13, 19, 28). Following an assurance of deliverance, the psalmist invites them to thank God for his steadfast love for his people. The repetition of both themes in each section creates a rich theological confession in this psalm. Following these four scenes, verses 33–41 serve as a hymn meant to praise the power of God at work in all aspects of creation on behalf of his people. The psalm concludes with an exhortation for the wise to consider the lessons in this psalm.

Theology and Application

Psalm 107 responds in part to the theological crisis precipitated by the Babylonian exile. The exile resulted in not only physical and economic devastation that led to considerable human suffering, but it also threatened to undercut many of Israel's foundational theological claims concerning God and his relationship with his people. So great was the trauma associated with those events that the people pondered whether God had rejected them forever in the book of Lamentations

(5:22). In response to this theological crisis, the psalmist affirms God's faithful commitment to his people. The steadfast love of God functions as the foundational theme for the entire psalm. The people are called to give thanks for the steadfast love of God in verse 1 and then throughout the four scenes (vv. 4–32), the community is asked to testify to the steadfast love of God in light of their deliverance (vv. 8, 15, 21, 31). The psalm concludes by defining the wise as those who consider the steadfast love of God (v. 43).

Following the opening celebration of the steadfast love of God in Psalm 107, the psalmist implores those redeemed by Yahweh (v. 2a) to give thanks because he has gathered them from the lands (v. 3a), that he has in fact responded to the plea uttered in Psalm 106:47. The testimony in 107:3 counters any claim that their sin has reduced them to a people literally exiled from the land forever, or worse yet, a people exiled from their God. Instead, the psalmist claims that from the east to the west, God's reach extends in pursuit of his people and that neither human threats from the "north" (*ṣāpôn*) nor the chaotic waters of the sea (*yām*) can cut short that reach. The four scenes in Psalm 107 give graphic testimony to the incomprehensible reach of God as a result of his steadfast love.

In addition to the repeated call to give thanks for the steadfast love of God, the psalmist also recalls the faithfulness of God to respond to the cries of his people. To cry out to God is to invoke memories of a redeeming God who has faithfully responded to the cries of his people before and to believe that this God is inclined to do so again because of his steadfast love.

For Those Who Sing Psalm 107

By their very nature, thanksgiving psalms are instructive. The psalm concludes with an invitation for the wise to reflect upon the lessons outlined in this psalm. Repeatedly, the psalmist reminds those who pray this psalm that God has heard the cry of his people, and because of his steadfast love, he has acted on their behalf to bring deliverance. God's actions in the past shape our hope for the future. The God who heard the cry of his people before will hear our own cries, and the steadfast love that brought redemption then will surely be the foundation of our hope for the future.

W. Dennis Tucker Jr.

They Cried Out to the Lord

Psalm 107:2-15

Brad Cawyer

Konstantin Zhigulin

So let them sing out thanks for his un - fail - ing
let them sing out thanks for his un - fail - ing love, for
love; praise to our God a - bove.
all that he has done, praise to our God a - bove.
a tempo
Sac - ri - fic - es of praise we bring un - to our Lord.
Let all pro - claim his ho - ly name!

Give Thanks to Jehovah for He Is Good

Psalm 107

Mark Shipp and Jerry Shipp | Ruth Ann Somervell

Give Thanks to Jehovah for He Is Good

Give Thanks to Jehovah for He Is Good

Psalm 108

Translation

A song. A psalm of David.

†1 My heart is resolved,[a] O God. I will sing and make melody; indeed, you are my glory.[b]
*2 Awake, O harp and lyre! I will awaken the dawn.
†3 I will give you thanks among the peoples, O Lord, and I will praise you among the nations.
*4 For your steadfast love is higher than the heavens; your faithfulness reaches to the clouds.

†5 Rise up over the heavens, O God! Let your glory be over all the earth!
*6 So that your beloved ones may be delivered, save with your right hand and answer me.

†7 God has spoken in his sanctuary, "I will triumph; I will parcel out Shechem; I will measure out the valley of Succoth.
†8 Gilead is mine; Manasseh is mine; and Ephraim is the helmet of my head; Judah is my scepter.
†9 Moab is my washbasin; against Edom I will hurl my shoe; I will shout in triumph over Philistia."

†10 Who can bring me into the fortified city? Who can lead me to Edom?
†11 Have you not rejected us, O God? You did not go out, O God, with our armies.

*12 Grant us help against the foe, for human help is futile.
*13 With God we shall do mightily; he will tread down our foes.

[a] The Hebrew term (*nākôd*) is sometimes translated as "steadfast," but the root means to be "established" or "to be firm." In this instance, the psalmist is resolute or resolved to call upon God, particularly given the presumed struggle mentioned in verses 10–13.

[b] A number of English translations emend *kəbôdî*, "my glory," to read *kəbēdî*, "my liver," understanding the latter term to refer to the seat of emotions, hence "with my whole heart" or "with all my soul" (NIV). In Psalm 3:3, however, Yahweh is referred to by the psalmist as *kəbôdî*, "my glory," and similar to Psalm 108, the psalmist in Psalm 3 was surrounded by threats. See also a similar use of "glory" in Psalm 106:20.

Structure and Poetry

In Psalm 108, two earlier psalms, Psalm 57:7–11 (an individual psalm of thanksgiving) and Psalm 60:5–12 (a communal lament), have been joined together to create a new composite psalm. The psalmist, however, did much more than simply "cut and paste" from earlier psalms. To the contrary, the psalmist adopted and adapted the earlier psalms to create a theological confession for the community.

Close attention to the structure of the psalm reveals the argument being constructed in the psalm. In the first strophe (vv. 1–4), the psalmist offers a song of praise celebrating the love (*ḥesed*) of God that extends "higher than the heavens." In the second strophe (vv. 5–6), the psalmist pleads with Yahweh to demonstrate his glory cosmically and, in so doing, to bring deliverance to his people. The third strophe (vv. 7–9) contains a divine oracle in which God, as the divine warrior, declares a coming military triumph. The shift to interrogative questions in verses 10 and 11 indicates another strophe in the psalm. In these verses, the psalmist pleads for Yahweh to act on behalf of the people in their struggles with Edom (and the nations writ large). The psalm closes with a communal plea for God to deliver his people from the foes (vv. 12–13).

Theology and Application

Although Psalm 108 comprises two former psalms, as noted above, the psalm does possess a certain sense of unity. A common thread is woven throughout all five strophes. In each strophe, the word for "God" (*'ĕlōhîm*) appears. It is found in the first line of each of the first three strophes and appears twice in verse 11 in response to the questions raised in that strophe. In the final strophe of the psalm (vv. 12–13), *'ĕlōhîm* is the first word in verse 13. The frequent use of *'ĕlōhîm* throughout suggests that the psalm is thoroughly theocentric in orientation, driving us to consider what the psalmist is confessing about Israel's God.

In the final two strophes of the psalm (vv. 10–13), the psalmist suggests that the life of the community remains under threat from enemies and foes. Despite this reality, however, the entire psalm demonstrates the psalmist's firm commitment to this God (v. 1). The psalmist begins the day singing to awaken the dawn in anticipation that God's steadfast love will unfold and be on demonstration (v. 6). Israel's God is not some regional deity, but instead is the one who is above the heavens and whose glory extends over all the earth. Deliverance is indeed possible for the community because *this* God is the God of Israel.

For Those Who Sing Psalm 108

Psalm 108 holds in tension the reality of the world and the certainty of our confession. Like many other psalms, this psalm acknowledges that human experience is far from idyllic and, at times, can border on the surreal as threats come from all sides. Yet we are not without hope. Our hope is in the steadfast love of God. And so, like the psalmist of old, we are to awaken the dawn with our songs as we live in anticipation of the unfolding of God's love in the brokenness of our existence.

W. Dennis Tucker Jr

Exalted Be Your Name, O God

Psalm 108

Glover Shipp (1927–2016) and Mark Shipp

Christiana Peterson
arr. Randy Daw

Ex - alt - ed be your name, O God,
Ex - alt - ed be your name, O God.
your glor - ies let us tell,
Your glor - ies let us tell,
that your be - lov - ed ones be saved; de - liv - er Is - ra - el.
that your be-lov-ed ones be saved;

Let Your Glory Be over the Earth, O Lord

Psalm 108

Brad Cawyer

Konstantin Zhigulin

Let Your Glory Be over the Earth, O Lord

Psalm 109

Translation

To the director of music. A psalm of David.

†1 O God of my praise, do not be silent.

†2 The wicked and deceitful have opened their mouths against me; they have spoken against me with a lying tongue.

†3 They have surrounded me with words of hate, and for no reason they have attacked me.

*4 In return for my friendship[a] they accuse me, but I continue to pray.

*5 They repaid me evil in place of good and hatred for my friendship.

†6 Appoint a wicked person against him, and let an accuser stand at his right hand.[b]

†7 When he is judged, may he be found guilty; may his prayers be counted as sin.

†8 May his days be few; may another take his position.

†9 May his children become orphans and his wife a widow.

†10 May his children wander about and beg; may they be driven[c] out of their ruined homes.

†11 May the creditor seize all that he owns; may strangers plunder his possessions.[d]

†12 May no one extend kindness to him, and may no one have compassion on his orphaned children.

†13 May his descendants be cut off; may their names be blotted out from the next generation.

†14 May the iniquity of his ancestors be remembered by the Lord; may the sins of his mother not be blotted out.

†15 Let their sins be before the Lord continually; may their memory be cut off from the earth,

*16 because he did not remember to show covenant loyalty, but instead pursued the poor, the needy, and the brokenhearted to their death.

†17 He loved to utter curses; may curses come upon him. He did not like to bless others, so may blessings be far from him.

†18 He clothed himself with curses like a garment; may they seep into his body like water and as oil into his bones.

†19 May the curse be like a garment one puts on or like a belt one wears continually.
†20 May this be the repayment of my accusers from the LORD, of those who speak evil of me.

*21 You, O sovereign LORD, help me for your name's sake; because your steadfast love is good, deliver me,
*22 for I am poor and needy, and my heart is pierced within me.
*23 Like a shadow at evening I am gone; I am shaken off like a locust.
*24 My knees are weak from fasting, and my body is gaunt, lacking fat.
*25 I am an object of scorn to my accusers; when they see me, they shake their heads.
*26 Help me, O LORD my God; save me according to your steadfast love.
*27 Let them know that this is your hand; you, O LORD, have done it.
*28 While they curse, you will bless! Let them arise and be put to shame, but your servant will rejoice.
†29 May my accusers be clothed in disgrace, and may they be wrapped like a robe in their own shame.
*30 With my mouth I will greatly confess[e] the LORD; I will praise him in the presence of the throng of worshipers.
*31 For he stands at the right hand of the needy, to save their lives from those who would condemn them.

[a] The verb *ʾāhab*, translated here as "friendship," means "to love." Frequently, this term can refer to covenant type relationships, whether between God and humans or humans and humans. The verse suggests that while the psalmist remained loyal to the relationship, the others did not.

[b] Although to stand at the right hand can have positive connotations, here the language invokes courtroom imagery. Both the wicked person and the accuser appear before the judge.

[c] The Hebrew reads *wədāršû*, "and they seek." While the verb *dāraš*, "to seek," appears to parallel nicely the previous verb *šāʾal*, "to ask," the resulting phrase is problematic. The LXX (Greek Septuagint) emends the verb to read *yəgoršû*, "let them be driven out."

[d] The Hebrew reads literally, "fruit of his labor."

[e] The Hebrew verb *yādâ* can mean "to praise, thank, or confess," as reflected in various translations. Here the psalmist promises to confess what he knows of God's redeeming work.

Structure and Poetry

Often termed an imprecatory or "cursing" psalm, this psalm employs language and imagery that appears to stand outside the bounds of what many readers would consider to be "appropriate" content for a prayer. As indicative of its treatment, or lack thereof, by Christians, Psalm 109 is one of the very few psalms that does not appear in the three-year lectionary cycle.

Structurally speaking, the psalm can be divided into three main strophes: verses 1–5, 6–20, and 21–31. It is generally agreed that the first and last sections of the psalm reflect the prayer of the psalmist. The speaker in the second strophe (vv. 6–20), however, remains a matter of some debate. In verses 1–5, the psalmist refers to the enemy using plural language ("they") and the psalmist returns to the use of plural language in verses 21–31. In the middle section, however, the enemy is referred to in the singular (i.e., "my enemy," v. 6). This shift in person has led some writers to contend that the middle section includes the charges leveled against the psalmist by the enemies. In other words, according to this interpretation verses 6–20 represent the words that the enemies used against the psalmist himself. This interpretation helps explain why the NRSV inserts the words, "They say" at the beginning of verse 6. In the Hebrew text, however, there is no introductory formula present in the text; the text simply begins with the imperative "appoint." Despite the troubling language in the second strophe, these verses are likely a series of curses spoken by the psalmist against the enemy.

Theology and Application

The rhetoric of Psalm 109 is a stumbling block for many readers. The explicit requests by the psalmist for God to destroy the enemy and make the enemy's family vulnerable leaves the modern reader uneasy at best, if not theologically flummoxed. Yet even in such a challenging psalm as this, the theological witness is rich.

In Psalm 109, the psalmist does not appeal to God because he believes that God is on his "side," nor does he appeal to God simply because he wants his enemy vanquished, if not completely destroyed. No, he lifts his voice in shrill prayer because he believes that God is a God of justice. In our world, we want to prove that we are in the right, that our argument trumps that of our opponents, that we can even exact vengeance in order to preserve our own honor. Yet the psalmist will have none of this. The psalmist implores God to act for the sake of God's name (v. 21). He asks that God act so that the workers of injustice will know that this is the work of God's hand (v. 27a), that he is the one who has done this (v. 27b). In short, this is not simply a prayer of someone who wants to be proven in the right; this is a prayer of a helpless person who wants nothing more than the God of justice to act and in so doing turn an upside-down world right side up—to create justice out of injustice.

While we are not privy to the circumstances that might have produced such an outpouring of pain, we do know that the psalmist feels helpless, utterly powerless, to change his situation. In the final strophe, the psalmist declares that he is "poor and needy," that his heart has been pierced through from the harangues of the enemy (vv. 1–5). We know that his life is ebbing away like the end of a day. And we know that physically his body has become weak and gaunt. That is not the picture of one capable of righting injustice or thwarting the ways of the godless; this is the image of one solely dependent upon the steadfast love of the God of justice.

For Those Who Sing Psalm 109

Psalm 109 confronts us with injustice, but for most people, our personal exposure to injustice is limited at best. Or put differently, few of us understand this psalm fully because few of us understand the impact of life-altering injustice. This psalm invites us into a world filled with injustice and invites us to join our voices with those weakened by injustice in calling out to God, the God of justice, and imploring him to turn an upside-down world right side up.

W. Dennis Tucker Jr.

For Your Sake

Psalm 109

Keith Lancaster — Keith Lancaster

For Your Sake

O Come to Save

Psalm 109

Matthew K. Porter

Matthew K. Porter

Psalm 110

Translation

A psalm of David.

†1 The LORD says to my lord, "Sit at my right hand until I make your enemies as a footstool for your feet."

*2 The LORD will stretch forth the power of your scepter from Zion; rule in the midst of your enemies.

*3 Your troops will be willing on the day you demonstrate your power.[a] In holy array, at sunrise, like dew your youth will come to you.

†4 The LORD has sworn and will not change his mind: "You are a priest forever in the manner of Melchizedek."

*5 The Lord is at your right hand; he has shattered kings in the day of his wrath.

*6 He will execute judgment against the nations, filling them with corpses; he will shatter heads over the wide earth.

*7 He will drink from the river by the way; therefore he will lift up his head.

[a] The psalmist is likely referring to battle or war (cf. NIV).

Structure and Poetry

Psalm 110 is typically classified as a royal psalm and understandably so. Royal imagery appears throughout the psalm, including references to footstools, scepters, battle, nations, kings, and rulers, imagery that is found in other royal psalms as well (e.g., Pss. 2, 18, 20, 21, 72, 101). The role of the king, and the divine king in particular, dominates the psalm. Although a human king or ruler is mentioned in verse 1, it is the divine king who serves as the principal figure in the psalm—he is the one who makes enemies a footstool, shatters kings, and executes judgment on the nations.

The structure of Psalm 110 provides further guidance in understanding the psalm. The psalm can be divided into two strophes (vv. 1–3, 4–7). Divine speech is recorded in the first verse of each strophe (vv. 1, 4), followed by verses that offer further commentary on the declaration of Yahweh. What unites both sections, however, is their common theme announcing the destruction of the king's enemies by Yahweh himself. For some, such rhetoric may prove theologically problematic (i.e., Yahweh's involvement in the destruction of others); but before the contemporary reader jettisons the psalm entirely due to that kind of rhetoric, the reader must realize that the psalmist is actually making a fundamental claim regarding Yahweh and his governance of the world.

Theology and Application

Psalm 110 focuses on the theme of God and his anointed in the midst of a hostile world. Like many psalms, this psalm speaks candidly about enemies and powers that resist the ways of God. Their continued opposition suggested that all was not right with the world; the enemies and nations were a constant threat, both literally and theologically. The continued presence of such hostile forces could have thwarted Israel's theological confession about Yahweh and his reign in the world, perhaps even leading them to wonder, "If there are still enemies, then perhaps God is less than we thought." The psalmist, however, rejected any such claim and instead moved in a very different direction. While the psalmist recognized those forces that threaten God's vision for the world, he also held firmly to the conviction that Yahweh was still king, and because he is king, the enemies will be vanquished. Israel's acknowledgment of a hostile world is always countered by their certainty of the kingship of God. One is as real as the other, but in the end, only one prevails.

For Those Who Sing Psalm 110

In the world in which we live today, power abounds; political, financial, and religious power threaten to unseat our vision of God's kingdom. Much like those who prayed Psalm 110 amid the threats of their day, we too may be inclined to wonder if "God is less than we thought." We may wonder whether God has the capacity to exact his divine rule over the world. We may wonder whether God can and will overcome such powers. In the face of such questions, Psalm 110 does more than simply remind us of the kingship of God; this psalm invites us to place our trust in the divine king, and even more, to trust that the divine king will act. Of that we can be sure because "The Lord has sworn" to it.

W. Dennis Tucker Jr.

The Lord Said to My Lord

Psalm 110

Mark Shipp and Randy Daw (1954–2019) Mark Shipp and Randy Daw (1954–2019)

Sit at My Right Hand

Psalm 110

Jack R. Reese

Jack R. Reese

Sit at My Right Hand

Psalm 111

Translation

†1 Praise the Lord!

(א, *aleph*) I will give thanks to the Lord with all my heart,
(ב, *bet*) in the company of the upright and in the congregation.

*2 (ג, *gimel*) Great are the works of the Lord,
(ד, *dalet*) sought after by all who take pleasure in them.

†3 (ה, *he*) His work is full of splendor and majesty;
(ו, *waw*) his righteousness endures forever.

*4 (ז, *zayin*) He has made his marvelous deeds a memorial;
(ח, *het*) the Lord is gracious and merciful.

†5 (ט, *tet*) He provides food to those who fear him;
(י, *yod*) he remembers his covenant forever.

*6 (כ, *kaph*) He has made known to his people the power of his works,
(ל, *lamed*) giving them the possession of the nations.

†7 (מ, *mem*) The works of his hands are faithful and just;
(נ, *nun*) all of his precepts are trustworthy.

*8 (ס, *samek*) They are sustained forever and ever,
(ע, *ayin*) to be performed with faithfulness and uprightness.

†9 (פ, *pe*) He sent redemption to his people;
(צ, *tsade*) he commanded his covenant forever;
(ק, *qoph*) holy and fearsome is his name.

*10 (ר, *resh*) The fear of the Lord is the beginning of wisdom;
(שׂ, *sin*) all who practice *his precepts*[a] have good understanding;
(ת, *taw*) his praise endures forever.

[a] The Hebrew literally reads "all who practice *them*."

Structure and Poetry

Psalm 111 begins and ends with praise to the Lord ("Hallelujah," v. 1,[3] and "his praise endures forever," v. 10). Structurally, the song unfolds as an acrostic, each line beginning with a successive letter of the Hebrew alphabet (twenty-two letters from *aleph* to *taw*; i.e., from "a" to "z"). The movement through verse eight occurs in couplets, the second line developing or restating the thought of the first. For example, "He has made known to his people the power of his works" is completed with "giving them the possession of the nations" (v. 6). The last two verses contain three lines, with the addition of declarative statements about the LORD: "holy and fearsome is his name" (v. 9) and "his praise endures forever" (v. 10).

Theology and Application

Apparently composed to be read with the following psalm (also an acrostic), Psalm 111 centers on the character of the LORD, while Psalm 112 focuses on the righteous who fear him. At the same time, the psalmist also addresses the upright in Psalm 111, with movement in the song toward those who fear him and practice his precepts (vv. 8, 10). This psalm is often labeled a wisdom psalm. The phrase in verse 10, "The fear of the LORD is the beginning of wisdom . . ." especially links this psalm with the book of Proverbs (cf. Prov. 1:7; 9:10; 30:3). With the emphasis in the psalm on the nature and character of the Lord, in fact, it is almost as if Psalm 111 further develops the thought in Proverbs 9:10 that "knowledge of the Holy One is insight" (NRSV) by reiterating the attributes of God that make him worthy of praise.

The Lord and his works are described directly and indirectly as great, full of splendor and majesty, righteous, marvelous, gracious, merciful, powerful, faithful, just, trustworthy, holy, to be feared, and worthy of praise. With an emphasis on what he has done, the Lord also emerges as one who causes his works to be remembered, provides sustenance, remembers his covenant, shows his power in his works, and sends redemption to his people. In addition, the psalmist portrays the Lord as unchangeable and therefore trustworthy by repeating the word "forever" (vv. 3, 5, 8, 10). One can always rely on the God of Israel.

Nevertheless, the wise do not just have knowledge of him. They fear (v. 10) the one whose name is "holy and to be feared" (v. 9) and faithfully obey. To emphasize this thought, the psalmist creatively employs the related words "work" and "to do" (*ma'aseh*, vv. 2, 6, 7, and *'asah*, v. 4) to call attention to what God has done and then uses the verb "to do" for the righteous who are "to perform" (*'asah*, v. 8) his precepts and "practice" (*'asah*, v. 10) wisdom.

[3]Like a superscription, "Hallelujah" in verse 1 is preliminary to the body of the psalm.

For Those Who Sing Psalm 111

Christians today who sing this psalm can with Mary in the *Magnificat* and with Zechariah in the *Benedictus* praise the Lord in his might who has "done great things" for us (Luke 1:49 NIV) and who has "redeemed his people" (Luke 1:68 KJV); however, to appreciate completely what the author of the psalm is expressing, one must recognize that the truly wise not only praise the LORD—they also perform and practice his precepts.

Jesse Long

Among the Faithful I Will Sing

Psalm 111

an alphabetic acrostic

Joseph Martin | Joseph Martin

Assemble the Righteous

Psalm 111

an alphabetic acrostic

Jerry Shipp — Ruth Ann Somervell

Assemble the Righteous

I Will Give Thanks to God with All My Heart

Psalm 111

Sarah Shipp — Ruth Ann Somervell

Psalm 112

Translation

†1 Praise the Lord!

(א, *aleph*) Blessed is the man who fears the Lord,
(ב, *bet*) who intensely takes pleasure in his commandments.

*2 (ג, *gimel*) His descendants will be mighty in the land;
(ד, *dalet*) the generation of the upright will be blessed.

†3 (ה, *he*) Wealth and riches are in his house,
(ו, *waw*) and his righteousness endures forever.

*4 (ז, *zayin*) Light dawns in the darkness for the upright;
(ח, *het*) he is gracious, merciful, and righteous.

†5 (ט, *tet*) Good comes to the man who is generous and who lends liberally,
(י, *yod*) who manages his affairs with justice.

*6 (כ, *kaph*) Because he will never be shaken,
(ל, *lamed*) the righteous will be a memorial forever.

†7 (מ, *mem*) He is not afraid of bad news;
(נ, *nun*) his heart is steadfast, trusting in the Lord.

*8 (ס, *samek*) His heart is sustained; he will not fear,
(ע, *ayin*) until he looks in triumph on his enemies.

†9 (פ, *pe*) He gives freely to the poor;
(צ, *tsade*) his righteousness endures forever;
(ק, *qoph*) his horn will be lifted high in honor.

*10 (ר, *resh*) The wicked man will see it and be angry;
(שׁ, *shin*) he grinds his teeth and despairs;
(ת, *taw*) the lust of the wicked will vanish.

Structure and Poetry

As the preceding psalm, Psalm 112 is constructed as an acrostic poem with eight couplets (vv. 1–8) and two triple-line cola (vv. 9–10). In each segment, the succeeding lines develop or restate the thought of the opening line. In verse 7, for example, "He is not afraid of bad news" is further developed with "his heart is steadfast, trusting in the Lord." "Hallelujah" in verse 1 functions as a preparatory exclamation which is followed by twenty-two lines that begin with successive letters of the Hebrew alphabet (see comments on Ps. 111).

Theology and Application

In the same way as in the foregoing song, Psalm 112 expresses wisdom themes. The contrast between the righteous and the wicked (vv. 9–10), for example, reflects a similar contrast in Proverbs (see, e.g., Prov. 10:3, 6–7, 11, 16, 20, 24–25, 28, 30, 32). With a broader stroke, however, the song also develops the thought of Psalm 111, almost like the second line in a poetic couplet. Psalm 111 ends with the declaration that "The fear of the Lord is the beginning of wisdom" (v. 10), and then Psalm 112 opens with "Blessed is the man who fears the Lord" (v. 1). While the second song in this psalm couplet develops the theme of the character of the righteous who fears the Lord, resonance between the two psalms adds theological depth to the ideas expressed.

The echoes from Psalm 111 occur in phrases like "Who intensely *takes pleasure* in his commandments" (112:1; cf. "Sought after by all who *take pleasure* in them," 111:2) and "His heart is *sustained*" (112:8; cf. "They are *sustained* forever and ever," 111:8). The artistry in these comparisons and theological significance of the two psalms as a couplet emerge when the same language that was used to describe the Lord in Psalm 111 characterizes the righteous who fear him in Psalm 112. As the Lord is gracious, merciful, and just (111:4, 7), so too are the upright who fear him (112:4–5). Psalm 112 also maintains that the righteous lends freely and gives to the poor (vv. 5, 9), which must also characterize the God of Israel.

The psalmist secures the resonance between the two psalms by proclaiming of both the Lord and the upright, "His righteousness endures forever" (111:3; 112:3, 9). Moreover, "He has made his marvelous deeds a memorial (*zeker*)" (111:4) in concert with "The righteous will be a memorial (*zeker*) forever" (112:6) implies that the righteous one who fears the Lord is also the work of his hands.

For Those Who Sing Psalm 112

Those who sing this psalm in dialogue with Psalm 111 should be encouraged in knowing that the righteous embody God's divine character. When we are gracious, merciful, and just, we display wisdom from God. In addition to the words we sing, the righteous lives we live give glory to the God we worship and serve.

Jesse Long

In the Dwellings of the Righteous

Psalm 112

an alphabetic acrostic

Rachel Shipp | D. J. Bulls

The Upright One

Psalm 112

an alphabetic acrostic

Jerry Shipp — Mark Shipp and Randy Daw (1954–2019)

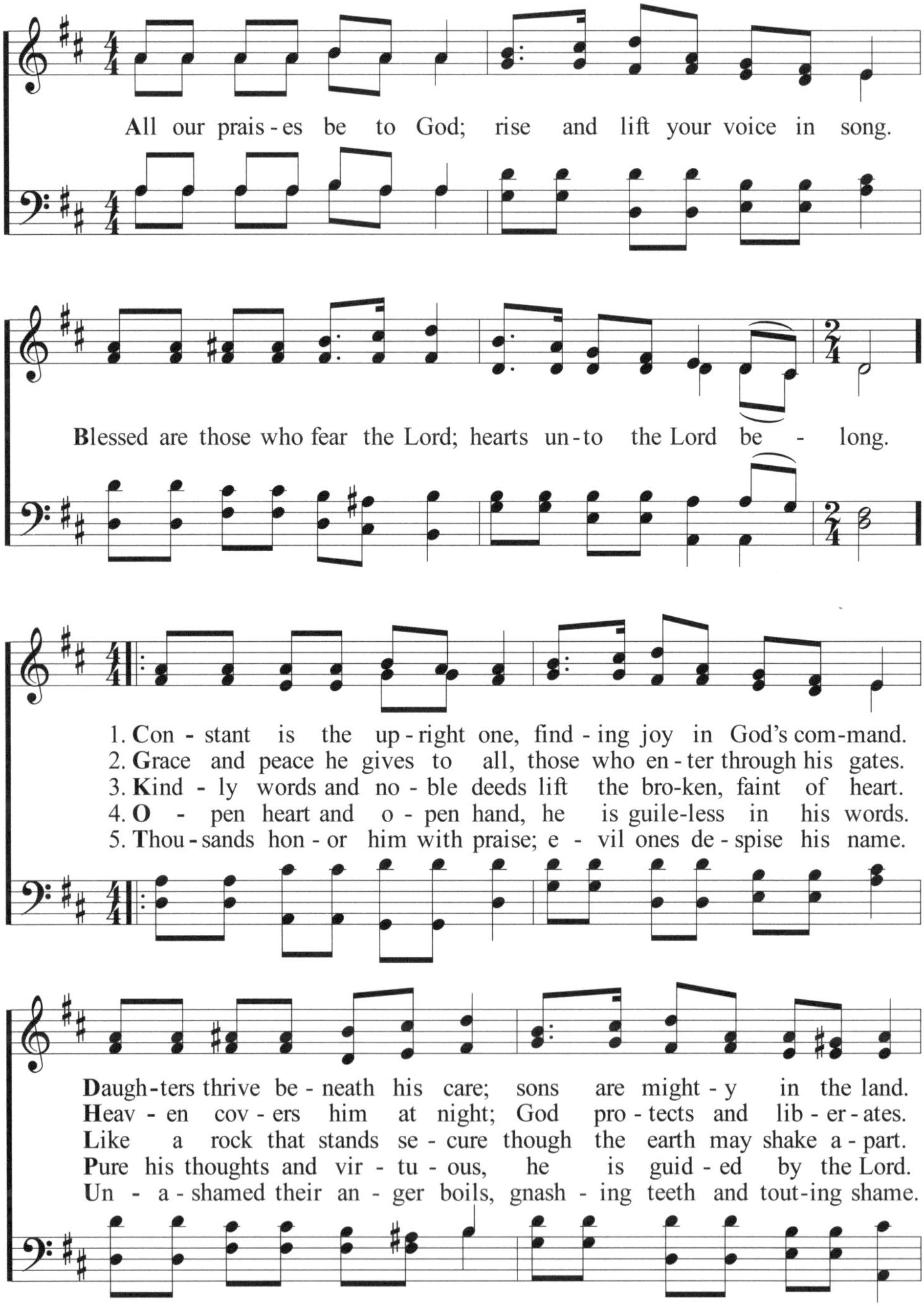

Each is blessed and gives with joy to all those who come for care.
In his house are grace and peace; all are safe who shel - ter there.
Man - y are his days on earth; right-eous-ness will be his guide.
Right-eous-ness his might - y shield, sav - ing him from eve - ry blow,
Vi - o - lence con-sumes their lives; hat - red spews with eve - ry breath.
Repeat for each verse
Fa - vor rests up - on his home— on the house-hold blessed with prayer.
Jus - tice guides his dai - ly path, gen - er - o - si - ty his care.
News of trou-ble brings no fear, for the Lord is at his side.
shel - ter-ing from storms of life, from the threats of eve - ry foe.
Wick-ed ones will dis - ap-pear, and their lives will end in death.
Last time only
Young ones, choose an up-right life; God will guide your steps a - right.

PSALM 113

Translation

†1 Praise the LORD!

† Praise, O servants of the LORD; praise the name of the LORD!
*2 Let the name of the LORD be blessed from this time forward
and forevermore.
*3 From the rising of the sun to its setting, let the name of the LORD be praised!

†4 The LORD rises high above all the nations, his glory above the heavens.
*5 Who is like the LORD our God, who dwells exalted on high,
*6 who humbles himself to look down on the heavens and the earth?

†7 From the dust he raises the poor; from the dung heap he lifts the needy,
*8 to make them dwell with princes, with the princes of his people.
*9 He makes the barren dwell in a house, the happy mother of children.

* Praise the LORD!

Structure and Poetry

Framed by the Hebrew imperative "Hallelujah!" (i.e., "Praise the LORD," vv. 1, 9), Psalm 113 emerges as a nine-line song of praise, each line with parallel segments, the second of which restates or develops the thought of the first. The nine lines thematically move in three stanzas from a call to praise the name of the Lord (vv. 1–3), and verses that extol the Lord as one who reigns on high and looks down on the earth (vv. 4–6), to lines that exalt him as one who lifts up the poor (vv. 7–9). He even makes the barren woman a mother of children (v. 9). In the Psalter, Psalm 113 opens the Psalms of *Hallel* (i.e., the "Psalms of Praise," Pss. 113–118), which are recited at all major Jewish festivals. In the Passover *seder*, the *Hallel* (called the Egyptian *Hallel* in that context) extols the God of Israel for what he has done to deliver God's people from slavery.

Theology and Application

The opening stanza (vv. 1–3) emphasizes "the name of the LORD," a phrase that occurs in each of the first three verses. While the divine name Yahweh (i.e., "LORD") occurs six times, all in the first half of the psalm (vv. 1[2x], 2, 3, 4, 5), the three-fold repetition of "the name of the LORD" resonates with the priestly blessing of Numbers 6:24–26, in which God's name is recited three times. In verses 2–3 of the psalm, blessing and praise to his name are connected in a concentric pattern: A) "Let the name of the LORD be blessed," B) "From this time forward and forevermore," B') "From the rising of the sun to its setting," A') "Let the name of the LORD be praised!" In the verse following the blessing in Numbers, the Lord informs Moses that in this way the sons of Aaron would put his name on the people of Israel (v. 27). For an implied audience, Psalm 113 begins with a call to praise the one whose name they wear, who in a covenant relationship has promised to bless them with his presence.

The central, second stanza contains the question of the psalm: "Who is like the LORD our God . . . ?" (vv. 5–6). Reminiscent of a similar query in the Song of Moses, which then lauds the God of Israel as "majestic in holiness, awesome in splendor, doing wonders" (Exod. 15:11 NRSV), Psalm 113 moves in another direction. Anticipating that move, the psalmist in verses 5–6 describes the Lord as one who "is seated on high/exalted" and who "looks far down/humbles himself," verbs that elsewhere convey raising up the lowly and bringing low the haughty (e.g., Ps. 18:28; Isa. 13:11; 26:5; Ezek. 17:24; 21:26[31]).

In the final stanza, the psalmist calls attention to how the Lord of Israel lifts up the poor and needy, even the barren. Calling attention to divine initiative, the word "dwell" ties the last two stanzas together. The one who *dwells* on high (v. 5) lifts up the poor to *dwell* with princes (v. 8) and makes the barren *dwell* in a house (v. 9). Resonance with Hannah's song, where verses 7–8a are a verbatim quotation of 1 Samuel 2:8a–b, conjures up the image of the distraught consort, cowering in shame without progeny, who petitions the God of Israel. She is then raised up to bear a son who will sit on a seat of honor with, and even anoint, princes in Israel. In the larger story, Mary epitomizes Hannah (note the allusions to Hannah/Samuel in the birth narratives in Luke; cf., e.g., 1 Sam. 1:10–11/Luke 1:13, 38; 1 Sam. 2:21, 26/Luke 1:80; 2:40, 52). In the Magnificat, Mary (with Hannah, 1 Sam. 2:1–8) verbalizes the divine reversal of Psalm 113 when she sings, "My soul magnifies the Lord, and my spirit rejoices in God my savior, for he has looked with favor on the lowliness of his servant. . . . He has brought down the powerful from their thrones, and lifted up the lowly" (Luke 1:46–48, 52 NRSV).

Psalm 113 ends where it began, in praise (v. 9); however, in this song the God of Israel is praised not because he *rises above* but, instead, because he *raises up*!

For Those Who Sing Psalm 113

Christians who sing Psalm 113 praise the Lord not only because he is an awesome, magnificent, and transcendent God who dwells on high. With Hannah, Mary, and the congregation of the righteous, we magnify the Lord our God because in Jesus he has come down and raised us up to one day dwell with him in glory.

Jesse Long

Arise

Psalm 113

Jack R. Reese

Jack R. Reese

glo - ry reigns a - bove cre - a - tion. All praise to him who
dwells ex - alt - ed on high.
A - rise, O peo - ple, from your bro - ken - ness.
God in glo - rious grace has cho - sen us, seized our hearts and
grants us glo - ry on high. A - rise!
3

Who Is Like Our God?

Psalm 113

Gary Pendergrass | Gary Pendergrass

Who Is Like Our God?

Psalm 114

Translation

†1 When Israel came out from Egypt, the house of Jacob from a people who spoke a foreign language,
†2 Judah became his sanctuary, Israel his dominion.

*3 The sea looked and fled; the Jordan turned back.
*4 The mountains skipped like rams, the hills like lambs.

†5 Why, O sea, do you flee? O Jordan, that you turn back?
†6 O mountains, that you skip like rams? O hills, like lambs?

*7 Tremble, O earth, at the presence of the Lord, at the presence of the God of Jacob,
*8 the one who turns the rock into a pool of water, the flint into a spring of water.

Structure and Poetry

The psalmist in Psalm 114[4] has composed an eight-line song (each line characterized by parallel segments) with rich imagery. The psalm poetically recalls events surrounding the Exodus by personifying "sea" as one who turns back, the "mountains" as "skipping like rams," and "the hills like lambs." These images recall the parting of the Jordan, and before that the "reed" sea (Josh. 3–4; Exod. 14–15), and the quaking of Sinai at the giving of the Law (Exod. 19–20; cf. Ps. 29:6). The overall structure of the psalm displays a concentric pattern, the center of which in parallel statements (vv. 3–4 and 5–6) describes and addresses the sea and the mountains. The framing verses (vv. 1–2, 7–8) proclaim that when Israel came out of Egypt, the land of Judah and Israel became the sanctuary and dominion of the God of Jacob, the God who miraculously sustained his people with water from a rock in the wilderness (Exod. 17:1–7; Deut. 8:15). At his presence the land should quake!

---

[4] While verses 1–8 are added to Psalm 115 and numbered as Psalm 113 in the Septuagint (LXX), Psalm 114 displays its own integrity and is better read as a separate psalm, as it appears in the Hebrew Masoretic text.

Theology and Application

One of the Psalms of *Hallel* which are read as part of the Passover *seder* ritual (see comments on Ps. 113), this psalm directly refers to the Exodus of Israel from slavery in Egypt (v. 1). The allusions to the parting of the Jordan at the entrance into Canaan, to the quaking of the mountains of Sinai at the presence of God, and to the miracle of bringing water from a rock in the wilderness recreate the supremacy and power of the God of Jacob. An original audience viewed "sea" as a deity (e.g., Yām who in Canaanite mythology was defeated by Ba'al) and mountainous areas as the realm of the gods (e.g., Ba'al of Mt. *Sapan*, modern Jebel Aqra, north of ancient Ugarit, modern Ras Shamra, Syria). With this language, the psalmist conjures up the image of the God of Israel as a divine warrior who led Israel against the nations and their gods to give them the land of Canaan. In terms of Israelite identity, the framing verses (vv. 1–2, 7–8) assert that the presence of this God means that Judah and Israel are the temple and dominion of the warrior God who delivers and sustains. Those who are not under his dominion should tremble (cf. Deut. 2:25).

References to the Exodus resonate with passages in the book of Isaiah which anticipate a second Exodus. Through the prophet, alluding to the Exodus, the Lord describes himself as one who "makes a way in the sea, a path in the mighty waters" who "will make a way in the wilderness and rivers in the desert. . . . For I give water in the wilderness, rivers in the desert, to give drink to my chosen people" (43:16, 19–20 NRSV; cf. Pss. 77:17; 78:15–16, 20; 105:41). In a direct parallel to Psalm 114, the Lord also says, "I will open rivers on the bare heights, and fountains in the midst of the valleys; I will make the wilderness *a pool of water*, and the dry land *springs of water*" (Isa. 41:18 NRSV, italics added; cf. 35:7; 48:21; Ps. 107:35). For Isaiah, the God of Israel would lead his people again from the waters of Exodus and give them water to drink in the wilderness. Through the gospel witness about Jesus,[5] Psalm 114 foreshadows the coming divine warrior who in a Moses-like second Exodus would deliver God's people from demonic powers, free them from the bondage of sin and death, and sustain them in the wilderness of life's trials.

The prophet Isaiah even petitions the Lord to "tear open the heavens and come down, so that the mountains would quake at your presence . . . . When you did awesome deeds that we did not expect, you came down, the mountains quaked at your presence" (64:1, 3 NRSV). As the very presence of God who has come to earth, Jesus redefines holiness from sacred place (cf. "sanctuary," Ps. 114:2) to sacred community, and authority (cf. "dominion," v. 2) from territory to hearts that are responsive to his reign.

---

[5]See, e.g., Sharyn Dowd, *Reading Mark: A Literary and Theological Commentary on the Second Gospel* (Macon, GA: Smyth & Helwys, 2000).

For Those Who Sing Psalm 114

When singing Psalm 114, Christians today as God's people remember the God who delivered us from slavery in Egypt, sustained us in the desert, led us into the land of promise, and through his death released us from the power of sin and death to new life in his presence as he reigns in our hearts. In this, we bow before him and sing with joy!

Jesse Long

Steeped in Mercy

Psalm 114

Kelly Cavender

Kelly Cavender

When Israel Departed from Egypt

Psalm 114

Mark Shipp | N. Lincoln Hanks

Psalm 115

Translation

*1 Not to us, O Lord, not to us, but to your name give glory, because of your
steadfast love and your faithfulness!
†2 Why should the nations say, "Where is their God?"
†3 Our God is in the heavens. He does whatever pleases him.

†4 Their idols are silver and gold, the work of human hands.
†5 They have mouths, but they do not speak; eyes, but they do not see.
†6 They have ears, but they do not hear; noses, but they do not smell.
†7 They have hands, but they do not touch; feet, but they do not walk. They
cannot make a sound in their throats.
†8 The ones who make them become like them, as are all who trust in them.

*9 O Israel, trust in the Lord! He is their help and their shield.
*10 O house of Aaron, trust in the Lord! He is their help and their shield.
*11 Those who fear the Lord, trust in the Lord! He is their help and
their shield.

†12 The Lord remembered us; he will bless us![a] He will bless the house of Israel.
He will bless the house of Aaron.
*13 He will bless those who fear the Lord, both the small and the great.
*14 May the Lord give you increase, both you and your children.
*15 May you be blessed by the Lord, the maker of heaven and earth.

†16 The heavens are the Lord's heavens, but the earth he has given to the children of mankind.
*17 The dead do not praise the Lord, nor all those who go down into the place
of silence.
*18 But we will bless the Lord, from this time forward and forevermore.

* Praise the Lord!

[a] The reading "bless us" corresponds with the Greek Septuagint (LXX). The object pronoun is missing in the Hebrew text.

Structure and Poetry

Another of the Psalms of *Hallel* (see comments on Pss. 113–14), Psalm 115 contrasts the God of Israel with the idols of the nations. The psalm is organized in five stanzas, in what can be read as a concentric arrangement. The framing verses (vv. 1–3 and 16–18) claim that the God of Israel lives in the heavens, evoking praise to the name of the Lord. The inside ring (vv. 4–8 and 12–15) contrasts the idols of the nations—which as objects created by humans cannot speak or even utter a sound—with the God of Israel who remembers and blesses his people. At the center of the psalm (vv. 9–11) the psalmist calls on Israel to trust in the Lord.

Theology and Application

Psalm 115 maintains that the God of Israel, the maker of heaven and earth, lives in the heavens where he does what he pleases. In contrast with the lifeless gods of the nations, the Lord blesses Israel, all who fear him. The description of idols (vv. 4–8) mirrors a similar portrayal in Psalm 135:15–18, a psalm which also maintains that the Lord does whatever he pleases (135:6). The caricature of idols and those who trust in them (vv. 4–8) also resonates with Isaiah 44:9–20, which mocks those who make and worship idols: "All who make idols are nothing, and the things they delight in do not profit" (v. 9 NRSV).

The contrast between the lifeless gods who cannot speak and the Lord who does as he pleases undergirds the threefold assertion that the God of Israel blesses the house of Israel, the house of Aaron (i.e., the priests), and all who fear him (vv. 12–13). This leads into the blessing of verses 14–15, an entreaty for the creator of heaven and earth to bless his people (cf. Num. 6:22–27). The contrast between the speechless idols and the creator frame a call for the house of Israel, the house of Aaron, and all who fear him to trust the Lord, their help and shield (vv. 9–11; cf. Ps. 33:20).

The worldview expressed in verse 17, that the dead who in *Sheol* (the realm of the underworld, a place of silence) cannot praise him (cf. Ps. 88:10–12), puts an exclamation on the contrast between those who make and trust in idols and become like them (v. 8) and those who trust in the Lord. Those who trust in lifeless idols are as dead men, unable to praise the maker of heaven and earth. With the repetition of the divine name *Yahweh/Yah* (i.e., LORD, twelve times), the psalm also enacts the opening overture—that because of his steadfast love and faithfulness, the name of the Lord deserves honor (v. 1). The moving initial words, "Not to us, O LORD, not to us" (v. 1), poignantly capture the song's theological declaration in poetry. Created objects—by extension including human beings—do not merit worship or praise. Fittingly, the psalm closes with praise, with blessing for the Lord "from this time forward and forevermore." With these words of benediction, the psalm becomes a call for God's people of every generation to worship their creator. Hallelujah!

For Those Who Sing Psalm 115

Psalm 115 calls singers today to worship not ourselves or the work of our hands but the creator of heaven and earth. He is our help and shield, the one who remembers and blesses, the one in whom we trust. Through the lens of Psalm 115, we sing not solely "Trust and Obey" (John H. Sammis, 1887), but "Trust, obey, and *praise* the name of the Lord our God!"

Jesse Long

Not to Us, O Lord

Psalm 115

Jerry Shipp

Debbie Dorman

Not to Us, O Lord

To Your Name May Glory Be Given

Psalm 115

Mel Witcher | Mel Witcher

Trust in the Lord, all God's peo - ple, for he is our hope and our shield!
All those who fear him, now trust him, for he is our help and our shield!
Yes, he is our help and our shield.

Psalm 116

Translation

†1 I love the Lord because the Lord hears my voice, my pleas,
*2 because he inclines his ear to me, and throughout my days I will keep calling on him.

†3 Death's bands had wrapped around me; the torments of *Sheol* had found me; I kept encountering anguish and grief.

*4 But I cried out in the Lord's name, "Please, Lord, rescue my life!"

*5 The Lord is gracious and just. Our God is one who shows tender compassion.
†6 The Lord is the protector of the naïve! I was abased but he saved me!
*7 Return, O my soul, to your repose, because the Lord replenished you,
*8 for you reclaimed my soul from death, my eyes from tears, my feet from stumbling.
*9 I will walk freely in the Lord's presence in the land of the living.

†10 I trusted even while saying, "I am severely oppressed,"
†11 though I even said in my alarm, "Everyone is a liar!"
*12 What shall I repay to the Lord for all his generosity to me?
*13 I will raise the cup of salvation, and I will call on the Lord's name.
*14 I will fulfill my vows to the Lord. I will do it in the sight of all his people.[a]
†15 The death of his faithful ones is weighty in the Lord's eyes.
†16 Oh, Lord, because I am your servant, because I am your servant, the son of your maidservant, you have opened my fetters.
*17 To you I will offer a thank offering, and I will call on the Lord's name.
*18 I will fulfill my vows to the Lord. I will do it in the sight of all his people,[a]
*19 in the courts of the Lord's house, in your midst, O Jerusalem.

* Praise the Lord!

[a] Reading with the suggestion in the apparatus of BHS. Note also that this verse is lacking in the Greek Septuagint (LXX). This applies also to this phrase's verbatim recurrence in verse 18. *Biblia Hebraica Stuttgartensia: with Werkgroep Informatica, Vrije Universiteit Morphology; Bible. O.T. Hebrew* (Werkgroep Informatica, Vrije Universiteit, 2006).

Structure and Poetry

Psalm 116 preserves the grateful praise of one who was spared from a life-threatening crisis. It bears all the marks of a thanksgiving psalm: opening summary, recollection of the crisis, appeal to God for help, description of deliverance, vows, and praise. Psalm 116 adheres fairly closely to this pattern, dividing into the following six sections.

Opening summary (vv. 1–2)
Recollection of the crisis (v. 3)
Appeal to God for help (v. 4)
Description of deliverance (vv. 5–9)
Vows (vv. 10–19a)
Praise (v. 19b)

The joyful relief the psalmist expresses, while conforming to traditional thanksgiving hymns, cannot quite be contained by their set structure. The various elements intermingle and even intrude on one another, giving the impression of excitement and spontaneity. For example, elements of praise interrupt the narrative of deliverance at key points (e.g., vv. 5–6, 9). Also, the psalmist's vows are derailed by invasive praise at vv. 15–16 only to be repeated in vv. 17–18 as if the psalmist, lost in the revelry of relief, suddenly remembered the train of thought and returned to the liturgical "script." The poetry, therefore, nicely balances the need for both order and spontaneity in worship.

The psalmist's description of the near-death experience is deliberately vague. Details are omitted in the interest of universalizing the psalm's appeal. Anyone who has ever been at death's door, by whatever means or for whatever reason, can relate to the psalmist's testimony. The lack of details, however, does not diminish the psalm's poignancy due to the strategic use of literary devices. The genuineness and palpability of the experience is captured by carefully crafted rhetoric. For example, the psalmist employs the imagery of bands and fetters to convey the sense of helplessness imposed by situations we can neither prevent nor rectify. The phrase "the bands of death" (v. 3) creates the impression of being tightly wrapped in a grave shroud as though being mummified alive.

A particularly powerful moment in the psalm occurs at verse 7, where the psalmist engages in a kind of soliloquy. Addressing his breath, which is still accelerated or perhaps frozen in fear, the psalmist calms himself. So sudden was the relief brought by the Lord's gracious intervention that the body's fight-or-flight response had not yet disengaged. The psalmist must convince himself that the crisis has truly abated, that life will go on thanks to God's salvation. As he processes what he has just experienced and audibly talks himself through it (something the psalms refer to as "meditation"), his breathing slowly returns to normal and his body relaxes.

This imagery continues into verse 8, though not as a soliloquy, where the psalmist addresses God in acknowledgment of his timely intervention. The psalmist paints a vivid picture of the Lord snatching his breath from death's clutches and restoring it.

The rhetorical question in verse 12 marks the transition to vows and expressions of gratitude. By opening this section with the question, "What shall I repay to the Lord for all his generosity to me?" the psalmist acknowledges that no amount of sacrifice, tithing, or praise is an adequate response to the lavish grace he experienced in his journey back from death's door. He cannot think of enough expressions of gratitude. Therefore, the clauses in this section seem to tumble in a cascade of thoughts alternately recalling the grace and generating new ideas for praising and serving the Lord.

Theology and Application

Perhaps the most famous line from this psalm is verse 15. It is often quoted in its traditional form, "precious in the eyes of the Lord is the death of his saints" (KJV). Unfortunately, stating it this way has led to a misunderstanding both of this psalm's message and of God's attitude toward death. Given the context of deliverance that dominates this psalm, it is more likely that the psalmist intends his readers to understand that the death of the Lord's faithful ones weighs heavily on the Lord. We know from Ezekiel 18:23 and 33:11 that not even the death of the wicked brings the Lord any delight, much less the death of his faithful children. His desire is always for life and flourishing.

The Scriptures generally portray death as an intruder to God's creation, the final, persistent foe of God and his people that will at last be defeated. The psalms contribute to this portrayal by constructing a polarity between the realm of the dead (*Sheol*), represented by the grave, and the Lord's dwelling, represented by the temple. These are opposite poles in the psalmists' universe. Life emanates from the divine presence experienced in the temple, whereas life dissipates as one nears the threshold of *Sheol*—the grave. Psalm 116 effectively employs this motif, but with an important twist. This polarity is no obstacle to God's intervention. His reach extends to *Sheol* despite his aversion to death, and he is more than capable of snatching his beloved even from that gaping abyss.

It is precisely this polarity between temple and *Sheol* that highlights the marvel of God's salvation in Psalm 116. Indeed, this is what motivates such exuberant praise and gratitude. If the Lord can save from death, then what enemy can possibly pose a threat to God's people? The psalmist simultaneously identifies with our propensity to fear and panic and supplies solid ground for security and recovery from such dismay. By expressing his own fear, the psalmist encourages us to express ours in worship, in the very presence of God. By exchanging fear for faith in the wake of the experience of salvation, the psalmist reminds us that in worship we, too, should exchange fear for faith and embrace the security offered us in God's supreme act of salvation through the death and resurrection of Jesus Christ.

In Jewish tradition, Psalm 116 constitutes one of the "Egyptian *Hallel* Psalms (Pss. 113–118) sung during Jewish festivals, particularly Passover. Together, these psalms commemorate Israel's Exodus from Egypt. Interestingly, Psalm 116 departs from the strident nationalism of the preceding *Hallels* to bring the significance of the Exodus to the personal level. Each instance of divine deliverance, whether individual or corporate, is a new chapter in the ongoing saga of Israel's gospel. Sharing such stories of God's salvation within the worshiping community reminds us that the God of the exodus is still at work in the world to revive the hope of the oppressed.

Perhaps this is the intended effect of the soliloquy in verse 7. We are encouraged to address ourselves with the gospel in worship as a means of calming our panicked hearts. The psalmist, however, did not stop at reminding himself of this salvation. He repays his vows and performs his thank offerings in full view of the community to share the peace and security. Worship should never be limited to personal devotion, as vital as that is. The true worshiper always longs to be joined by others so that security can be shared and the praises to God be multiplied.

For Those Who Sing Psalm 116

Our culture is robbing us of times and places where we can calm ourselves with the recollection of God's faithful acts of deliverance. With the intrusion of electronic devices and social media into our every waking moment, we find it harder and harder to address our interior lives. Psalm 116 directs us to the worship assembly as the one remaining refuge where we may still remind ourselves and others of God's saving acts. The psalmist teaches us to share our stories, fulfill our vows, and offer our thanks in full view of the community that we may all regain a sense of the peace and security offered us in the promise that God delivers even from death.

Kevin Youngblood

Thank Offering

Psalm 116

Keith Lancaster

Keith Lancaster
arr. Keith Lancaster & Mike Rogers

Thank Offering

I Love the Lord Who Hears My Voice

Psalm 116

Randy Daw (1956–2019)

Clyde H. Slimp
Harm. Randy Daw

Psalm 117

Translation

†1 Praise the LORD, all nations! Extol him, all peoples!

*2 For his loyal love has prevailed[a] over us, and the LORD's faithfulness
endures forever.

* Praise the LORD!

[a] This phrase has traditionally been translated something like "his steadfast love is great toward us." The Hebrew verb employed here, however, clearly denotes conquering and overpowering (*gavar*). Furthermore, this emphasis seems central to the psalm's message as the commentary explains.

Structure and Poetry

Psalm 117 is the shortest psalm in the entire Psalter. Despite its brevity, it is remarkable for its beautiful and bold summons to all nations to acknowledge the goodness and glory of Israel's God.

Though extremely concise, the psalm betrays the structure and features of a praise psalm or hymn. Notable characteristics of hymns include a preponderance of commands (e.g., praise, extol), typically followed by reasons for the commands introduced by the conjunction "for" or "because." Psalm 117 is framed by the plural command "Praise the LORD"—a refrain of Psalms 113–118 collectively known as the Egyptian *Hallel* Psalms ("Hallelujah" is Hebrew for "praise the LORD"). Within this frame is the additional command to extol the Lord, after which two reasons are offered for the propriety of international acknowledgment of the Lord's greatness. A suitable outline is as follows.

- v. 1: Summons to nations to worship the Lord
- v. 2a–b: Reasons why nations should worship the Lord:
    - The prevailing power of his love
    - The everlasting endurance of his fidelity
- v. 2c: Repetition of summons to worship the Lord

Theology and Application

Psalm 117 is a fitting sequel to Psalm 116. Whereas Psalm 116 appropriates the story of the Lord's salvation for the individual in a very personal testimony of deliverance, Psalm 117 appropriates the story of the Lord's salvation for the international community. This suggests that they too, and not just Israel, may participate in the ever-expanding effects of his redemption. The interpretation of the psalm turns on one's understanding of the "us" in the phrase, "For his love has prevailed over us." If this pronoun is inclusive of the nations who are summoned to join in praising the Lord, then the psalm makes a truly remarkable claim. Ultimately, the nations are subordinated to the Lord's rule not by military conquest—indeed, not by coercion of any kind—but rather by the compelling nature of divine love and fidelity. The psalm, therefore, anticipates the universal scope of the work of Christ and the inclusion of Gentiles in his church. While directly summoning the nations to add their voices to the adoring throng of worshipers, the psalm also indirectly summons the church to embody the compelling love of God in the world and to seek no other means of bringing the nations into his kingdom. In fact, Paul quotes the first verse of this psalm in Romans 15:11 in support of his argument that the strong should defer to the weak as a demonstration of Christ's love, so that all nations might come to know and praise the God and Father of the Lord Jesus Christ.

For Those Who Sing Psalm 117

Probably nothing seems more remote to God's people today than does universal acknowledgment of the greatness and goodness of the one true God and of his Son, Jesus Christ. Indeed, it seems presumptuous, even offensive, to issue the kind of international call to render praise to God we find in this psalm. This scenario is no more remote today, however, than it was at the time Psalm 117 was first sung. It is the very nature of biblical faith to make wildly counterintuitive and countercultural claims precisely because we are convinced of the universality of divine love and of its power to prevail over cynicism, suspicion, and hostility in the international community. As the hymnists Matthew Bridges and Godfrey Thring ("Crown Him with Many Crowns," 1851) have put it,

> Crown him the Lord of peace
> whose power a scepter sways
> from pole to pole that wars may cease
> absorbed in prayer and praise!

Kevin Youngblood

Praise the Lord, Praise the Lord

Psalm 117

Glover Shipp (1927–2016)

Debbie Dorman

Praise the Lord, All You Nations

Psalm 117

Jack R. Reese — Jack R. Reese

O Praise the Lord Our God

Psalm 117

Konstantin Zhigulin

Konstantin Zhigulin

Begin with the bass alone, adding the tenor the second time, and then all parts together twice. After this sing Alleluias, repeating as desired.

Psalm 118

Translation

†1 Give thanks to the Lord for he is good, for his loyal love endures always.
†2 Let Israel now say, "His loyal love endures always."
†3 Let the household of Aaron now say, "His loyal love endures always."
†4 Let those who fear the Lord now say, "His loyal love endures always."

†5 In dire straits I cried to the Lord. He answered me from the Lord's palatial dwelling.[a]
*6 The Lord is for me, I will not fear. What can any mortal do to me?
†7 The Lord is for me as my helper, and I, I will look triumphantly over those who hate me.
*8 It is better to take refuge in the Lord than to trust in mere mortals.
†9 It is better to take refuge in the Lord than to trust in princes.
*10 All the nations surrounded me. It is in the name of the Lord that I repelled them.
†11 They surrounded me, indeed, they surrounded me. It is in the name of the Lord that I repelled them.
*12 They surrounded me like bees; they were extinguished like a fire among thorns. It is in the name of the Lord that I repelled them.
†13 I was forcefully pushed toward my fall, but the Lord helped me.

*14 The Lord is my strength and my song. He has become my deliverance.
*15 The sound of victorious shouting is in the tents of the righteous. The Lord's right hand is acting valiantly.
*16 The Lord's right hand is exalted. The Lord's right hand is acting valiantly.
*17 I will not die. Instead, I will live so that I might recount the Lord's deeds.
†18 The Lord will surely discipline me, but for death he has not appointed me.
†19 Open for me the gates of righteousness that I may enter them, that I may thank the Lord.
*20 This is the Lord's gate. The righteous may enter it.
*21 I will thank you because you answered me. You became my deliverance.
†22 A stone that the builders rejected has become the cornerstone!
*23 Because of the Lord this has happened, a miracle before our very eyes.
*24 This is the day the Lord has made. Let us celebrate and rejoice in it.

†25 O Lord, we beg of you, please save us! O Lord, we beg of you, please grant us success!

*26 Blessed is the one who comes in the LORD's name! We bless you all from the LORD's house.
†27 The LORD is God. He enlightened us. Bind a festive sacrifice with ropes up to the horns of the altar.
*28 You are my God, and I will give you thanks. O my God, I will exalt you.
*29 Give thanks to the LORD for he is good. His loyal love endures always.

[a] Most English translations render this as "and set me free" or "and brought me into a broad place." In the Hebrew text, however, this clause has no verb, and its syntax suggests that the "broad place" is the Lord's heavenly dwelling whence he heard and responded to the psalmist's cry. See D. J. A. Clines, ed., *The Dictionary of Classical Hebrew*, vol. 5 (Sheffield: Sheffield Academic, 2001), 484.

Structure and Poetry

Psalm 118, the final psalm in the series of Egyptian *Hallels* (Pss. 113–118, see discussion in *Theology and Application* section on Psalm 116), is framed by a summons to all Israel to offer grateful praise (vv. 1–4, 28–29). This framework suggests that it is a communal thanksgiving hymn. Within this framework, however, elements of other genres intrude. For example, the psalmist's anticipation of divine discipline (v. 18) is reminiscent of a penitential lament. Excerpts from a victory song suddenly appear in verses 7 and 15, while verses 19–27 sound like an entrance liturgy that might be sung by pilgrims en route to one of the annual festivals. This conglomeration of genres leaves the impression of a song sung in gratitude for a recent victory over an enemy God raised up to discipline his wayward people. Its music appears to accompany a march to the sanctuary in anticipation of a worshipful celebration of yet another instance of divine deliverance. The psalm is a good example of an important subtype of thanksgiving hymn, the song of confidence. As such it is a fitting conclusion to the series of *Hallel* Psalms commemorating the exodus as the paradigm of God's cyclical saving activity and the basis for Israel's renewed faith in the Lord.

Songs of confidence, like most hymns, typically consist of three basic elements: a summons to the community to praise God, a list of reasons why praise is appropriate, and a renewed, often expanded, summons to praise. In the case of songs of confidence, however, a particular experience of salvation serves as the basis for more general affirmations of divine attributes. In other words, a historical experience provides the occasion for theological reflection in musical form. Psalm 118 may be outlined as follows.

- vv. 1–4: Summons to praise God
- vv. 5–13: Description of the salvation experience
  - v. 5: Summary of experience
  - vv. 6–9: Expressions of confidence
  - vv. 10–13: Description of deliverance from global conspiracy

vv. 14–24: Affirmation of divine deeds & qualities
- vv. 14–16: Praise of the divine warrior
- vv. 17–18: Acknowledgment of the Lord's death-defying deliverance
- vv. 19–20: Entrance liturgy
- vv. 21–24: Praise for the Lord's exaltation of the rejected and marginalized

v. 25: Appeal for future salvation

vv. 26–29: Summons to join a pilgrim festival

Psalm 118 begins and ends with the same summons to worship: "Give thanks to the LORD for he is good, for his loyal love endures always." In fact, the last part of that summons serves as a refrain that unites the psalm's first stanza (vv. 1–4) and brings the psalm to a fitting conclusion (v. 29). Repetition is a chief characteristic of this psalm. Verbatim repetition of key phrases marks its emotional zeniths. For example, the psalm's central section (vv. 8–16) contains a number of repeated phrases as the tension peaks with the climactic confrontation between the psalmist and hostile nations followed by the LORD's miraculous deliverance. The following list enumerates each of these key phrases and their frequency.

"His loyal love endures always." (5x)
"(The nations) surrounded me." (4x)
"It is in the name of the LORD that I repelled them." (3x)
"The LORD's right hand is exalted/acting valiantly!" (3x)
"It is better to take refuge in the LORD than . . ." (2x)

The effect of such repetition is to impress upon the worshiper key truths the psalmist learned from his experience: the endurance of divine love, the reliability of God as a refuge, the impossibility of defeating our foes apart from divine aid, the power the Lord's name, and the prowess of the divine warrior in battle.

Psalm 118 revisits the polarity common in the psalms between God's dwelling represented by the temple and the realm of the dead (*Sheol*) represented by the grave. The psalmist uses this polarity to highlight both the severity of the crisis from which he was delivered and the surprising, even miraculous, nature of God's intervention. A good example of this motif occurs in verse 5. The psalmist says, "In dire straits I cried to the LORD. He answered me from the LORD's palatial dwelling." The coupling of the phrases "dire straights" (the Hebrew term includes the definite article, suggesting the ultimate crisis of death) and "the LORD's palatial dwelling" represents this polarity and underscores how close to death the psalmist was and what a great chasm the Lord crossed in order to rescue him.

The prevailing imagery of the psalm celebrates the Lord as a victorious war hero whose emancipated people greet his return from battle with a full ticker-tape parade. The imagery derives primarily from the song the Israelites sang after successfully crossing the Reed Sea (Exod. 15) and serves as a fitting climax to the series of Egyptian *Hallel* psalms (Pss. 113–118).

Theology and Application

Psalm 118 celebrates the Lord's inexhaustible love for his people by emphasizing the Lord's prowess in battle. The surprising link the psalm creates between divine love and the Lord's role as the divine warrior challenges overly sentimental and anemic conceptions of God's love. It also challenges the tendency to pit divine wrath against divine love. The Lord's entrance into the fray is motivated by his profound love for his people, which expresses itself in outrage toward their oppressors. Divine wrath, therefore, is a reflex of divine love. As any parent knows, love for one's children triggers an intense anger toward anyone who threatens them. We deem such a response not only appropriate but necessary for keeping such threats at bay. From the psalmist's point of view, therefore, the Lord's assault against the oppression perpetrated by the enemies of his people is evidence of God's love and reason for singing his praises. As the Lord said to Pharaoh, "Israel is my firstborn son. I said to you, 'Let my son go'" (Exod. 4:22–23 NRSV). It is in the context of this relationship that the plagues against Egypt should be understood. The Lord loves too intensely to stand idly by while his creation is ravaged by oppression and injustice.

A common concern is that conceptions of God as divine warrior encourage violence. Scripture, however, suggests just the opposite. Those who have faith that God will redress the wrongs that they endure in this life are far less likely to resort to vigilantism. They believe that God means it when he says, "Vengeance is mine. I will repay" (Deut. 32:35; Rom. 12:19; Heb. 10:30). Only God has the wisdom and the restraint to administer justice appropriately. Ironically, it is the imagery of God as the divine warrior, who alone has the right to judge and punish, that encourages believers to love and to forgive their enemies, to reject retaliation and to encourage the wicked to repent (Rom. 12:18–21).

The effect of the Lord's warfare is the exaltation of the marginalized and the neglected. Unlike human warfare that often worsens the plight of those at the margins, divine warfare actually establishes those that the world has rejected as the very foundation of God's kingdom (v. 22). The supreme example of this is Jesus Christ. Though rejected by Jew and Gentile alike, Jesus was raised from the dead and was established as the very foundation of God's new temple, where Jew and Gentile alike are invited to worship him (Matt. 21:42; Mark 12:10; Luke 20:17; Acts 4:11; 1 Pet. 2:4–8).

For Those Who Sing Psalm 118

All over the world huddled bands of believers meet secretly each Sunday, carefully evading the watchful eyes of powerful persecutors. They worship at great personal risk, comforting each other with words like these: "The LORD is for me, I will not fear. What can any mortal do to me?" Many of those who have been caught willingly embraced death rather than capitulate or retaliate. Their souls join the rest of the martyrs under God's altar with this song on their lips, "I will not die. Instead, I will live so that I might recount the LORD's deeds." Such persecuted believers rightly feel rejected by the world. They also, however, firmly stand on the cornerstone of the Lord Jesus Christ who, like them, was rejected and yet now serves as the eternal foundation of a living temple consisting of all those who will join him in his priestly service to the Father. This is the only structure that, like God's love, will endure forever.

Kevin Youngblood

His Kindness Forever Endures (Refrain)

Psalm 118

Mark Shipp

Mark Shipp & Michael E. Showalter

His Kindness Forever Endures

Psalm 118

Mark Shipp

Michael E. Showalter

His Kindness Forever Endures

His Love Endures

Psalm 118

Marva L. Hughes | Marva L. Hughes

Psalm 119

Translation

Aleph

†1 Blessed are those who are on the path of integrity, who are in step with the Lord's law.
†2 Blessed are those who keep his testimonies; with full devotion they seek him.
†3 They also commit no injustice. They follow his ways.
†4 You have commanded that your principles be carefully observed.
*5 Oh that my ways might be established in keeping your decrees!
*6 Then I will not be ashamed when I consider your commandments.
*7 I will praise you with integrity of heart once I learn all of your just ordinances.
*8 I will keep your decrees; don't abandon me completely.

Bet

†9 How shall a young man cleanse his path so as to bring it into keeping with your word?
†10 I have treasured your word in my heart, so that I might not sin against you.
†11 With all of my devotion I have sought you. Do not let me stray from your commands.
†12 Blessed are you, O Lord. Teach me your decrees.
*13 With my lips I relay all of the ordinances that come from your mouth.
*14 In the path marked by your testimonies, I rejoice as much as in all wealth.
*15 I will meditate on your principles, and I will consider your ways.
*16 I will delight myself with your decrees. I will not forget your word.

Gimel

†17 Deal generously[a] with your servant, that I might live and keep your word.
†18 Open my eyes, that I might see the wonders of your law.
†19 I am an alien in the land. Don't conceal from me your commands.
†20 I am crushed with longing for your ordinances at all times.
*21 You have rebuked the accursed, insolent ones who stray from your commands.
*22 Roll away from me reproach and shame, for I keep your testimonies.
*23 Indeed, princes have sat down together to conspire against me. Your servant still meditates on your decrees.
*24 Yes! Your testimonies are my delight. They are my advisors.

Dalet

†25 My life clings to the dust. Revive me according to your word!
†26 I have made known my ways, and you answered me. Teach me your decrees!
†27 The path marked by your principles instructs me. I will meditate on your wonders.
†28 My life is draining away due to grief. Raise me up according to your word.
*29 Remove from me the false path; by your favor show me compassion.
*30 I have chosen a reliable path. I have set your ordinances before me.
*31 I cling to your testimonies, O Lord. Don't put me to shame.
*32 I will run in the path marked out by your commands, for your have set my heart free!

He

†33 Instruct me, O Lord, in the way of your decrees, so that I may follow it to the end.
†34 Teach me that I might follow your instruction, that I might keep it with all my heart.
†35 Direct me in the way marked by your instruction, for I delight in it.
†36 Bend my will to your testimonies and away from plunder.
*37 Divert my attention from futile fixations. Revive me with your word.
*38 Confirm for your servant your word, which is for the one who reveres you.
*39 Remove my reproach that I fear, for your ordinances are good.
*40 See how I desire your principles? Revive me with your justice.

Waw

†41 And let your loyal love come to me, O Lord, your salvation in keeping with your promise,
†42 that I may answer the one who taunts me with words, for I have trusted in your word.
†43 Do not remove completely from my mouth a sure word, for I have been awaiting your judgment.
†44 I always keep your instruction forever and ever.
*45 I will roam freely because I seek your principles.
*46 I will speak of your testimonies before kings, and I will not be ashamed.
*47 I will delight myself with your commands which I love.
*48 I will lift my hands to your commands which I love, and I will meditate on your decrees.

Zayin

†49 Remember your promise to your servant by which you have offered me hope.
†50 This is my comfort in my affliction, that your word revives me.
†51 Insolent men mock me incessantly. From your instruction I will not depart.
†52 I have remembered your ordinances from long ago, Lord, and I am comforted.

*53 Zealous rage has gripped me because of the wicked who forsake your instruction.
*54 Your decrees have become my songs in the house where I reside.
*55 At night I have remembered your name, O LORD, that I may keep your instruction.
*56 This is my possession, that I observe your principles.

Het

†57 My allotment, O LORD, as I have said, is to keep your words.
†58 I have wholeheartedly entreated your favor. Be gracious to me according to your word.
†59 I considered my ways so that I may return my feet to your testimonies.
†60 I have hastened without hesitation to keep your commandments.
*61 The ropes of the wicked have restrained me, but your law I have not forgotten.
*62 In the middle of the night, I rise to praise you because of your just ordinances.
*63 I am friend to all who revere you and to those who keep your principles.
*64 Your mercy, LORD, has filled the world. Teach me your decrees.

Tet

†65 You have treated your servant well, O LORD, according to your word.
†66 Teach me goodness, discernment, and knowledge, for I have trusted in your commands.
†67 Before I endured affliction, I was wayward; but now I keep your word.
†68 You are good and perform good deeds. Teach me your decrees.
*69 Insolent men have smeared me with lies. I, however, remain totally devoted to observing your principles.
*70 Their minds are dull like fat; I, however, have found delight in your instruction.
*71 It is to my benefit that I was afflicted, so that I might learn your decrees.
*72 Instruction from your mouth is more valuable to me than thousands of gold and silver pieces.

Yod

†73 Your hands made me and established me. Teach me that I may learn your commands.
†74 Those who fear you see me and rejoice that I wait on your word.
†75 I know, O LORD, that your ordinances are just, and you have faithfully afflicted me.
†76 Let your loyal love be ever present to comfort me according to your promise to your servant.
*77 May your compassionate acts come my way that I may live, for I have found delight in your instruction.
*78 May the insolent be put to shame because they have discredited me falsely. I, however, will meditate on your principles.

*79 Let those who fear you turn to me, that they may know your testimonies.
*80 Let me be blameless to your decrees, so that I need not be ashamed.

Kaph

†81 I have reached my limit waiting for your deliverance. I have waited for your word.
†82 My eyes are exhausted looking for your promise, saying, "When will you comfort me?"
†83 Though I am like a wineskin in hot smoke, I have not forgotten your decrees.
†84 How many days does your servant have? When will you administer justice to my pursuers?
*85 Insolent men have dug pits for me, which is not in keeping with your law.
*86 All of your commands are reliable. Falsely do they pursue me. Help me!
*87 They have nearly eradicated me from the earth. I, however, have not forsaken your principles.
*88 Revive me according to your mercy that I may keep the testimony that comes from your mouth.

Lamed

†89 Your word, O Lord, is established in heaven forever.
†90 Your faithfulness endures throughout all generations, just as you established the earth and it stands.
†91 By your decrees they stand today, because all things are your servants.
†92 Had your instruction not been my delight, I would have already perished in my affliction.
*93 I will never forget your principles, for by them you revive me.
*94 I am yours. Save me, for I seek after your principles.
*95 The wicked lie in wait for me to destroy me. I still give all of my attention to your testimonies.
*96 To all perfection I see a limit, but the breadth of your commandment is immeasurable.

Mem

†97 How I love your instruction! All day long it is my meditation.
†98 Your commands make me wiser than my enemies. Indeed, they are mine forever.
†99 I have more insight than all of my teachers, for your testimonies are my meditation.
†100 I am surpassing the aged in understanding because I keep your principles.
*101 From every evil way I withhold my feet so that I might keep your word.
*102 From your ordinances I have not strayed, because you were the one who taught me.
*103 How sweet to my palate is your word, more so than honey to my mouth.
*104 Because of your principles I have insight; therefore, I hate every deceptive detour.

Nun

†105 Your word is a lamp for my feet and a light for my path.
†106 I swore an oath to keep your just ordinances, and I fulfilled it.
†107 I have been utterly afflicted. O Lord, revive me according to your word.
†108 Please accept freewill offerings from my mouth, O Lord, and teach me your ordinances.
*109 My life is always in jeopardy, but I have not forgotten your instruction.
*110 The wicked set a snare for me, but from your principles I have not strayed.
*111 I have inherited your testimonies forever, for they are the joy of my heart.
*112 I have inclined my will to perform your decrees forever, until the end.

Samek

†113 I hate duplicitous people, but I love your instruction.
†114 You are my hiding place, my shield; I hope in your word.
†115 The wicked turn away from me, but I keep observing my God's commands.
†116 Support me with your word that I might survive, and that you might not put me to shame because of my hope.
*117 Sustain me that I might be delivered, that I might ever fix my sights on your decrees.
*118 You have disregarded all who stray from your decrees, for they are false and deceitful.
*119 You have destroyed like dross all of the wicked of the earth. Therefore, I love your testimonies.
*120 My body trembles from awe of you, and because of your ordinances I revere you.

Ayin

†121 I have acted justly and rightly. Don't leave me to my oppressors!
†122 Ensure the prosperity of your servant. Let not the insolent oppress me.
†123 My eyes have wearied of looking for your deliverance, for the promise of your vindication.
†124 Treat your servant mercifully, and teach me your decrees.
*125 I am your servant; instruct me that I may know your testimonies.
*126 It is time for the Lord to act; they have violated your instruction.
*127 This is why I love your instructions more than gold, more than the finest gold.
*128 This is why with all of your principles, with all of them I have aligned myself; every deceptive path I hate.

Pe

†129 Your testimonies are wonderful; therefore, I have kept them.
†130 The revelation of your words illuminates, making the simple discerning.
†131 I opened wide my mouth and panted, because I desired your commands.
†132 Turn toward me and be gracious to me, according to the justice due to those who love your name.
*133 Establish my steps in your word, and let no wickedness dominate me.

*134 Ransom me from a human's oppression, that I may keep your principles.
*135 Shine the light of your face upon your servant, and teach me your decrees.
*136 Streams of water pour from my eyes, because people do not observe your instruction.

Tsade

†137 Righteous are you, LORD, and your ordinances are right.
†138 You decreed your testimonies in righteousness; they are utterly reliable.
†139 My zeal has consumed me, because my adversaries have forgotten your words.
†140 Your word is very refined, and your servant loves it.
*141 Though I am insignificant and despised, I have not forgotten your principles.
*142 Your righteousness is an eternal righteousness, and your instruction is truth.
*143 Trouble and anguish have found me, but your commands are my delight.
*144 The righteousness of your testimonies is eternal. Grant me insight that I might live.

Qoph

†145 I cried out with all of my heart, "Answer me, LORD, that I may keep your decrees!"
†146 I have summoned you, "Save me that I might observe your testimonies."
†147 I woke before dawn and cried out; I hoped in your word.
†148 My eyes opened before the end of the night watches to meditate on your sayings.
*149 Hear my voice according to your mercy. According to your justice, revive me!
*150 Those who pursue an evil plan draw near, but they are far from your instruction.
*151 You are near, O LORD, and all of your commands are truth.
*152 I have long known about your testimonies, because you founded them in eternity.

Resh

†153 Notice my affliction and deliver me, for I have not forgotten your instruction.
†154 Defend my cause and redeem me; revive me with your word.
†155 Deliverance is far from the wicked, because they do not seek your decrees.
†156 Many are your acts of mercy, O LORD; revive me according to your ordinances.
*157 My aggressors and adversaries are many. From your testimonies, however, I have not veered.
*158 I have observed those who commit treachery, and I loathe them, because your word they do not observe.

*159 See how I love your principles, O LORD! Revive me in keeping with your mercy.
*160 Your word is truth from the start. Every one of your righteous judgments lasts forever.

Sin

†161 Princes have pursued me for no reason, but my heart is in awe of your word.
†162 I rejoice over your sayings like one who finds great plunder.
†163 I hate, even abhor, deception, but I love your instruction.
†164 Seven times a day I have praised you for your just ordinances.
*165 Great peace belongs to those who love your instruction; nothing causes them to stumble.
*166 I have been awaiting your salvation, LORD, and I have performed your commands.
*167 I have kept your testimonies, and I have loved them immensely.
*168 I have kept your principles and your testimonies, because all of my ways are before you.

Taw

†169 Let my cry reach you, O LORD. Instruct me with your word.
†170 Let my petition enter your presence. According to your promise, deliver me!
†171 May my lips erupt in praise, because you teach me your decrees.
†172 May my tongue sing your word, because all your commands are righteous.
*173 May your hand be there to help me, because I have chosen your principles.
*174 I long for your salvation, O LORD, and your instruction is my delight.
*175 I live on and praise you, and your ordinances help me.
*176 I have wandered off like a lost sheep. Seek out your servant, for I have not forgotten your commands.

[a] The Hebrew verb used here means "repay" and is typically in reference to punishment for evil. When combined with the preposition *'al* ("upon" or "with"), however, it takes on the sense of dealing generously with someone. See D. J. A. Clines, ed., *The Dictionary of Classical Hebrew*, vol. 2 (Sheffield: Sheffield Academic, 1995), 363.

Structure and Poetry

Psalm 119, by far the longest psalm in the entire collection, is one of three that have traditionally been designated as "Torah psalms." The other two are Psalms 1 and 19. What these psalms have in common is an unmistakable emphasis on the perfections and pleasures of divine law (Heb. *torah*). The word "law," however, does not really do justice to the Hebrew word *torah*. A better equivalent would be "instruction," because it is broad enough to include all of the content implied by the word, much of which is not at all legal (e.g., stories, songs, oracles, and liturgies).

Torah psalms, unlike other psalm types, do not have a set structure. Rather, they are identified by certain common features. For example, Torah psalms frequently contain beatitudes or blessings (cf. Ps. 1:1; Ps. 119:1, 2, 12), are more instructional in tone than the other psalms, and typically employ mnemonic devices to facilitate memory and meditation. In fact, meditation is an important and frequent theme in such psalms (Ps. 1:2; Ps. 119:15, 23, 27, 48, 78, 148).

Psalm 119's most obvious feature, other than its length, is its elaborate acrostic structure. An acrostic is a poem that uses the order of the letters of the alphabet as a structuring and mnemonic device. Usually this involves beginning each line of the acrostic with a word that starts with the successive letter of the alphabet. In the case of Psalm 119, however, each of the eight lines of its 22 stanzas begins with the same letter of the Hebrew alphabet, with each stanza advancing to the next letter. Most English translations draw attention to this structure by prefacing each stanza in Psalm 119 with a heading indicating the letter of the Hebrew alphabet featured in its stanza. This is why the translation above is punctuated by the headings *aleph, bet, gimel, dalet,* etc. These are the names of the letters of the Hebrew alphabet in their traditional order. The visual and auditory effect of this device is striking and is approximated in the diagram below.

A______________________________
A______________________________
A______________________________
A______________________________
A______________________________
A______________________________
A______________________________
A______________________________

B______________________________
B______________________________
B______________________________
B______________________________
B______________________________
B______________________________
B______________________________
B______________________________ . . . etc. to Z

The poetic significance of such a tight, stable, and predictable structure is that it suggests both orderliness and comprehensiveness (everything from A to Z)—two attributes that are consistently ascribed to the Torah (119:9–10, 18, 27, 30, 46, 66–67, 70, 89, 91–92, 96, 98–100, 104–5, 128–29, 137–38, 142, 144, 152, 160, 165, 172). God's instructions in the Torah have the power to order our chaotic lives, and they are encyclopedic in the wisdom they offer regarding the varied issues we face. Furthermore, the psalm exhausts the vocabulary for God's written revelation, employing every conceivable synonym for Torah in its 176 verses. Each synonym, however, has its own connotation, thus underscoring both the Torah's diversity and its universal scope.

The psalm is replete with colorful images celebrating the power and perfection of divine instruction. God's word is compared to wealth and treasure (119:14, 72, 112, 127, 140, 162), to wise advisors (119:24), to a broad highway on which one can run free (119:32, 45), to delicious, nourishing foods that incite longing (119:20, 103, 131), and, of course, to a bright light that guides travelers in the darkness (119:105, 135).

Theology and Application

This psalm surprises and perplexes Christians with its unrestrained enthusiasm for Torah. As far as this psalmist is concerned, God's law is no burden; rather, it is the greatest delight life can offer. Christians have often thought of the Old Testament law as a tightrope that Israel had to walk with painstaking care without the assurance of a net to catch them should they fall. By contrast, the psalmist here describes the Torah as a broad highway on which one can freely run and frolic. This psalm suggests that Christians may have misread and misconstrued Paul and other New Testament authors who appear at times to be critical of the Torah. God's law is liberating and life-preserving when properly understood and applied. The guardrails it provides on the road of life actually enable and encourage free, productive, and enjoyable living by alerting us to danger and keeping us on track toward our destination—permanent rest in God's presence.

The psalm, however, is also noticeably tinted with a dark hue. The psalmist is clearly threatened by powerful enemies whose designs spell the psalmist's doom (Ps. 119:23, 98, 121, 161). Throughout the ordeal, the psalmist has remained a faithful adherent of divine revelation and instruction, but his situation seems only to worsen. The reader can sense that the psalmist is in crisis and wonders why God, who promised deliverance to those who remain faithful, has not yet intervened in this situation. The psalmist fears that little time remains before either death or desertion from the faith wins out (119:25, 40, 43, 61, 69, 77, 81–82, 84, 87–88, 95, 107, 109, 116, 121–123, 126, 134, 153–154, 157, 170).

In the context of such intense oppression, the psalmist's praise of Torah is all the more remarkable. It is a bold, even defiant, assertion of faith in the face of dire circumstances, but not one based on denial or intellectual dishonesty. The psalmist is honest with himself and us regarding what is at stake and how fragile his faith and hope are at the moment. His praise of Torah, therefore, is his meditation that bolsters his resolve in the face of such fierce opposition. It also forms the basis of his appeal to God. He reminds God of promises that God has made, especially to people, like the psalmist, who have committed themselves to God's ways.

Two important principles emerge from the psalmist's struggle. First, devotion to God's word is no protection against pain and persecution. Indeed, it can often be a magnet for such trials. One's motivation for obedience must be deeper than the expectation that such obedience will provide a smooth, pain-free, uncomplicated life. The psalmist maintained his integrity despite his trials, and the testimony he has left us in this psalm inspires us to do the same.

The second principle is that affliction, while not always instigated by God, can always be an instrument of God for our spiritual formation. The psalmist reached this conclusion at a certain point in his own suffering. With considerable maturity he states in verse 67, "Before I endured affliction, I was wayward; but now I keep your word." Similarly, in verse 71 he states, "It is to my benefit that I was afflicted, so that I might learn your decrees." Such sentiments resonate with the example of our Savior of whom it was said, "Although he was a Son, he learned obedience through what he suffered" (Heb. 5:8 NRSV).

For Those Who Sing Psalm 119

What a gift God's word is! God's instruction (Torah) is no dry, boring "law" as we think of the term. Indeed, Torah can be sung! It inspires singing even in the darkness of oppression. It has the power to sustain those who must endure long bouts of suffering. More than that, it can even change our perspective on suffering to the point that we can value it as a catalyst for our sanctification. Far from depriving life of joy, it is the very source of life's joy even in the midst of intense trials. We live in a time when God's word is maligned because its principles run counter to cultural trends. Perhaps we ourselves are tempted to question its relevance and power in such a rapidly changing world, particularly when open devotion to God's word runs the risk of inviting persecution and pain. Psalm 119 reminds us that whatever the cost, God's word is worth it. It is more valuable than the finest gold and more pleasurable than the richest delicacies.

Kevin Youngblood

Blessed

Psalm 119:1-16

Mark Shipp

Ruth Ann Somervell

ho - ly and true. Then I would praise with heart that is blame - less;
right-eous de - crees, and I will keep your sta - tutes and judg - ments.
keep his way sure? Let me not wan - der from your com-mand-ments;
guide me a - right. I med - i - tate on all of your pre - cepts,
1, 3
(1) my eyes are fixed, O Lord, u - pon you.
(3) hide them with - in, that I may be pure.
2
D.C.
Do not for - sake, but vin - di - cate me.
4
D.C. al Fine
and in your words of truth I will de - light.

I Am a Stranger on the Earth

Psalm 119:17-32

Jerry Shipp

Michael E. Showalter

Instruct Me in Your Righteous Ways

Psalm 119:33-48

Mark Shipp

Mark Shipp and Randy Daw (1954–2019)

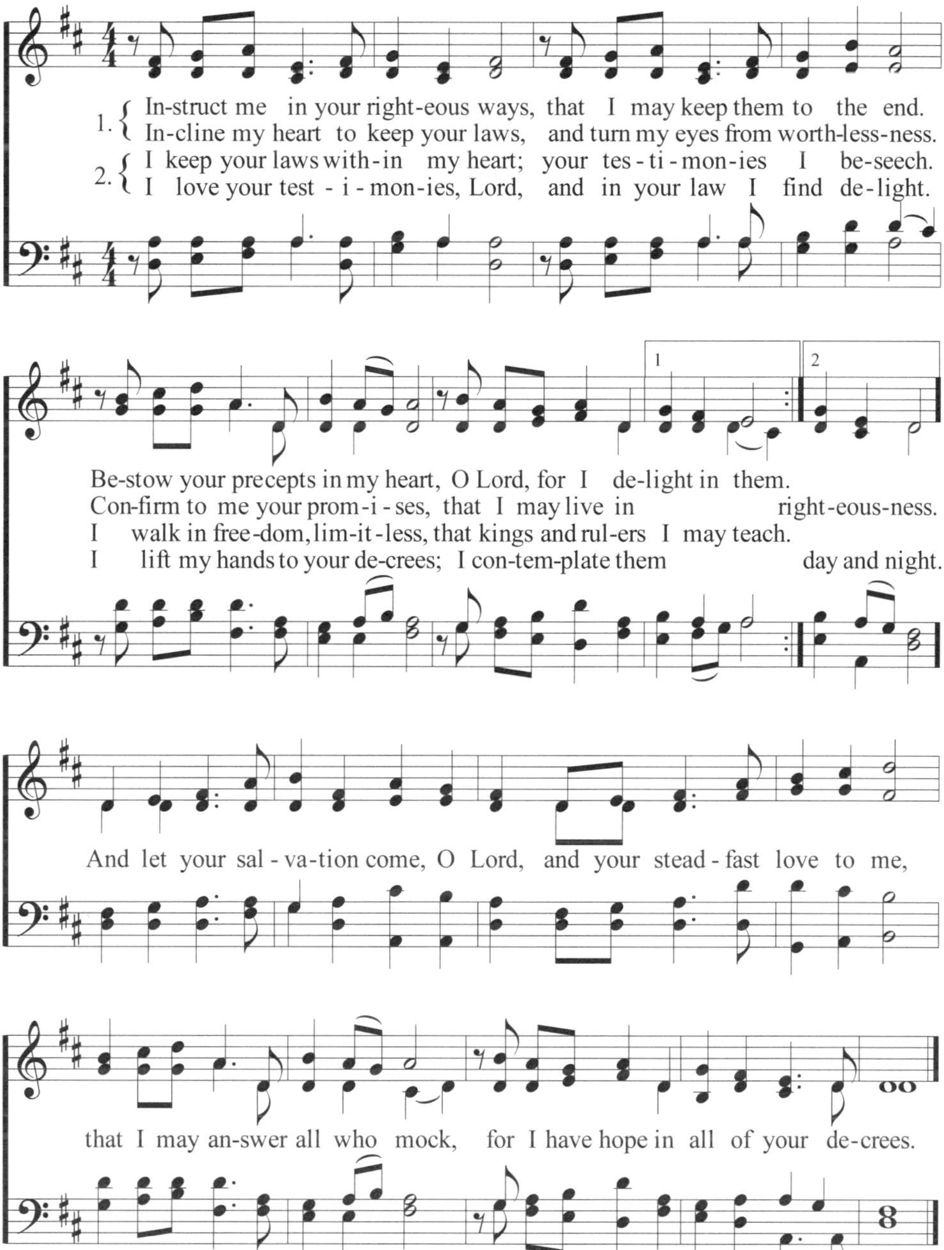

Hold to Your Promise, Lord

Psalm 119:49-64

Jack R. Reese — Jack R. Reese

Hold to Your Promise, Lord

You Have Dealt Well with Me

Psalm 119:65-80

Mark Shipp

Debbie Dorman

Your law is great - er far than all the plans that they de - vise.
but put the ar - ro - gant to shame, and their de - ceit re - quite.
Their hearts are cold and hard, un - feel - ing is their soul,
Let those who fear the Lord your tes - ti - mon - ies claim.
but I de - light to do your will; your pre - cepts make me whole.
And may I nev - er be a - shamed, but praise your ho - ly name.
Faith - ful the af - flic - tion that you did not with - hold,
bet - ter far than sil - ver, more pre - cious far than gold.
bet - ter far, more pre - cious far than gold.

My Soul Cries Out for My Release

Psalm 119:81-96

Jerry Shipp | Mel Witcher and Ruth Ann Somervell

My Soul Cries Out for My Release

How I Love Your Law

Psalm 119:97-112

Mark Shipp

Michael E. Showalter

turned a - side from you. Sweet up - on my pal - ate are your
ev - er in my hands, and the wick - ed laid a snare be -
ev - er, to the end; nev - er let me wan - der from your
pre - cepts! They are al - to - geth - er just and true.
fore me, though I have not strayed from your com - mands.
path - way; on your tes - ti - mo - nies I de - pend.
How I love your law, my med - i - ta - tion through the day and
watch - es of the night! How I love your ho - ly in - spi -
ra - tion, shep - herd - ing my feet and giv - ing light!

I Love Your Steadfast Law, O God

Psalm 119:113-128

Jack R. Reese

Debbie Dorman

I Love Your Steadfast Law, O God

Righteous Lord

Psalm 119:129-144

Mark Shipp & Randy Daw (1954–2019) | D. J. Bulls

life hold sway. From op - pres - sive deeds re -
ev - er right. Grant me wis - dom, Lord, that
deem my life; shine your light; let me see your way.
I may live; in your teach - ing I find de - light.
You are al - to - geth - er right - eous, Lord, and your tes - ti -
mo - nies with - out flaw; my eyes o - ver - flow with bit - ter
tears, for the man - y who pro - fane your law.

Give Me Life

Psalm 119:145-160

Jerry Shipp

Jack R. Reese

just; you fash - ioned them to last for - ev - er.
dain. Your laws are al - ways true and ho - ly.
Give me life ac - cord - ing to your stead - fast love.
Give me life ac-cord-ing to your prom-ise. Time-less and en - dur - ing is your
poco rit.
right-eous-ness, O Lord. Give me life ac - cord - ing to your mer-cy.

I Await in Hope

Psalm 119:161-176

Mark Shipp | Ruth Ann Somervell

Psalm 120

Translation

A Song of Ascents.

*1 I cried out to the Lord in my distress and he answered me.
*2 O Lord, save my life from lying lips, from treacherous tongues.

*3 What will he repay you and how much more will he do to you, O treacherous tongue?
*4 The warrior's arrows are sharpened with flaming juniper kindling.

†5 Woe is me that I have sojourned in Meshech,[a] that I have dwelt with the tents of Kedar.[b]
†6 I have dwelt with those who hate peace longer than I can stand.
†7 I want peace, but whenever I speak of it, they want war.

[a] See the commentary that follows for geographical details and explanation.

[b] See the commentary that follows for geographical details and explanation.

Structure and Poetry

Psalm 120 is the first in a series of related psalms (Pss. 120–134), all of which share the same heading: "a song of ascents." The title suggests that these were songs pilgrims sang as they made their way up to Zion for festivals.[6] The term "ascent" occurs also in Ezra 7:9 in reference to a return from captivity and may have become a technical term for homecoming in the postexilic period. If this is the case, these psalms may well have been compiled in the postexilic period to commemorate Judah's return from captivity.

The psalm takes the form of a lament consisting of four parts: an acknowledgement of an answered prayer (v. 1), a petition (v. 2), a mild imprecation or curse (vv. 3–4), and a complaint (vv. 5–7). It appears that the psalmist was the victim of malicious and false accusations from which he had asked God for deliverance. The psalmist proceeds to address the accusers directly with a curse expressed as a rhetorical question. Verse 5 becomes more introspective as the

[6] The precise meaning of this title is debated. Others have suggested that it refers to the fifteen-step climb that the Levitical singers made to their posts in the temple. Still others suggest that the songs were composed to celebrate Nehemiah's rebuilding of the walls of Jerusalem in 445 BCE.

psalmist reflects on a prolonged sojourn amidst violent tribes with whom the psalmist has attempted to broker peace. Supposedly, these are the "lying lips" and "treacherous tongues" mentioned in verse 2.

The references to the place names Meshech and Kedar are somewhat mysterious. Their precise locations are not known for certain, though Meshech derives its name from one of Japheth's sons and is often associated with the region of Lydia in Western Anatolia (cf. Gen. 10:2; Ezek. 38:1–2). Kedar was a son of Ishmael and subsequently an Arabian tribe (cf. Gen. 25:13; Isa. 21:13–16). Together, the terms mark the farthest northern point and farthest southern point in the psalmist's geographical consciousness, thus forming a *merism*. A merism is a poetic device in which the extremes are used to represent the whole. In this case, violent tribes and nations in general are represented by their northern and southern extremities with, perhaps, a particular emphasis on Babylonian hegemony.

Theology and Application

The psalm laments a failure of diplomacy and its deterioration into false accusations used as an excuse to foment war. As a song sung during pilgrimage to the temple, it cultivated both a deep desire for peace and a deep sadness for its elusiveness in the worshiping community. It may also have reminded them that the temple was a refuge of peace in a violent world, anticipating the time when God's universal sovereignty would eventually lead to the beating of swords into plowshares and spears into pruning hooks. Worship should always include prayers for peace and for the coming of God's kingdom, without which there can be no lasting peace. Perhaps Judah's prolonged exile at the hands of a cruel imperial power (Babylon) soured her on imperial ambitions pursued by violent means.

The New Testament suggests that the church (the community, not the building) is the new temple (1 Cor. 3:16; 1 Pet. 2:4). As such, it should be the new refuge of peace in a violent world. The church should be desperately attempting to broker peace amid estranged and antagonistic parties as we anticipate the consummation of God's kingdom and the perfect, everlasting peace that it brings to all nations (Eph. 2:14–17). Certainly, within the church itself one should see a model of peaceful and harmonious community that stands in stark contrast to our fragmented and feuding world. We, like Israel before us, are called to be the first fruits of the new creation characterized by God's final, eternal peace.

For Those Who Sing Psalm 120

As the church conducts her pilgrimage toward the New Jerusalem through the wastelands of a war-torn world, she is constantly being tempted to take sides in worldly conflict. Furthermore, her violent surroundings more often than not have a greater influence on her than she does on her violent surroundings. As a result, we see a balkanized church divided into warring factions that reflect rather than reform the world. A good way to begin healing these rifts is to lead the church and the world in the right kind of songs. Songs are powerful and may be used to facilitate alienation or to facilitate reconciliation. Let's pay attention to what we sing, and let's be sure that we are singing songs that the Spirit can use to broker peace, to heal, and to reconcile rather than to foment war, to wound, and to alienate.

Kevin Youngblood

I Cry unto the Lord

Psalm 120

Marva L. Hughes | Marva L. Hughes

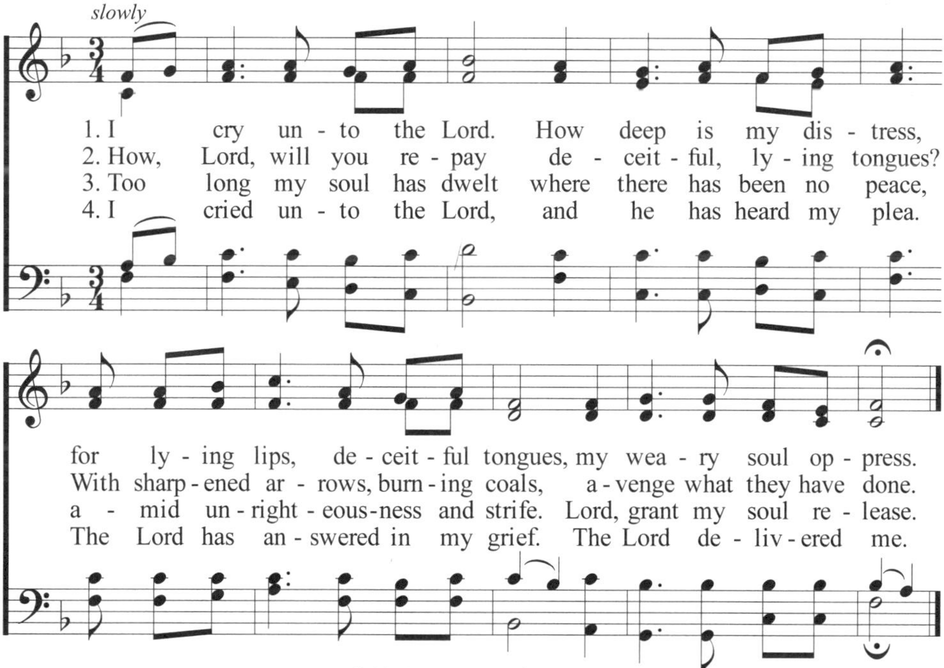

In My Day of Distress

Psalm 120

Gary Pendergrass Gary Pendergrass

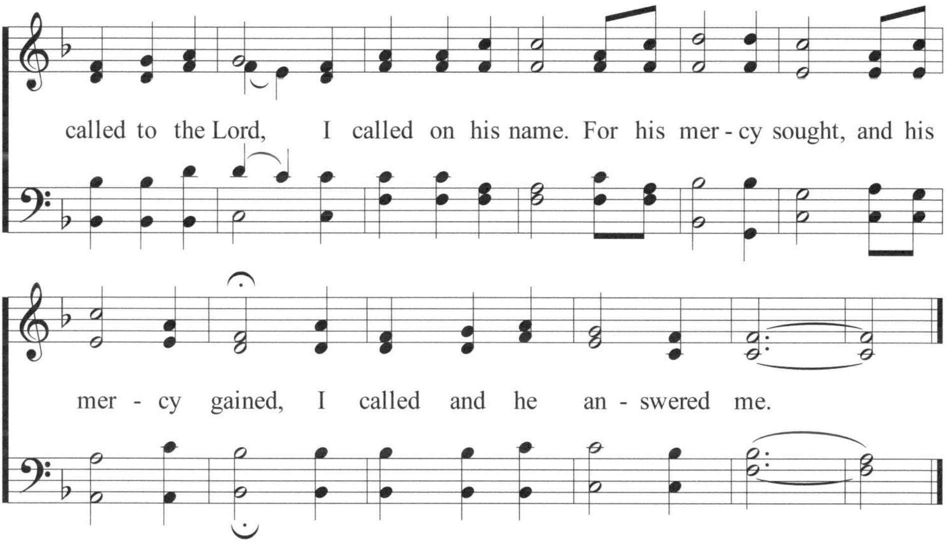
called to the Lord, I called on his name. For his mer - cy sought, and his
mer - cy gained, I called and he an - swered me.

Psalm 121

Translation

A Song of Ascents.
†1 I lift my eyes to the mountains. From where does my help come?
*2 My help is from the LORD, maker of heaven and earth.

†3 May he not let your foot slip; may your keeper not slumber.
*4 Indeed, Israel's keeper neither slumbers nor sleeps!
†5 The LORD is your keeper; the LORD is your shade at your right hand.
*6 By day the sun will not strike you, nor the moon by night.

†7 May the LORD keep you from all evil; may the LORD keep your life.
*8 May the LORD keep your going out and coming back, now and forevermore.

Structure and Poetry

Second of the "Psalms of Ascents" (Pss. 120–134), Psalm 121 was part of a traveling liturgical collection probably used by pilgrims on their way to (and perhaps from) festival worship at the temple in Jerusalem.

In two different ways, the structure of Psalm 121 can be laid out to show its function as a farewell liturgy of sorts.

The first approach follows the two voices in the psalm:

Voice 1, in vv. 1–2, marks the beginning of the sojourn.
Voice 2, in vv. 3–8, is a prayer and a blessing by the one (or ones) who stays behind.

It is possible that this psalm was used responsively, by the one (or ones) about to depart for the temple, and those who were staying, a sort of liturgy of farewell and safe travels.

The second approach identifies three different emphases in the psalm:

A statement of confidence in the Lord	vv. 1–2
A seconding of that confidence	vv. 3–6
A benediction or blessing, calling upon that confidence	vv. 7–8

This progression is built upon the claim that the Lord is the "keeper" of this people (strikingly, both "Lord" and "keep/er" appear six times in the psalm's 8 verses). While the word "keep" or "keeper" does not appear in the original statement of confidence, it peppers the remainder of the psalm. One might paraphrase each section as follows:

Who is my keeper?	vv. 1–2
The Lord is the one who keeps	vv. 3–6
May the one who keeps Israel, keep you	vv. 7–8

Either of these structural views of Psalm 121 is served poetically by the basic pattern of extension from verse to verse, which follows the shape of generic parallelism. Verse 2 answers the question of verse 1: "From where does my help come?" From the Lord; verse 4 extends verse 3: may your keeper never slumber, our keeper neither slumbers nor sleeps; and verses 6 and 8 amplify verses 5 and 7.

The overarching protective sense of the psalm is brought home in the final verse, which calls upon the Lord to "keep your going out and your coming back." If this is a pilgrimage psalm, then the going out and returning suggest that the protection invoked will cover the whole of the journey to Jerusalem. At the same time, this bidding is for "now and forevermore," in other words, for every day, and for every journey.

Theology and Application

Psalm 121 paints the theological picture of a God who is tireless in keeping the divine eye on all of Israel and the individual; of a God who provides places of safe travel ("lest you dash your foot against a stone," to borrow from Ps. 91), and of rest and safety (shade and shelter from sun and moon) day and night; and of a God who is comprehensive in care, protecting "from all evil," "now and forevermore."

These are bold theological claims, which for the one who is stumbling, or lost, or struggling may ring hollow. But the psalm begins with hopefulness, with the positive assertion that help is found in the Lord, and ends with the fervent wish of others on behalf of the traveler through this life, that the Lord will be ever present to help and keep.

For Those Who Sing Psalm 121

For one who is on a journey, whether literal or metaphorical, this psalm offers the hopeful and encouraging vision of a God who keeps the divine eye open and on us. This psalm invites us to keep our eyes open and up as well. While one may look to the mountains with either trepidation or confidence—*From where will my help come?* or *From there my help comes!*—the hopeful tone of the prayer is predominant. This is the song of one who is confident that in all circumstances the Lord is present and potent to help. It also serves as an exhortation to such hope. Mendelssohn's soaring "Lift thine eyes to the mountains" makes of this description an exhortation, turning description, "I lift my eyes . . ." to direction, "Lift thine eyes . . . ."

> Lift thine eyes, O lift thine eyes to the mountains, whence
> cometh help.
> Thy help cometh from the Lord, the Maker of heaven and earth.
> He hath said, thy foot shall not be moved. Thy Keeper will
> never slumber.

This is the hopeful posture to which Psalm 121 calls us in our journeying.

Rolf and Karl Jacobson

He Watches Over You

Psalm 121

Jerry Shipp | Ruth Ann Somervell

I Lift Up My Eyes to the Hills

Psalm 121

Michael E. Showalter | Michael E. Showalter

Psalm 122

Translation

A Song of Ascents. Of David.
†1 I rejoiced when they said to me, "Let us go up to the house of the LORD!"

*2 Our feet are standing within your gates, O Jerusalem!
*3 O Jerusalem! You are built as a city which is joined together well,
*4 to which the tribes go up, the tribes of the LORD!

† It is a commandment for Israel to give thanks to the name of the LORD,
5 for there the thrones for judgment sit, the thrones of the house of David.

*6 Pray for the peace of Jerusalem! "May those who love you be at ease.
*7 May there be peace within your walls, and rest within your towers."
*8 For the sake of my family and my neighbors, may I ask for peace within you.
*9 For the sake of the house of the LORD our God, may I seek good for you.

Structure and Poetry

If Psalm 121 had two voices speaking (in vv. 1–2 and 3–8), Psalm 122 seems to be a single voice speaking first of "I," then of a "we," and addressing others, a "you."

In its opening verse, the psalm recalls the invitation to join in a pilgrimage to the temple in Jerusalem, to "the house of the Lord." This invitation brought joy to the psalmist's heart. There is a jump in both space and time between verses 1 and 2, with verses 2–4 amounting to a "we have arrived." Now standing within the walls of Jerusalem, the psalm becomes an ode to the city which houses the house of the Lord. The fifth verse is something of a pivot or hinge, turning from reflection on the sojourn and arrival, to the invitation to join in prayer that makes up the psalm's remaining four verses (vv. 6–9). Verses 4b–5 bear rereading at this point:

> It is a commandment for Israel
> to give thanks to the name of the Lord.
> For there the thrones for judgment sit,
> the thrones of the house of David.

Notice that the commandment for Israel is to "give thanks," which is the purpose of the pilgrimage. There is a debate about the meaning of this verb. Many scholars have argued that Hebrew does not have a verb that specifically means "to give thanks," and argue here that the meaning should be understood as "to confess" or "bear witness." But Patrick Miller noted, "The dimension of thanksgiving need not be played down in the Psalter or in Hebrew thought generally."[7] The point is that the psalmist and others have come to Jerusalem to exalt God, thank God, and confess his name. The psalmist has come to Jerusalem in response to the religious expectation that pilgrimage be made. Thematically, religiously, and structurally, verse 5 is central.

A striking poetic feature of this psalm is that (not unlike the Songs of Zion, see Psalms 46, 48, 76, 84, and 87) it addresses itself directly to the city of Jerusalem: "O Jerusalem" (vv. 2–3), and "May those who love you." The city itself is lauded for its beauty, as the honored and honorable place where God's house is located, and where the "tribes of the Lord," i.e., all Israel, gather together. This poetic address is not unique to Psalm 122 (compare Pss. 116:19; 137:5–7; 147:12; contrast Ps. 125, in which Jerusalem is exclaimed *about*, rather than to), but here it serves to emphasize the locus of well-being found in, and desired for: the "holy city."

Theology and Application

On the surface, there may seem to be little that is explicitly theological in this psalm. The psalm appears to be an ode to Jerusalem, like the Songs of Zion. But there is, in biblical theology, a strong connection between God and the place where God's name dwells or on which it rests. This is made explicit in several psalms:

Psalm 76:1–2	In Judah God is known, his name is great in Israel. His abode has been established in Salem, his dwelling place in Zion. (NRSV)
Psalm 74:2	Remember Mt. Zion, where you [O God] came to dwell. (NRSV)

It is possible, then, that in the address to "Jerusalem," we may hear an address to God (i.e., "Jerusalem" may be a poetic reference to Yahweh).

Verse 5, the central verse of the psalm both structurally and religiously, characterizes the sojourn to Jerusalem as a "commandment" (which may also be translated as "decree" or "statute") for Israel. This psalm, then, chronicles a response to the command in Exodus 23:14–19 and Leviticus 23:14–43 for Israel to come to Jerusalem during the three major festivals of the year, Passover, Pentecost, and

[7] Patrick Miller, *Interpreting the Psalms* (Philadelphia: Fortress Press, 1986), 4.

Booths. This same "commandment" is referenced elsewhere in the psalms, see in particular Psalm 81:1–5, in which festal worship with singing, trumpet-sounding, and other instrumentation gives rise to praise of the Lord. Psalm 122 identifies the commandment as being, specifically, to "bear witness" to God's name, without any reasons or examples given. The content of the commanded witness is absent. Psalm 81 offers a fruitful comparison at this point, where praise of God's name is descriptive of God's activities and deeds in Israel's story, explicitly. While there is no description in Psalm 122, that praise is implicit in the yoking of bearing witness with the command to make pilgrimage.

For Those Who Sing Psalm 122

Psalm 122 is an invitation into the presence of God—first answered by the psalmist and then echoed by him. This invitation is for a purpose, praising the name of the Lord. It is in the praising of God's name that peace and ease and rest are to be found, and it is to this peace-bringing praise which the psalm now invites, or perhaps better, commands those who read it. In a sense, Psalm 122 serves as a sort of summary psalm for the whole of the Psalter, the "hymnbook of the temple," which, as the collection is called in Hebrew, "Praises" (*tehilim*).

Rolf and Karl Jacobson

May There Be Peace

Psalm 122

Jack R. Reese | Jack R. Reese

May There Be Peace

I Was Glad When They Said unto Me

Psalm 122

Mark Shipp

Chris Stivers
Arr.: D. J. Bulls

I Was Glad When They Said unto Me

Psalm 123

Translation

A Song of Ascents.

†1 To you I lift my eyes, O you who sit in the heavens!

*2 Indeed, as the eyes of servants to the hand of their masters, as the eyes of a maid to the hand of her mistress, so are our eyes to the LORD our God, until he has mercy on us!

†3 Be gracious to us, O LORD, be gracious to us! For we have had more than our fill of contempt.

*4 Our very soul has had more than our fill of the scorn of those who are at ease, of the contempt of those who are proud.

Structure and Poetry

Psalm 123 begins in a fashion similar to Psalm 121, with a "lifting of the eyes." While for Psalm 121 it leads to an immediate question, "from where will my help come," here the question, or better, request, is delayed for a few verses: the imploring "be gracious to us" of verse 3. Again, where in Psalm 121 the eyes are lifted "to the hills" (and perhaps implicitly beyond, to the help that comes from the Lord), here the lifting is explicitly beyond the hills, up to the one "who sits in the heavens."

After this familiar introduction, the psalm moves quickly into a poetic comparison after the style of as "A," so "B." In order to communicate just how the psalmist waits for the Lord to answer, a comparison is made with servants and masters. As a servant waits for his master, eyes on his hands, and as a maid waits upon her mistress, eyes on her hands, so the author of the psalm watches and waits for God. Whether fearfully or faithfully is not specified, nor is that necessary, as awaiting the Master's mercy may well be either or both.

It is interesting that the "hand" of God does not occur here (as it does frequently in the Psalms, cf. 10:12; 20:6; 31:5; 75:8; 77:2; 109:27; 118:15–16, etc.), as the parallelism would be fuller. Perhaps this an intentional elision, where dropping the expected parallel feature serves to magnify it.

This waiting is insistent, desperate, even hungry—feelings which resonate with us. In the *Table Talks*, there is a recollection of Martin Luther and his dog, who sat at his feet beside the table, begging for scraps. Luther said of this begging, "Oh, if I could only pray the way this dog watches the meat! All his thoughts are concentrated on the piece of meat. Otherwise he has no thought, wish, or hope." This, again, is the kind of expectant "eyeing" of the Lord which the psalmist models.

As with many lines of Hebrew poetry, there is also clear parallelism in verses 2–4, which serves first to extend the "as . . . so" comparison, and second to amplify the intensity of that which has been "more than our fill." Servants . . . maids . . . we . . . contempt . . . scorn . . . contempt (again) . . . These extending parallels draw the reader of the psalm on, and, ending as it does without resolution (i.e. "and the lord answered," cf. Ps. 18:6ff), intensifies the sense of tireless waiting which the psalm embodies.

Theology and Application

As with Psalm 122, we encounter another of the sojourner-psalms which does not employ much in the way of explicitly descriptive theology. If we were to limit ourselves to what the psalm explicitly says about God, we could say only that God "sits in heaven." But there is, implicitly, a critical theological argument at work in this psalm. Implicit in the expectant watching and waiting, the continued "lifting of the eyes" to the heavens, is that the God "who sits in the heavens" is not simply far removed, distant, or disinterested in the plight of God's servants. The expectation implies a great deal about God, first and foremost that God can be waited upon hopefully. What is more, this God can be expected to be merciful and gracious, and to care that the proud, and those who sit at their ease, have neither care nor compassion for those who suffer.

Here again, this psalm may well assume a great deal of the reader, namely some familiarity with the common comparison of the wicked and the righteous, the proud and the faithful, the foundational contrasting image with which the Psalter begins (cf. Ps. 1).

As we read this psalm, we are invited into the shared interpretive space. Through this psalm we are invited to reflect on what we wait for, upon whom we are waiting, and how we await it/him.

There is a legend about Alexander the Great receiving requests from his subject. One man who had traveled for many miles and waited for many days, when he finally stood before the great king, asked him for land to start a farm, money for seed to plant, and livestock to tend. To the surprise of his advisors, Alexander granted each of the man's requests. When asked why he did it, Alexander replied, "Because he treated me like a king, he asked of me as though I were a king, how could I act otherwise?"

For Those Who Sing Psalm 123

Psalm 123 imagines waiting for God, a waiting that is of a particular nature, a persistent waiting, an expectant waiting, which will endure "until God has mercy on us." The conviction which this psalm would engender in us is that God's mercy will be ours, because while the Lord sits [enthroned] in the heavens, the Lord is not blind to the contempt that is heaped on his people. As the old hymn by Isaac Watts puts it:

> Those that in wealth and pleasure live,
> Our daily groans deride,
> And thy delays of mercy give
> Fresh courage to their pride.
>
> Our foes insult us, but our hope
> In thy compassion lies;
> This thought shall bear our spirits up,
> That God will not despise.

Rolf and Karl Jacobson

Have Mercy on Us

Psalm 123

Gary Pendergrass | Gary Pendergrass

To You I Lift Up My Eyes

Psalm 123

Mark Shipp | D. J. Bulls

Psalm 124

Translation

A Song of Ascents. Of David.

†1 If it had not been the LORD who was for us, let Israel now say:
*2 "If it had not been the LORD who was for us," when human beings rose
against us,
*3 then they would have swallowed us alive, when their anger burned
against us!
*4 Then the waters would have overwhelmed us, the river would have come
over our very soul!
*5 Then the raging waters would have come over our very soul!

†6 Blessed be the LORD, who did not give us over to be prey for their teeth!
*7 Our very soul is like a bird that has escaped from the snare of the trappers.
The snare is shattered and we have escaped.

*8 Our help is in the name of the LORD, maker of heaven and earth.

Structure and Poetry

As the beginning of Psalm 123 mirrors Psalm 121:1, so the ending of Psalm 124 (v. 8), mirrors Psalm 121:2:

Our help is in the name of the LORD, maker of heaven and earth.	My help is from the LORD, maker of heaven and earth.

The main difference between the two verses is clear, the shift in the opening from "my" to "our." This pattern is common in the Psalter (cf. Pss. 78:1–8 and 106:4–8), and in the Songs of Ascent as well (Pss. 122:1–2; 123:1–2). Here, this shift may serve to amplify the echoing invitation that stands between verse 1a and verse 2a, "let Israel now say." If earlier in the use of these psalms it was the "I" of the psalmist who spoke, "*my* help comes from the LORD," the invitation is now extended to include all of Israel, "let Israel now say," in response to God's deliverance of the people, which leads to the statement of confidence that concludes the psalm, "*Our* help is in the name of the LORD" (for a similar shift see Ps. 122:6–9).

The other difference, emphasizing the "name of the Lord," echoes Psalm 122:4, and in and of itself is not necessarily vital, although it does highlight once again a shared emphasis of this group of psalms.

Taking these beginnings and endings together, one can certainly see that there are common themes and terms within the Songs of Ascent. What is more, the dual mirroring may invite a reading of Psalms 123 and 124 as an exploration of the introductory theme set out in Psalm 121:1–2. The lifting of the eyes to the hills in Psalm 121:1 leads to a question, "From where will my help come?" Psalm 123 picks up on that question and becomes a more prolonged reflection on the need for an active and merciful God without resolving the question. Psalm 121:2 is, again, a statement of confidence, "My help comes from the Lord . . . ." Psalm 124, then, seems to suggest a looking back upon how God "was for us"—that is, how God has shown up, been gracious and merciful, and delivered the psalmist (and the psalmist's people) during times of trouble. The structure of such a reading would look like this:

Psalm 121:1
  Psalm 123:1
  Psalm 123:2–4
  Psalm 124:1–7
  Psalm 124:8
Psalm 121:2

It is not certain, by any means, that these two psalms were intentionally composed to be read against Psalm 121:1–2, but it is certainly plausible to do so, and this may make for a fruitful reading.

Theology and Application

The theology of this psalm is, in comparison at least to Psalm 123, wildly explicit. God is the "maker of heaven and earth," who is "for us," and who "shatters the snare" so that one may escape (cf. Ps. 91:3).

It is important to note that the profound hopefulness of this psalm is not "pie in the sky," or Pollyanna; this psalm cannot be read as encouraging or assuming perfect safety in all things, at all times, as though God's provision were a shield against all that might come. Rather, the psalm identifies what has happened as being God's will. Verses 1–6 of the psalm offer an extended "if . . . then . . ." reflection. This "if . . . then . . ." is doubled and tripled as it grows into a full-blown hymn of praise, "If . . . If . . . Then . . . then . . . then . . . ." If God had not been for us, the psalm argues, if God had not been for us, *then* we would have been swallowed alive, *then* we would have been overwhelmed, *then* "our very soul," our whole life, would have been lost. The psalmist remembers and celebrates what God has done by imagining what would have happened if God had done nothing.

In other words, the theology of this psalm is not forward-looking in a simplistic way, rather it is looking backward in a faithful way. The life-experience of the psalmist (and the psalmist's people) is examined through the eyes of faith, and what God has done for this people is declared. It is this God, this active, for-us God, which the psalm praised and in so praising, recommends to the one who reads, hears, or prays it as her own.

For Those Who Sing Psalm 124

The phrase "Let Israel now say" was, as noted above, likely an invitation for the worshiping congregation to respond antiphonally. Here the explicit saying that we are invited to join in is the proposition, "If it had not been the Lord who was for us . . . ." This proposition prompts faithful theological reflection on God's providence in our own lives. If it had been some other "god" or some other thing—wealth, status, our own bootstraps—that we had to rely on, what then might have been the outcome? In putting this reflective phrase on our lips, Psalm 124 invites us to join our voices in looking back on the blessings, the triumphs, the recoveries, etc., that we have known in our lives and to see them as what God has done for us. This will not only allow us proper theological perspective on our lives so far, but will enable us to face all that might come our way moving forward. As Bishop Robert Lowry's great hymn has us sing,

> No storm can shake my inmost calm while to that Rock I'm clinging. Since Christ is Lord of heaven and earth, how can I keep from singing?

Rolf and Karl Jacobson

Had It Not Been the Lord

Psalm 124

Debbie Dorman | Debbie Dorman

Bless-ed be the Lord who would not give us up.
Bless-ed be the Lord for his un-fail-ing love.
The snare is bro-ken, and we have es-caped.
1st time D.C.
Last time Fine
Our help is in the name of the Lord. Bless-ed be the Lord!

Our Help Is the Name of the Lord

Psalm 124

Zach Olson | Julianne Grace Brown and Mel Witcher

Psalm 125

Translation

A Song of Ascents.

†1 Those who trust in the Lord are like Mount Zion; it cannot be moved and remains forever.

*2 Jerusalem! The mountains surround her and the Lord surrounds his people, now and forevermore.

†3 For the scepter of the wicked shall not rest upon the land allotted to the righteous ones,
in order that the righteous ones might not reach out their hands to sin.

*4 Do good, O Lord, to the good, and to the upright of heart,

*5 but to those inclined to their crooked ways, the Lord will lead away those who do evil.

* Peace be upon Israel!

Structure and Poetry

This psalm begins with an interesting comparison, one that is perhaps unique in the Psalter, saying that the righteous, "those who trust in the Lord," are "like Zion." In the Psalms, Zion is almost always a location from which, for example, God "shines forth" (50:2), and from which the Lord's help comes (14:7). In other places, "Daughter Zion" is a metonym for the people of Israel (cf. Ps. 9:14; Lam. 2:18; Mic. 4:10). Here, however, the strength and security of Mt. Zion is a simile for those who trust in the Lord. Those who trust are like the mountain, specifically the mountain where the Lord dwells (cf. Pss. 122:3–4; 9:11). In other words, those who trust in the Lord find themselves in the presence of the Lord.

This opening comparison is seconded and extended in the second verse. "Jerusalem!" may well be read as having an ellipsis before it, suggesting a second simile, in which those who trust in the Lord are like the holy city, surrounded and protected by the mountains. In the second simile, the mountains are the Lord, not those who trust. These two similes set the stage for the parallelism and contrast that make up the rest of the psalm.

Because those who trust in the Lord are like Zion, which cannot be moved, and like Jerusalem, which is surrounded by the Lord's protective ranging:

v. 3: the wicked shall not rest // the land belongs to the righteous ones
v. 3: so that the righteous ones // might not be led to sin
v. 4: the Lord will do good to the good and the upright of heart
//
v. 5: to those who walk crookedly, along with all who do evil, the Lord will lead them away

These several contrasting statements paint a picture of the security and stability that those who trust in the Lord will enjoy, and in which they will be "kept" (to borrow language from Psalm 121). The thrust of these poetic parallels is that the wicked will be removed from the land (vv. 3a, 5), which belongs, properly, to the righteous (v. 3, i.e., those who trust in the Lord [v. 1]); this leading away of those inclined to crooked, wicked, evil ways prevents the righteous ones from falling into sin.

The contrasting parallelism of verses 3–5 drives the reader from the opening affirmation to the goal, which is declared in the last line of the psalm, that "Peace be upon Israel." This is more than a goal, more than a bidding, or a hope; it is a reality, joyfully exclaimed: "Peace be . . . peace *is* . . . upon Israel."

Theology and Application

The theology of Psalm 125 is driven by its opening similes, showing us a God who is trustworthy and in whom stability and endurance for this life may be found. Because God is trustworthy, those who trust God are made worthy, i.e., become the righteous ones (cf. Gen. 15:6; Rom. 4:3).

While the extended contrast of the ways of the wicked and the ways of the righteous (not to mention their sharply differing ends) found in Psalm 1 are not so neatly balanced in this psalm, the comparison is similar. Those who trust in the Lord are firm and enduring, like Mt. Zion ("They are like trees planted by streams of water, which yield their fruit in its season, and their leaves do not wither," Ps. 1:3 NRSV), not so those whose ways are crooked ("The wicked are not so, but are like chaff that the wind drives away," Ps. 1:4 NRSV). Furthermore, the comparison of the righteous and the wicked is not simply laid out for the reader to understand based on that comparison. Rather, the reader is told that the Lord will prevent the wicked from resting their scepter on the land, in order that the righteous not fall prey to temptation or be led astray.

Psalm 125 describes, and thereby prescribes, the kind of righteousness that comes only through trusting in the Lord. It is that kind of trust, that kind of uprightness of heart, to which the psalm calls us.

For Those Who Sing Psalm 125

In the life of faith there are those "wicked" who oppose us, whose evil challenges us and at times entices us. Jesus said, "you always have the poor with you" (Mark 14:7 NRSV), but he may well have said the same of this psalm's wicked ones. There will be those who would lead the faithful astray, whether in explicit terms, tempting God's people, or through example. "Scepter" in this psalm almost certainly has to do with leadership. When the leaders of the people set a poor example or chart a faithless road, the people are certainly bound to follow in one way or another. But Psalm 125 offers a different theological worldview, one in which God will be an ever-present help in trouble, even when that troubling comes from our leaders. The promise that this psalm sings is that the one who trusts in the Lord and in the Lord's way "cannot be moved."

Rolf and Karl Jacobson

Peace upon Israel

Psalm 125

Marva L. Hughes | Marva L. Hughes

for in his right - eous - ness they dwell,
em - braced by his ev - er - last - ing pres - ence.
1, 2
3
Peace up - on Is - ra - el! el!
Peace up - on Is - ra - el!

We Pray for Peace

Psalm 125

Matthew K. Porter

Matthew K. Porter

Psalm 126

Translation

A Song of Ascents.

†1 When the Lord restored those who were returning[a] to Zion, we were like
those who dream.

*2 Then our mouth was filled with laughter and our tongue with a ringing cry
of rejoicing. Then it was said among the nations, "The Lord has done great
things among these *people*."

*3 The Lord did great things among us; we were joyful.

†4 Restore us who are returning,[b] O Lord, like the water channels in the
Negev.[c]

*5 Those who sow in tears with a ringing cry of rejoicing will reap the harvest.

*6 Indeed, the one who goes out weeping, carrying seeds for sowing,

* will come in with a ringing cry of rejoicing, carrying the sheaves.

[a] The NIV and NRSV translations render this phrase "the fortunes of," while the NASB renders it "the captive ones of." The KJV has "the captivity of," however. Whatever the exact interpretation of this phrase, it undoubtedly refers to the Israelites' return to Jerusalem at the conclusion of the Babylonian captivity. See the further comment on verse 4.

[b] The phrase translated here as "those who were/are returning" is a difficulty in the Hebrew text. Most translations harmonize their renderings of verse 1—thus "the fortunes of," "the captivity of."

[c] The Negev is the desert area in the southern portion of Palestine. Thus many translations render the word as "the south."

Structure and Poetry

Psalm 126 is the seventh psalm in the collection of psalms in Book Five of the Psalter designated "Songs of Ascents" (Pss. 120–134). It is classified as a community lament, a psalm in which the gathered community of faith calls on God to come to its aid as it struggles through a difficult situation. The psalm opens with the community remembering a time in its past when God restored them to Zion and did great things among them. It continues with a petition to God to once again restore the community so that it may rejoice in God's good provisions. The psalm's structure, thus, may be outlined as follows:

Verses 1–3:	Praise for God's provisions in the past
Verse 4:	Cry to God in a new situation
Verses 5–6:	Praise for God's provisions in the future

Theology and Application

One psalm scholar characterizes Psalm 126 as "joy remembered and joy anticipated."[8] The community of faith recalled their restoration to the land after the exile, an event that brought about "laughter" and a "ringing cry of rejoicing" by the community of faith and awe among the "nations" because of what God did on their behalf. Now, in another difficult circumstance, the community once again calls on God to restore them.

The format of Psalm 126 is typical of the community psalms of lament in the Psalter. The people find themselves in a distressful situation, and so they cry out to God for deliverance. But an essential element of that crying out, that of asking for help, is the recollection of what God has done for them in the past—assurance that God is able and willing to come to the aid of God's people once again. An interesting element of Psalm 126 is that the psalm singers repeat the words of verse 1's memory of past deliverance in verse 4's plea for help in the present circumstance.

Three powerful images bring Psalm 126 to life. First, we find a threefold repetition of "ringing cry of rejoicing" (vv. 2, 5, and 6). The Hebrew word used here suggests a loud and emotive celebration of God's goodness. This word is used in the book of Psalms to describe the actions of all of God's creation, not just humanity. In Psalm 96:12, for example, we read, "then shall all the trees of the forest give a ringing cry of rejoicing," and in Psalm 98:8, "let the hills give a ringing cry of rejoicing" (translations mine). Thus, humanity, along with all creation, is encouraged to celebrate God's care.

Second, water is a powerful image in Psalm 126, as it is in many other psalms—see especially Psalm 42. In Psalm 126, the water channels in verse 4, those seasonal wadis that fill with nourishing water in the rainy season in the desert of the Negev, give way to the tears of those sowing the arid fields in hopes of a good crop that will feed their households.

And, third, the agricultural imagery that we find in verses 5–6—that of sowing and reaping—is what those who analyze literary structures call a "merism." The words "sow" and "reap," indicating the beginning and the end of the farming process, are meant to be understood as representative of the whole season's process: the planting, the watchful care, the weeding, and finally the harvest. The

---

[8] James L. Mays, *Psalms*, Interpretation: A Bible Commentary for Teaching and Preaching (Louisville: John Knox Press, 1994), 399.

psalmist employs day-to-day images of human toil in these verses to describe God's restorative work.

God's deliverance, God's good care, may very well feel like refreshing water of the Negev turned to tears of struggle to plant a good crop. Sowing is always an act of anticipation, and so Psalm 126 tells us that those tears will give way to the gift of a good crop to feed, nourish, and restore the people of God, and that, in the end, all creation can and will give a "ringing cry of rejoicing" to this good God.

For Those Who Sing Psalm 126

In a world so increasingly divided between the "haves" and the "have nots," the "citizens" and the "immigrants," the "insiders" and the "outsiders," the words of Psalm 126 are a powerful reminder of the importance of "place." So many people in the world today have been "displaced" and struggle to find a place to once again call their own. Without "place," how can parents provide for their children? Without "place," how can people reap a good "crop"? Without "place," how can people "dream and laugh and give a ringing cry of rejoicing"? The words of Psalm 126 remind us that God's good provisions extend to and are available to all.

Nancy deClaissé-Walford

Restore Us, O Lord

Psalm 126

Jack R. Reese — Jack R. Reese

like rain in a des - o - late land.
Your mer - cy a - dored, your king - dom re - stored
rit.
with joy by your gra - cious hand.
Optional CODA
Lord of mer - cies, im - plore us, your king - dom be - fore us.
rit.
Re - store us by your gra - cious hand.

The Lord Has Done Great Things

Psalm 126

Debbie Dorman

Debbie Dorman

Psalm 127

Translation

A Song of Ascents. Of Solomon.

†1 If the Lord does not build a house, the ones building it toil uselessly. If the Lord does not keep watch over a city, the ones keeping watch over it keep watch uselessly.

*2 It is useless for you to rise early and go late to your rest, all the while eating the bread of anxious labor, for *the* Lord gives sleep to the one he loves.

†3 Behold, children are a gift from the Lord, a reward, the fruit of the womb.

†4 Like arrows in the hand of a mighty one, so are the children of your youth.

*5 Happy will be the mighty one who has filled his quiver with them; they will not be ashamed when they speak with enemies in the *city* gate.

Structure and Poetry

Psalm 127 is the eighth psalm in the collection of psalms in Book Five of the Psalter designated "Songs of Ascents" (Pss. 120–134). It is classified as a wisdom psalm, the first of three in the Songs of Ascents,[9] and is the only psalm in the Psalter ascribed to Solomon except Psalm 72. A wisdom psalm provides instruction in right living and right faith in the tradition of the other wisdom writings of the Old Testament—Job, Proverbs, and Ecclesiastes. Two themes appear in the two sections of Psalm 127, which many scholars suggest are two "proverbial" sayings that have been joined together. Other scholars maintain that the psalm is a unity with a single theme running through it. Nevertheless, we may outline its simple structure in the following way:

Verses 1–2: The house
Verses 3–5: The children

Theology and Application

Verses 1–2 address the uselessness of various human undertakings—building a house, safeguarding a city, working long hours—unless the Lord is involved in those undertakings. "House" (v. 1) is a rich and multivalent word in Hebrew.

[9] The others are Psalms 128 and 133.

It certainly refers to family dwellings, as we see, for instance, in Genesis 19:2 and Judges 11:31. It can also indicate extended families (Exod. 40:38; Josh. 24:15; Ezek. 36:22); ruling dynasties (2 Sam. 3:1; 1 Kings 16:3); or the temple in Jerusalem (2 Kings 22:3; Jer. 7:2).

Since the Songs of Ascents are thought to be pilgrimage songs that the people of Israel sang as they made their way to Jerusalem to celebrate various festivals, we may picture the house of verse 1 as the temple, just as we may picture the city referenced there as Jerusalem. But we may also picture the "house" in verse 1 as a family that one strives to "build" and the "city" as the immediate environs of that family. In either instance, the message is clear. Unless the Lord is involved in such undertakings, all our striving is useless.

In like manner, verse 2 cautions against anxiously working long hours, since the Lord gives rest to those he "loves." The basic meaning of the Hebrew word has to do with a mutual and favorable relationship between two parties. God loves humanity, and if humanity reciprocates that love, God will give rest and rejuvenation for the tasks of our daily lives. Further, in the context of Psalm 127, the words of verse 2 may be understood as a caution against neglecting home and family as one works to provide for that home and family.

Verses 3–5 stress the importance of one's family above all else. The word translated as "children" in verses 4 and 5 is *baniym*; the word translated as "build" in verse 1 is *banah*. The acoustic similarity between the two words helps tie the two sections of the psalm together and reinforces the suggestion above, that one understanding of the "house" being built in verse 1 is a family.

The language of verses 4 and 5 can be somewhat problematic in our gender-sensitive twenty-first century context. If, though, we can keep in mind the original context in which the words of this psalm were sung and know that we are permitted to sing these songs in our own contexts, then we can widen the scope of meaning for the "mighty one" to include both women and men.

The final words of Psalm 127 have been interpreted in two distinct ways based on the translation of the pronouns in the last strophe of verse 5. The pronouns are plural in the Hebrew text ("they"), suggesting that the referent is "the children" rather than "the mighty one." The gate of a city in the ancient Near East was the gathering place for the elders and judges who settled disputes, rendered judgment, and made important decisions regarding the life of the community. Thus the children of the "mighty one," the one who wisely builds and guards a house and who works diligently but embraces the soothing rest of God, can stand tall and proud in their community.

For Those Who Sing Psalm 127

Psalm 127 is a wonderful advocacy for and celebration of family life, tinged with the reminders of the dangers of how we go about "family building." What we build and keep watch over, what we rise early for and stay up late tending only matters if God is intimately involved in what we do.

Second, children are indeed a "building project" of life. But as we see more couples struggling with fertility, more persons choosing a single lifestyle, more broken families, and more nonconventional relationships, we are called to expand the term "children" to include far more than our biological offspring. My "child" might be my niece or nephew who can no longer live with his or her biological parent, a project aimed at reducing childhood hunger in my inner city, volunteering to tutor children in my local community, visiting with seniors who wait anxiously for my weekly visits, fostering a child who needs a stable home life, or mentoring the teen down the street who seems to have lost his way. These children, these "building projects," are the sources of our happiness in life (v. 5) for which God gives us restful sleep (v. 2).

Nancy deClaissé-Walford

If the House Is Not Built by the Lord

Psalm 127

Marva L. Hughes | Marva L. Hughes

rest. Do not anx - ious - ly toil, for the Lord pro -
shame, for the Lord has con - struct - ed their dwell - ing
vides, and those whom he loves will be blessed. And
place; the Lord has es - tab - lished their name. The
rit.
those whom he loves will be blessed.
Lord has es - tab - lished their name.

If the Lord Builds Not the Dwelling

Psalm 127

Jack R. Reese | Jack R. Reese

Psalm 128

Translation

A Song of Ascents.
†1 Happy are all who reverence the Lord, who walk in his ways.
*2 What you produce with your hands, that you will eat; you will be happy, and
it will be good to you.
†3 Your wife will be like a fruit-bearing vine in the inner chambers of
your house;
your children will be like the shoots of the olive tree all around your table.
*4 For in this way the mighty one will be blessed, the one who reverences
the Lord.

†5 May the Lord bless you from Zion, and may you see[a] the goodness of
Jerusalem all of your days.
*6 May you *live* to see your children's children; *and may there be* well-being
for Jerusalem!

[a] The verbs "see" here and in verse 6 are in the imperative form. A jussive translation seems most appropriate in the context.

Structure and Poetry

Psalm 128 is ninth in the group of the fifteen psalms in Book Five of the Psalter designated in their superscriptions as "Songs of Ascents." It is classified as a wisdom psalm, the second of three in the Songs of Ascents.[10] Wisdom psalms, like the other wisdom writings of the Old Testament—found in Job, Proverbs, and Ecclesiastes—provide instruction in right living and right faith. While scholars offer a variety of structures for Psalm 128,[11] the most straightforward is two strophes, the first of which Samuel Terrien calls "sapiential salutations," and the second of which he calls "priestly blessing"[12]:

[10] The others are Psalms 127 and 133.

[11] Samuel Terrien, *The Psalms: Strophic Structure and Theological Commentary* (Grand Rapids: Wm. B. Eerdmans, 2003), 832; Leslie C. Allen, *Psalms 101–150*, Word Biblical Commentary, vol. 21 (Waco: Word Books, 1983), 185; and J. Clinton McCann Jr., "The Book of Psalms: Introduction, Commentary, and Reflections," in *The New Interpreter's Bible: A Commentary in Twelve Volumes*, ed. Leander E. Keck, vol. 4 (Nashville: Abingdon Press, 1996), 1200.

[12] Terrien, *The Psalms*, 832.

Verses 1–4:	Wisdom words
Verses 5–6:	Priestly words

Theology and Application

The words of verses 1–4 use much of the vocabulary contained in Psalm 127, permitting us to read the two as "twin psalms," with the words of Psalm 128 reinforcing those of Psalm 127. Their shared vocabulary includes "happy" (127:5; 128:1); "house" (127:1; 128:3); "eat" (127:2; 128:2); "children" (127:3, 4; 128:3, 6); "behold" (127:3; 128:4); and "mighty one" (127:4, 5; 128:4).

The psalm opens with the word "happy," the same word we find in the last verse of Psalm 127. Some Bible versions translate the word as "blessed." It conveys a sense of deep-seated contentment at doing what is right and good. It is the same word used by Jesus in the Sermon on the Mount in the gospel of Matthew (5:3–11). Psalm 128 states that "all" who reverence the Lord are "happy."

While the words of Psalm 127:2 suggest that anxious human toil is useless, verse 2 of Psalm 128 promises that you will eat what you produce with your hands. While the message of Psalm 127 is that a satisfying life is a gift from God, regardless of human toil, Psalm 128 reminds us that we can and must contribute to attaining that satisfied life.

Verse 3 celebrates a "good" family environment to the one who reverences the Lord, depicting one's wife as a fruitful vine and one's children as olive shoots, and the words "the inner chambers of your house" and "your table" in verse 3 suggest the intimacy of family relationships. Verse 6 completes the blessing of the Lord with the confident anticipation of seeing one's children's children.

As is the case with its "twin psalm," Psalm 127, the words of Psalm 128 seem to be very androcentric. We must respect the culture out of which these psalms grew but recognize the timelessness of their messages and permit ourselves to appropriate their words to their twenty-first century context. The words of verse 3 have to do with the flourishing of one's family, whatever form that family takes—the fruit of the labor of one who reverences the Lord and walks in his ways.[13] That person is called "the mighty one" in verse 4 and in verses 5 and 6 receives a twofold blessing: to see the good of Jerusalem and to see one's children's children.

[13] Recall the opening words of the psalm: "Happy are *all* who . . ."

For Those Who Sing Psalm 128

The twofold blessing of Psalm 128:5–6 reminds us of the basic components of "happiness" in life—that deep-seated sense of contentment that one has done and continues to do the right things. Jerusalem, in the context of Psalms 127 and 128, represents the center, the grounding of faith for the psalm singers. The hope for Jerusalem's good in verse 5 and the prayer for well-being (*shalom*) in verse 6 signal the hope for the good and well-being of the faith of one being blessed.

The hope of seeing one's children's children (v. 6) is not just the hope for a long life, but perhaps, more precisely, the hope for a fulfilled life in relationship with one's family—in whatever form that family exists. The singers of Psalm 128 thus remind us that a solid and well-grounded faith and a strong and healthy relationship with our families are the basics, the essentials, of right living with God and with humanity.

Nancy deClaissé-Walford

How Blest Are All Who Fear the Lord

Psalm 128

M. W. Bassford

Michael E. Showalter

Respect the Lord

Psalm 128

Jerry Shipp

James W. Tackett

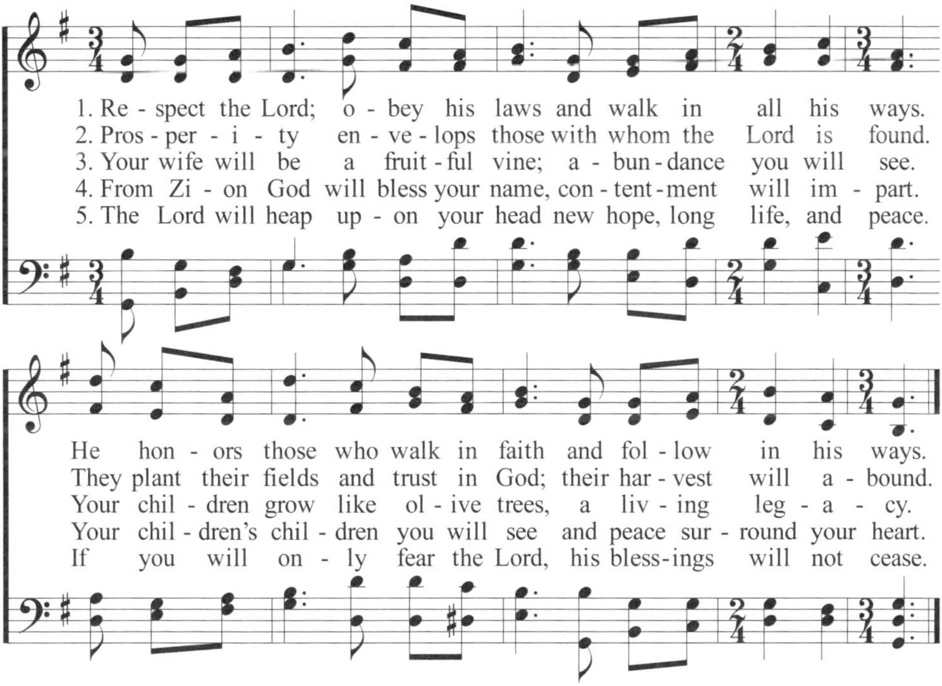

Psalm 129

Translation

A Song of Ascents.

†1 Many times they have oppressed me from my youth. Let Israel say:

†2 Many times they have oppressed me from my youth, but they have not overpowered me.

†3 Their oppression feels like someone plowing a field up and down my back, up and down, over and over.

*4 But the LORD is righteous; he cuts through the ropes that the wicked use to keep me prisoner.

†5 Let the ones who hate Zion be ashamed and go away.

†6 Let them be like wheat seeds growing on a rooftop that wither before they ever have a chance to grow.

†7 Let the ones who go to reap that harvest find nothing and those who come to gather up the produce go away empty-handed.

*8 Let those who pass by and see, not say, "The blessing of the LORD be upon you. We bless you in the name of the LORD."

Structure and Poetry

Psalm 129 is the tenth of the "Songs of Ascents" in Book Five of the Psalter. It continues the agricultural theme of Psalms 126–128, but its tone is quite different. It has been variously categorized as a community lament, an imprecatory psalm, and a hymn of trust. A lament psalm calls on God to right a wrong that has come to the psalm singer(s); an imprecatory psalm calls on God to not just right a wrong, but to inflict the oppressor(s) with grievous harm[14]; and a hymn of trust is one in which the psalm singer(s) thanks God for anticipated deliverance from a harmful situation. How one interprets the psalm depends on how one chooses to translate the verbs in verses 5–8. Following the New Revised Standard Version and the New International Version, I have chosen to translate the verbs as a call to God to act in a vengeful way toward the psalmist's oppressors, nullifying for

[14] See, for instance, Psalms 83, 94, and 137.

them Psalm 128's promise of a blessed life to those who reverence the Lord and walk in his ways.

Another way to understand the psalm is to translate the verbs as assurance of future action on God's part—"God will cut through the ropes; the ones who hate Zion will be ashamed; they will be like seeds growing on a rooftop." With this rendering, the psalm would be understood as a hymn of trust. Whatever its categorization, Psalm 129 may be divided into three parts:

Verses 1–3:	The account of past suffering
Verse 4:	The account of divine rescue
Verses 5–8:	Imprecatory words (or, words of trust)

Theology and Application

The opening words of Psalm 129 appear to be a call to the people of Israel to speak as with one voice about the ongoing oppressive situation in which they find themselves. The word rendered here in verses 1 and 2 as "many times" is translated in the NRSV as "often," and the same Hebrew word is translated in Psalm 120:6 as "too long" and in Psalm 123:4 as "more than enough." The singers of Psalm 129 express a sense of endless and relentless oppression, from their early times as a people ("from my youth"). But the psalm singers state, "they have not overpowered me."

Verse 3 employs an agricultural metaphor to express Israel's oppression: the relentless movement of the plow through the soil, churning up buried soil, bringing it to the surface, and then returning it, broken apart, to the depths from which it came. Here is a powerful image of oppressors continually opening old wounds, pouring salt in them, and then returning them to the depths of the oppressed one's soul.

Verse 4 is the turning point in the psalm. The singers express words of hope that the oppressor will not ultimately prevail with the words, "The LORD is righteous." The word "righteous" has a very simple meaning in Hebrew—"to do the right thing." The Lord is righteous; he will do the right thing by "cutting through the ropes of the oppressors." The word "rope" continues the agricultural imagery of verse 3, suggesting the ropes used by farmers to tether and guide the plow animals through the fields.

Verses 5–8 outline the fate of the oppressors. "Hate" is a powerful word in Hebrew, conveying emotion as well as act. In the act of "hating," persons distance themselves from the object of their hatred, both emotionally and physically. In that emotive act, the oppressors are set apart from, contrasted to, those who reverence the Lord and walk in his ways in Psalm 128:1.

Thus the oppressed express confidence[15] that God will not provide a harvest for the oppressors' undertakings, and that no one will bless their efforts to bring in a bountiful harvest.

For Those Who Sing Psalm 129

The message of Psalm 129 is straightforward. One of my German aunts or uncles said to me once, "Was auch immer du säst; dass du ernten wirst": "Whatever you sow; that you will reap." Oppression is a pervasive presence in our world today—child and spousal abuse, discrimination against "the other," economic injustices that range from lack of food in developing countries to food deserts in developed ones, political corruption, the fallout of warfare, and so forth. The words of the singers in Psalm 129, "Many times" (vv. 1, 2) "from my youth" (vv. 1, 2), remind us that oppression is an age-old human phenomenon. And they remind us that we cannot rest until all such oppression is addressed at its root cause and quashed—until the oppressors are "ashamed and go away" (Ps. 129:5) and never plant their seeds again.

Nancy deClaissé-Walford

[15] Either as realized condemnation, making Psalm 129 a hymn of trust, or as expected condemnation, making Psalm 129 an imprecatory psalm.

How Many Are My Enemies

Psalm 129

Mark Shipp

Michael E. Showalter

Let Israel Confess and Proclaim

Psalm 129

Mark Shipp James W. Tackett

Psalm 130

Translation

A Song of Ascents.

†1 Out of the depths I cry to you, O Lord.
*2 My Lord, listen to me. Be attentive to my entreaties.

†3 If you kept track of wrongdoings, O Lord, then, my Lord, who could stand?
*4 But you offer forgiveness, so you are reverenced.

†5 I wait for the Lord, my whole being waits, waits expectantly for his word.
*6 My whole being *waits expectantly* for my Lord, more so than the guards of the city who wait for the morning, those who wait for the security of the light of day.

†7 Wait expectantly for the Lord, O Israel, for the Lord offers steadfast love and abundant deliverance,
*8 and he will deliver Israel from all of its wrongdoings.

Structure and Poetry

The eleventh of the "Songs of Ascents" in Book Five of the Psalter, Psalm 130 is usually classified as an individual lament, in which a psalm singer calls on God for deliverance from some threatening life situation. Five components make up an individual lament in the book of Psalms[16]:

An invocation, calling on God to hear the words of lament
A complaint, telling God what the cause of the lament is
A petition, telling God what the psalmist wants God to do
An expression of trust, stating why the psalmist believes God will act
An expression of praise, stating the psalmist's intention to praise God

Psalm 130's lament structure is outlined as follows:

Invocation:	Verses 1, 3, 5, 7
Complaint:	Verse 1

[16] Few lament psalms incorporate all the elements of lament; these five elements, however, constitute the genre called "lament."

Petition:	Verses 1, 2
Expression of Trust:	Verses 3–6

Expressions of trust abound in Psalm 130, calling into question the categorization of the psalm as an individual lament. And, in addition, the psalm singer speaks of personal wrongdoings, rather than of oppression by another. Thus we might read Psalm 130 as a hymn of trust, in which the psalm singer speaks of wrongdoing, but of forgiveness and then offers words of admonition to the community of Israel to acknowledge their own wrongdoings and to wait expectantly for deliverance from the Lord.

The psalm divides into four two-verse sections:

Verses 1–2:	A cry to the Lord to listen
Verses 3–4:	A statement of trust in the Lord
Verses 5–6:	A statement of hopeful expectation
Verses 7–8:	An invitation for all Israel to join the hopeful expectation

Theology and Application

Psalm 130 begins with the words, "out of the depths," used elsewhere in the Old Testament in reference to the sea, specifically the Mediterranean, a place of watery storm and potential death.[17] The psalmist likens the current situation to that of one lost at sea, one caught up in a life-threatening situation.

Psalm 130 employs, in verses 1–3 and 5–6, two words used to address God: LORD and my Lord. The word translated "LORD" is *Yahweh*, while the word translated "my Lord" is *Adonai*. Both are common ways of addressing the God of Israel in the Old Testament.

"Entreaties" in verse 2 is a Hebrew word that means "a request to look kindly upon/to be gracious to." It is one of the self-descriptive words spoken by God in Exodus 34:6 as he passes by Moses: "The LORD, the LORD, a God merciful and gracious" (NRSV). The psalm singer asks God to be "gracious" and heed the psalmist's "entreaties."

Verse 3 contains the reason for the psalmist's request—wrongdoings. The Hebrew word occurs often in the Old Testament and is the primary word used to describe human sin and guilt. Its basic meaning is "to bend, curve, turn aside, or twist,"[18] providing a concrete image of what it means to "do wrong"—perhaps an echo of the legal system's charge of "perverting justice."

Verses 5–6 narrate the psalm singer's expectant waiting for God to act. The verses use three Hebrew words to convey the full intent of the psalm singer. In

[17] See Isaiah 51:10; Ezekiel 27:34; Psalm 69:2, 14; Jonah 2:2–6.

[18] E. Jenni and C. Westermann, eds., *Theological Lexicon of the Old Testament*, vol. 2 (Peabody, MA: Hendrickson, 1997), 863.

verse 5, the singer states that she "waits" for the Lord (*qavah*) and "waits expectantly" for his word (*yahal*). Verse 6 describes the waiting (*shamar*) of the guards of the city for the security of daylight, when the possibility of attack from enemies was lessened.

In verses 7–8, the psalm singer turns from self-reflection to all Israel and admonishes them to "wait expectantly" (*yahal*) for the Lord, who offers to them "steadfast love" and "abundant deliverance." "Steadfast love" is rendered in various translations as "faithful love," "lovingkindness," "unfailing love," and "mercy." The Hebrew word has to do with the covenant commitment between God and Israel, and thus may also be translated as "covenant love." Pairing the word with "abundant deliverance" recalls God's past acts to deliver the people as part of the covenant commitment and God's continuing commitment to "abundantly deliver."

For Those Who Sing Psalm 130

Psalm 130 is one of the seven penitential psalms sung during the season of Lent in the medieval church.[19] The psalms were prayed while kneeling each day of the Lenten season, reminding the singer of the great divide between humanity's wrongdoing and God's goodness. But Psalm 130 also reminds the singer of God's offer of "forgiveness" (v. 4), "steadfast/covenant love" and "abundant deliverance" (v. 7). One of Martin Luther's most well-known hymns is his metrical version of Psalm 130. John Wesley wrote, after hearing Psalm 130 sung at St. Paul's Cathedral in London, that his heart was "strangely warmed," much like the two disciples on the Emmaus Road in Luke 24 who felt their "hearts burning within" them as they talked with Jesus about "the law of Moses, the prophets, and the psalms."[20]

As we sing the words of Psalm 130, let us remember those who have walked the paths of faith before us, and let us recall the strength they drew from Psalm 130's admonition to "wait expectantly" for the "steadfast/covenant love" and "abundant deliverance" of the Lord.

Nancy deClaissé-Walford

[19] The others are Psalms 6, 32, 38, 51, 102, and 143.

[20] See, further, J. Clinton McCann Jr., "The Book of Psalms," in *The New Interpreter's Bible*, vol. 4 ed. Leander E. Keck (Nashville: Abingdon Press, 1996), 1,206.

Out of the Depths

Psalm 130

Marva L. Hughes

Marva L. Hughes

From the Depths I Cry to You

Psalm 130

Glover Shipp (1927–2019) and Rachel Shipp

Mark Shipp

My Soul Waits

Psalm 130

for Randy Daw

Sarah Shipp & Jack R. Reese

Jack R. Reese

My Soul Waits

PSALM 131

Translation

A Song of Ascents.

†1 O LORD, my heart is not proud, nor are my eyes arrogant, nor do I walk[a] among things too great or marvelous for me.

†2 Instead, I am calm and stilled like one who is weaned on his mother, like a weaned child upon his mother, like a weaned child is my soul within me.

*3 Israel, wait for the LORD from now on and forevermore.

[a] I prefer the more literal translation "I walk among" to the NASB's "I involve myself" or the NRSV's "occupy myself" because it extends the imagery of the human body in the verse. See Proverbs 21:4, 8.

Structure and Poetry

Many interpreters find it difficult to classify Psalm 131, though some regard it as a hymn of praise that expresses trust in the Lord. This short poem, only three verses in total, neatly divides into two parts. The first part, verses 1–2, contrasts the humility of the psalmist with those who are proud. The second section, verse 3, is a call to Israel to demonstrate patience with regard to the Lord. Verse 1 expresses the Psalmist's position toward the Lord in negative terms: The psalmist's heart is *not* proud, the poet's eyes are *not* exalted. Finally, by using the metaphor of walking, the singer refers to his or her feet and states that they do not walk among things too great. Heart, eyes, and implied feet all bear the mark of humility, rather than pride in relation to God. This humility extends into verse 3, where a new metaphor emerges—a weaned child. The psalmist compares himself or herself to a contented child at the mother's breast. Though difficult to translate, the last half of verse 2 may indicate the posture of trust of a child who has eaten its fill and is now ready to rest in the arms of his or her parent. In the final verse, the psalmist urges the community of Israel to place its hope in the Lord (Isa. 30:15).

Theology and Application

Humility is a key characteristic of the faithful life, especially in the prophetic literature centered around the exilic and postexilic periods (Isa. 66:2; Zeph. 3:11–13). One may also recall the description of Moses (Num. 12) and depiction of Jesus in John 13 and Mark 10:33–45. In contrast to self-reliance and autonomy, Psalm 131 speaks to the heart of human existence as we find our confidence in God rather than the self.

In addition, the psalm uses maternal imagery to describe the Lord and the worshiper's relationship with the deity. Images that are similar to the contentment found on the face of child at their mother's breast can be found in Isaiah:

> As a mother comforts her child,
> so will I comfort you;
> and you will be comforted over Jerusalem. (Isa. 66:13 NIV)

These maternal images of God would prove especially helpful to a people who have suffered tremendously (exile?) and are trying to put the pieces back together in a postexilic setting. The need for humility and calmness is especially prevalent in situations where the believer seems overwhelmed and may even question the Lord's care and provision in difficult times. Such times existed in Israel's life and they also occur in the lives of believers today. This psalm reminds and reassures the faithful that God is the ultimate comforter in times of trouble.

For Those Who Sing Psalm 131

Songs that bring a sense of quiet calmness and contentment will be the types of songs that best reflect the mood of this psalm. Many of us come to worship frazzled and frenetic, worried and anxious about Monday. As such, we have little time for calm and repose on Sunday. A practical, as well as spiritual, benefit of worship should be that we are reminded that God cares for us as a mother cares for her newborn child. One may also hear in this psalm Jesus's call to be like a child (Mark 9:33–37; 10:13–16) and Paul's reminder to the Corinthian church that they are not from the elites of society (1 Cor. 1:26–31).

Rodney Ashlock

In You, O Lord

Psalm 131

Dedicated to Randy Daw

Michael E. Showalter | Michael E. Showalter

My Heart Is at Peace

Psalm 131

Mel Witcher | Mel Witcher

Psalm 132

Translation

A Song of Ascents.

†1 O Lord, remember David and all who have afflicted him,

†2 that he swore to the Lord, he made a vow to the Mighty One[a] of Jacob:

†3 "I will surely not[b] enter the tent of my house or go up upon the couch of my bed,

†4 or give sleep to my eyes or slumber to my eyelids,

†5 until I find a place for the Lord, a dwelling place for the Mighty One[a] of Jacob."

†6 Behold! We heard it was in Ephrathah; we found it in the fields of Jaar.

†7 Let us bring it to its dwelling place; let us bow down before the footstool of his feet.

*8 Arise, O Lord, to your resting place, you and the ark of your strength.

*9 Your priests are dressed in righteousness, and your faithful ones sing out.

*10 For the sake of David your servant, do not turn away the face of your anointed one.

†11 The Lord has sworn to David; truly he will not turn from it. "I will set one from your offspring on your throne.

†12 If your sons will keep my covenant and my testimony, which I will teach them, even their sons forever will sit on your throne."

†13 Surely the Lord has chosen Zion; he desires it for his dwelling place.

*14 "This is my resting place forever; here I will dwell, for I desire it.

*15 I will surely bless its food supply; its poor I will satisfy with bread.

*16 Its priests I will dress with salvation, and its faithful ones will surely sing out."

*17 There I will cause the horn of David to sprout; I will set a lamp for my anointed.

*18 I will dress his enemies with shame, but I will cause his crown to shine!"

[a] "The Mighty One" or "Bull," is likely an old, poetic reference to God. It was also a term used by the ancestor Jacob when he blessed his son Joseph (Gen. 49:24).

[b] Here David makes a vow. Literally, verses 3 and 4 begin with "If I will," but since verses 3–5 take the form of an oath, the sense is, "I will surely not."

Structure and Poetry

Interpreters commonly classify this psalm as a royal psalm that either prays for the continuance of the Davidic covenant or its restoration. It neatly divides into two parts. Verses 1–10 petition the Lord to remember David and the choice to make him king. Verses 2–7 rehearse the vow David made to the Lord (here referred to as "the Mighty One of Jacob," or "the Bull of Jacob") and the effort he and the people expended to bring the ark to Jerusalem. The phrase "the Bull of Jacob" may recall the time when the ark was located in Shiloh and before it was lost to the Philistines in 1 Samuel 4. Verse 6 recounts the return of the ark by the Philistines and the journey it took as it was pulled by two cows back to the Israelites. Eventually, it made its way to Kiriath-Jearim (1 Sam. 7:1–2) and stayed there until David brought it to Jerusalem in 2 Samuel 6. Traditions surrounding the ark go back to the days of Moses and the wilderness wandering. It was a part of the furnishings of the tabernacle. Most likely it represented the footstool of God as it was carried through the wilderness and into battle (Num. 10; Josh. 6). Verses 11–18 contain the response of the Lord to the petition and a reiteration of the promise God made to David in 2 Samuel 7. In addition, verse 13 stresses God's choice of Zion as well as David, and the following verses emphasize God's promise to bless Zion and the offspring (horn) of David. It is difficult to tell whether this psalm was written before or after the exile, but in its current context within the Songs of Ascents it certainly continues to express the concern for the fate of Zion and hope for the Davidic monarchy.

Theology and Application

Psalm 132 celebrates the Lord's selection of both David and Jerusalem. As a backdrop to the psalm, the careful interpreter might want to spend some time reading 2 Samuel 5–7, which narrates the story of David's capture of the city of Jerusalem from the Jebusites, the entry of the ark of the covenant into the city, and the covenant between God, David, and David's descendants. In addition, while Psalm 132 recalls the glory of the covenant between God and David, Psalm 89 reflects the tragedy of the destruction of the temple and the end of the Davidic line in 587 BCE by the Babylonians. Perhaps this psalm was written and sung during the postexilic period when the temple had been rebuilt and hope renewed. In fact, the phrase "Bull of Jacob" is mentioned twice in the psalm (vv. 2 and 5) and is a metaphor to describe God's power. For Christians, we may find several parallels with the gospel story. The apparent defeat on the cross is followed by a tremendous demonstration of God's power on the cross. In fact, Paul refers directly to God's power in Romans: "For I am not ashamed of the gospel; it is the power of God for salvation to everyone who has faith, to the Jew first and also to the Greek" (Rom. 1:16 NRSV) In addition, we might see in this psalm the type of celebration associated with Jesus's entry into Jerusalem as the Son of David (Matt. 20:29–21:9 and Mark 10:46–11:10).

For Those Who Sing Psalm 132

Celebration is the theme and mood of this psalm, and those who lead and sing it should join in this chorus of praise. The worship leader may want to tap into this heritage of unabashed praise and lead the congregation in a worship song that is both celebratory and reflective. The psalm may give us some cues as it asks God to remember (petition) the past relationship the Lord established with Israel (Jacob) and then rehearses the faithful acts of David. As if on cue, the Lord responds and promises to restore the glory associated with David. Perhaps our worship would have more meaning and relevance if we sang and prayed as confidently as the psalmists. And why shouldn't we? The Living One, the Son of David, is with us even when only two or three of us are gathered together (Matt. 18:20).

Rodney Ashlock

In Royal David's City

Psalm 132

Michael Morgan (1948-2022) D. J. Bulls

Remember Us, O God of Grace

Psalm 132

M. W. Bassford | M. L. Daniels

Psalm 133

Translation

A Song of Ascents. Of David.

†1 Behold, how good and how pleasant are brothers and sisters[a] dwelling in unity,

*2 like good oil upon the head, dripping down the beard—the beard of Aaron—which goes down in front of his garment,

*3 like the dew of Hermon that descends upon the mountains of Zion. For there the LORD issues the blessing, life forevermore.

[a] Literally, "brothers."

Structure and Poetry

Many interpreters classify Psalm 133 as a wisdom psalm. Its structure appears to center on the use of two metaphors—oil and dew—both symbolizing fertility and blessedness. Verse 1 may be using a proverb or maxim that highlights the blessedness of brothers dwelling together (in my translation above I have included sisters along with brothers). Verse 2 utilizes the first of two images to depict the generosity of God, which is portrayed as olive oil rolling down the head, through the beard, and onto the front of the garment. Olive oil symbolizes hospitality and luxury and would serve as a sign of happiness and fellowship. The land of Israel is arid to semiarid, and at certain times of the year the only consistent form of precipitation would be the early morning dew. This dew would keep certain forms of plant life alive, which, in turn, would keep herds and flocks alive. A difficulty does arise when we realize that Mount Hermon is north of the land of Israel, but now it applies to Mt. Zion and the blessing that issues from it on the land as a whole. The final thrust of the Psalm is to stress that both oil and dew are good gifts from the hand of God (for Israel's difficulty in grasping this concept see Hosea 2).

Theology and Application

From a theological perspective, the placement of this psalm is instructional. It follows Psalm 132, which describes David's bringing the ark into Jerusalem, and precedes Psalms 134 and 135, which call for those who are standing in the temple to praise the Lord. This psalm may have been written following separation and forced migration as the Assyrians and Babylonians deported the Israelites and Judahites respectively. Thus, what a sight it must have been to see God's people from different corners of the globe gathered together in one place to dwell and worship in community! This psalm celebrates that experience.

Furthermore, deportees may have seen exile as a time of barrenness and lack. The metaphors of oil and dew speak to the fertility and abundance that the Lord provides for Israel in the land. Life itself comes from God both in antiquity and today. Christian interpreters and readers of this psalm might recall Jesus's words to the crowds in the Sermon on the Mount not to be anxious about food or clothing, but to rely on the goodness of God and the gifts the Lord provides (Matt. 6:25–34). In addition, Paul stresses the provision of God to the Philippian church when he states that the Lord "satisfies every need" (Phil. 4:10–20). With regard to unity, Jesus emphasizes the bond he shares with the disciples when he "eagerly desired" to eat the Passover meal *with* them (Luke 22:15) and when he calls them "friends" in John 15:14–15.

For Those Who Sing Psalm 133

The blessing of fellowship, unity, and community can never be overstated, and worship should help us never to take life together for granted. Songs that emphasize community and fellowship would fit nicely with a worship service that highlights this psalm. In addition to the unity theme, worshipers may also enjoy and benefit from celebrating the bounty that the Lord provides. In the Christian tradition, our unity might be best expressed in our gathering around the table to commemorate the death, burial, and resurrection of our Lord and Savior Jesus Christ. Perhaps the reading of this psalm and a hymn based upon it can help us to imagine bread and wine as oil and dew—the very sources of our life together.

Rodney Ashlock

How Good and How Pleasant

Psalm 133

Mark Shipp

Michael E. Showalter

Behold, How Good and Pleasant

Psalm 133

Barbara Little

Ruth Ann Somervell

he gives them life for - ev - er - more and saves them by his grace.
Their sus - te - nance is from the Lord while they are in this place;
he gives them life for - ev - er - more and saves them by his grace.

Psalm 134

Translation

A Song of Ascents.

†1 Behold, bless the LORD, all you servants of the LORD, the ones who stand in the house of the LORD by night.
†2 Lift your holy hands and bless the LORD.
*3 May the LORD bless you from Zion, the maker of heaven and earth.

Structure and Poetry

Only three verses long, this psalm marks the end of the collection known as the Songs of Ascents and functions as a concluding doxology. The psalm should be read as one piece, stressing the importance of praise as the appropriate response to the works and wonders of God, who continues to bless Jerusalem. The phrase "the ones standing in the house of the LORD" is, more than likely, a technical term used to denote those who minister before the altar or serve in some capacity in the temple area, as it parallels the phrase, "servants of the LORD." The flow of the psalm calls for the priests to bless the Lord, which would lead to the entire community of faith worshiping the Lord. One blesses through both the use of the voice and uplifted hands. This posture suggests the notion of supplication and also stresses the location from whence God will bless—Zion.

Theology and Application

Blessing is a reciprocal activity. As worshipers, we bless God with our presence together in sacred space. The lifting of hands suggests a posture of supplication and adoration toward God. Voice and hands join together and incline the worshipers toward God and with each other. In return, this psalm reminds us that God continues to bless us from the divine abode. In Luke 11:9–10 (NRSV), Jesus stresses that we must approach God with confidence,

> So I say to you, Ask, and it will be given you; search, and you will find; knock, and the door will be opened for you. For everyone who

> asks receives, and everyone who searches finds, and for everyone who knocks, the door will be opened.

One may even hear an echo of Paul's wish in Romans 15:5–6 (NRSV),

> May the God of steadfastness and encouragement grant you to live in harmony with one another, in accordance with Christ Jesus, so that together you may with one voice glorify the God and Father of our Lord Jesus Christ.

For Those Who Sing Psalm 134

Psalm 134 is the final psalm in the Songs of Ascents collection. Its doxological nature suggests that an extremely appropriate way to end our time of worship is with praise. Gathering and sending are key movements of many worship services, and this collection of psalms bears witness to this rhythm and movement. One can easily imagine Psalm 134 as a "closing song" that encourages all the believers in the sanctuary to join voices and hands in unabashed praise of the Lord. What better way to send God's people out into the world than a hymn based on this psalm!

Rodney Ashlock

Come and Bless the Lord Forever

Psalm 134

Jack R. Reese

Jack R. Reese

Come and Bless the Lord Forever

Bless the Lord

Psalm 134

Gary Pendergrass

Gary Pendergrass

O Come to Bless the Lord

Psalm 134

Konstantin Zhigulin
Translation by Brad Cawyer

Konstantin Zhigulin

Leader's Note: Can be done as a 2 or 3 part canon, if preferred.

How to enter the canon — start "O come" at the beginning when the part that entered before you reaches ❇"Lord" in the first phrase.

How to end the canon — hold the note on "name" until all parts join you on "name."

Psalm 135

Translation

†1 Praise the LORD!

* Praise the name of the LORD; praise him[a] O servants of the LORD,
†2 who are standing in the house of the LORD, in the courts of the house of our God.
*3 Praise the LORD, for the LORD is good; sing praise to his name, for it is pleasant.

†4 For the LORD has chosen Jacob for himself, Israel, for his treasured possession.
*5 Surely I know that the LORD is great, and our Lord is above all gods.
*6 All that he desires, the LORD has done, in the heavens and on the earth, in the seas and all the deep.
†7 He causes vapors to ascend at the end of the earth; he makes lightning for rain; he causes the wind to go out from his storehouses.
*8 He smote the firstborn of Egypt, both human and beast.
†9 He sent signs and wonders in the midst of Egypt, against Pharaoh and against all of his servants.
*10 He struck many nations and killed mighty kings,
†11 even Sihon, king of the Amorites, and Og, king of Bashan, and all the kingdoms of Canaan;
*12 and he gave their land as an inheritance, an inheritance for Israel his people.

†13 O LORD, your name is forever; O LORD, your memorial is from generation to generation.
*14 For the LORD will judge his people, and upon his servants he will have compassion.
†15 The idols of the nations are silver and gold, the work of the hands of human beings.
*16 They have mouths, but do not speak; they have eyes, but do not see;
†17 they have ears, but do not hear. Surely there is no breath in their mouth.
*18 Their makers shall be like them, all those who trust in them.
†19 O house of Israel, bless the LORD; O house of Aaron, bless the LORD.
†20 O house of Levi, bless the LORD; those who fear the LORD, bless the LORD.
*21 Blessed be the LORD from Zion, the one who dwells in Jerusalem.

* Praise the LORD!

[a] The Hebrew text does not have the word "him."

Structure and Poetry

This psalm, like Psalm 134, is usually classified as a hymn of praise and can be divided into three units. Verses 1–3 form an opening summons to praise that urges the members of the temple community to praise (Hallelujah) the Lord because of God's goodness and the fact that the divine name is pleasant. Verses 4–12 recount the mighty acts of God, who has chosen Israel and considers Jacob a "treasured possession" (see Exod. 19:6–7). Within this second section, God should be praised because of the power the Lord demonstrated in creation (vv. 5–7). Next, the psalmist recites the salvific acts done in Egypt, the wilderness, and among the enemies of Israel in the Transjordanian region (vv. 8–12). The final section of the psalm, verses 13–21, bursts into praise of the one true and living God. It denounces, in the manner of Hosea 14 and Isaiah 44, any reliance on idols and any attribution of power or life to them (vv. 15–18). Finally, in a steady four-fold progression, the houses of Israel, Aaron, Levi and all those who fear the Lord (even non-Israelites?) are enjoined to bless and praise the Lord. Thematically, this psalm is linked to the previous psalm by the phrase, "those who are standing in the house of the Lord," which emphasizes the importance of the temple in ancient Israel's worship experience. Psalm 135 moves the reader closer to the final section of the Psalter and the concluding chorus of praise hymns—Psalms 145–150.

Theology and Application

Memory—it's important. This psalm, which focuses on the attendants in the temple, is a doxology, or call to praise. The two primary reasons given to praise are the creative and saving acts of God. This psalm recounts God's activity in the world and his "delight" in it (v. 6). The psalm also reminds us that the Lord is good and even his name should be pleasant to our ears (v. 3). But the primary focus of this psalm is the saving acts of God and the role they play in the relationship between the Lord and Israel. Beginning with Israel's experience in Egypt, Psalm 134 follows the basic storyline of exodus, wilderness wandering, defeat of the kings Sihon and Og, and the gift of land. Furthermore, like Psalms 78 and 105–106 before it, this psalm draws upon Israel's memories and traditions to tell a story—a story of God's saving activity and Israel's response, wonder, praise, and trust (Exod. 14:1–15:21). It also contrasts the living God of Israel with the idols of other nations as a reminder to God's people to whom their devotion, loyalty, and trust belong. In a world filled with distractions and appeals to pursue the modern idols of self and money, Psalm 134 reminds us once again who the only God is and in whom we need to place our trust and express our praise and adoration.

For Those Who Sing Psalm 135

Every once in a while, you just have to praise the Lord (Hallelujah). Psalm 135 is an excellent example of a call to praise, or doxology, and it continues to summon believers to do the same today. Reasons to praise God are numerous, and this psalm surfaces several. We may praise God for his work in creation, but we may also recall God's saving acts for members of our worshiping community. Sometimes it is good simply to recite what God has done for us. Perhaps a worship leader could lead the congregation in a recitation of God's saving activities among the people in their congregation. As the first psalm after the collection of the Songs of Ascents, we might view it as an opening song or call to worship. Why are we here rather than somewhere else? Why are we singing, praying, reading Scripture, and gathering around the table? Because we believe that the God who created this world and who saved in the past remains the only true God, and the Lord will continue to save and create anew. Let us join our voices together to recite and praise the Holy One of Israel.

Rodney Ashlock

The Lord Is Great, above All Gods

Psalm 135

Jerry Shipp

Konstantin Zhigulin

The Lord Is Great

Psalm 135

Jerry Shipp

Michael E. Showalter

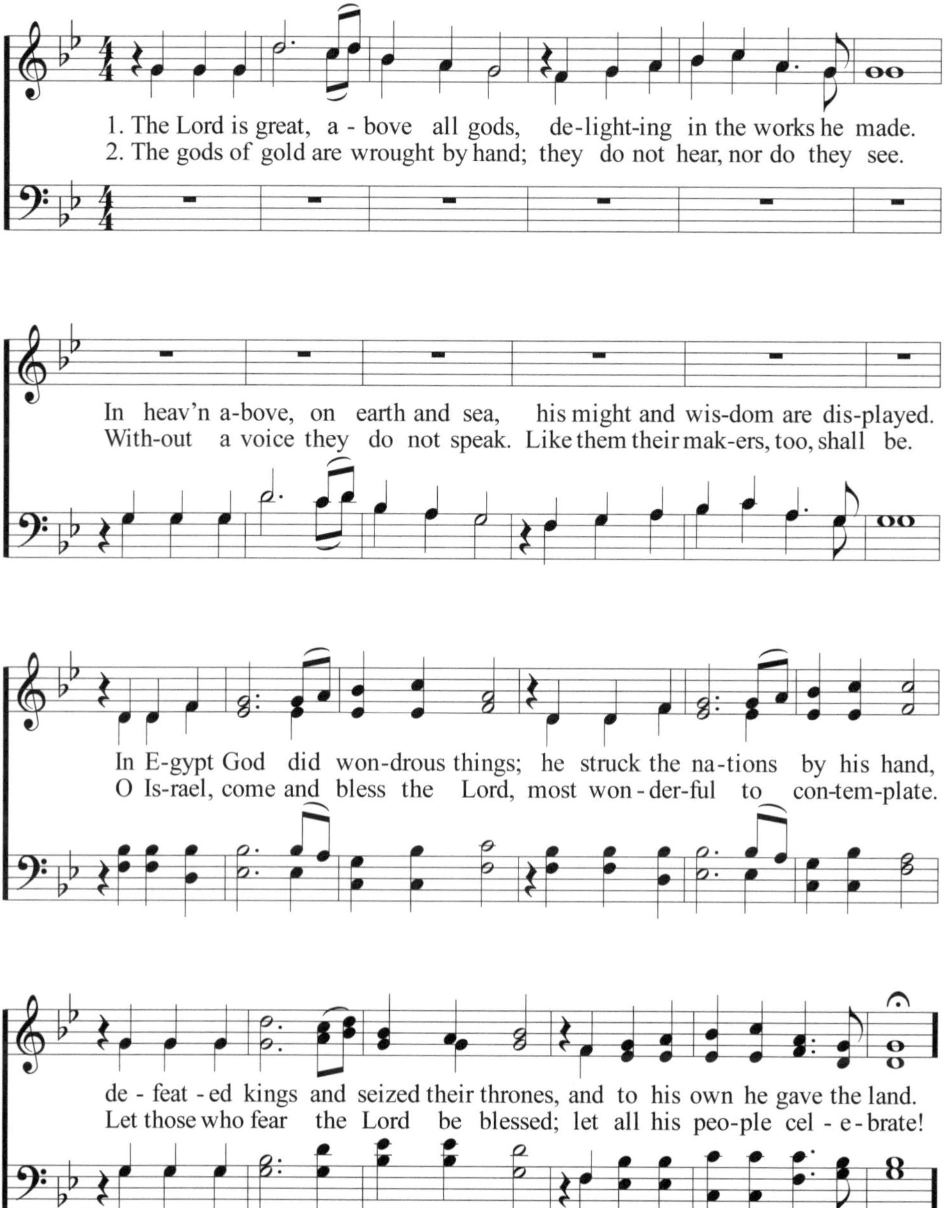

The Lord Is Great

O Praise God's Name Together

Psalm 135

Michael Morgan (1948–2022)

Randy Daw (1954–2019), D. J. Bulls, and Mark Shipp

Psalm 136

Translation

†1 Confess[a] the Lord for he is good,
 * for his steadfast love is enduring.
†2 Confess the God of gods,
 * for his steadfast love is enduring.
†3 Confess the Lord of lords,
 * for his steadfast love is enduring.

†4 Who alone performs great wonders,
 * for his steadfast love is enduring.
†5 Who made the heavens with wisdom,
 * for his steadfast love is enduring.
†6 Who spread out the earth over the waters,
 * for his steadfast love is enduring.

†7 Who made the great lights,
 * for his steadfast love is enduring.
†8 The sun to rule the day,
 * for his steadfast love is enduring.
†9 The moon and the stars to rule the night,
 * for his steadfast love is enduring.

†10 Who struck down the Egyptians through their firstborn,
 * for his steadfast love is enduring.
†11 Who led Israel out from their midst,
 * for his steadfast love is enduring.
†12 With a powerful hand and an outstretched arm,
 * for his steadfast love is enduring.

†13 Who split the Reed Sea asunder,
 * for his steadfast love is enduring.
†14 And made Israel pass through its midst,
 * for his steadfast love is enduring.
†15 And shook off Pharaoh and his force,
 * for his steadfast love is enduring.

†16 Who led his people through the wilderness,
 * for his steadfast love is enduring.

†[17] Who struck down great kings,
 * for his steadfast love is enduring.
†[18] And killed prominent kings,
 * for his steadfast love is enduring.

†[19] Sihon, king of the Amorites,
 * for his steadfast love is enduring.
†[20] Og, king of the Bashan,
 * for his steadfast love is enduring.

†[21] And gave their land as a heritage,
 * for his steadfast love is enduring.
†[22] A heritage for Israel his servant,
 * for his steadfast love is enduring.

†[23] Who remembered us in our lowliness,
 * for his steadfast love is enduring.
†[24] And redeemed us from our adversaries,
 * for his steadfast love is enduring.
†[25] Who gives bread to all flesh,
 * for his steadfast love is enduring.

†[26] Confess the God of the heavens,
 * for his steadfast love is enduring.

[a] The basic meaning is "to confess" (God, God's greatness, gratitude, sin, human condition, etc.), and hence may also be translated as "acknowledge" (LXX), "give thanks" (NIV, NRSV), or "praise." It is juxtaposed with Hebrew *hll*, "praise" (Pss. 106:1; 109:30; 111:1).

Structure and Poetry

There is no superscription for this psalm in the Hebrew text, but it is so closely associated with the preceding one in themes, vocabulary, and structure that the two may have been read together. If so, the superscription of Psalm 135—"Praise the LORD!"—serves as well for Psalm 136, these two psalms together constituting an appendage to the Songs of Ascent beginning in Psalm 120. Indeed, the Septuagint and the Vulgate take "Praise the LORD!" at the end of the previous psalm as the beginning of this one. Whatever the original may have been, this psalm came to be known among Jews as "the Great *Hallel*"(that is, "the Great Praise"). Here it is praise in the sense of a confession of God's goodness, as also in Psalm 106:1,"Praise the LORD, confess, for he is good/for his steadfast love is forever."

This obviously liturgical psalm consists of twenty-six couplets, each consisting of an identical second line in an unwavering refrain: "for his steadfast love is enduring." The refrain follows every new line, as if in response to it. It is likely that the psalm was intended to be read antiphonally, or in a call and response pattern. The first three verses constitute the invocation that calls upon worshipers to confess the Lord (v. 1), whom the poet acknowledges as "the God of gods" and "the Lord of lords," which is the Hebrew way of saying "quintessential God and Lord" (vv. 2–3). The content of this confession is introduced in verse 4 as "great wonders," the details of which the rest of the psalm will spell out.

The bulk of the psalm appears to be a liturgical recounting of the Torah story—the Pentateuch in a nutshell, as it were: creation of the cosmos (vv. 5–9), deliverance from bondage (vv. 10–15), guidance through the wilderness (vv. 16–20), and the giving of the promised land (vv. 21–22). We may recognize seven stanzas from the invocation to the giving of the land to Israel, with seven being a number for completeness. Yet the psalm does not end with the seventh stanza as the expected climax of the story. Rather, there is an eighth stanza, where the recitation of wonders for Israel told in the third person gives way to the first person plural ("us"/ "our"), namely, those who are present and now participating in the liturgy (vv. 23–25). The concluding couplet harks back to the beginning, as it reiterates the summons to confess God (v. 26), just as the preceding psalm opens and closes with summons to "praise the Lord!"(Ps. 135:1, 21).

Theology and Application

The precise wording of the first couplet is found in Psalms 106:1; 107:1; 118:1, 29; 1 Chronicles 16:34; and 2 Chronicles 20:21, altogether indicating a topic familiar in the context of worship (compare also Jer. 33:11; Ezra 3:11; 1 Chron. 16:41; 2 Chron. 5:13; 7:3, 6). At issue is the goodness of the Lord, as manifest in God's "steadfast love," a theologically-loaded term in the Hebrew that is critical in the Psalms, where it recurs 124 times in reference to divine love—a figure unmatched in any other portion of the Bible. And nowhere else is there as great a concentration of the term as in this psalm, which may be viewed as a liturgical exposition of the goodness of divine character manifest in this enduring divine love. This exposition begins with the Lord's supremacy as God and Lord (vv. 2–3), and it ends with the deity as "the God of heaven" (v. 26). These theological conceits thus frame the narrative that the liturgy recounts, which itself holds together God's "great wonders" in creation and in history, in matters universal and particular, not least God's involvement with a particular people (vv. 4–22). Yet the liturgy does not dwell on the triumphalism of the promised land. Far from being in a triumphant state, those who sing this song are in lowliness and beset by adversities, though they recognize that God has remembered them and redeemed them from their plights.

While the election theology that undergirds the Torah story is manifestly exclusivist in that it highlights divine favor of Israel at the expense of other peoples, the liturgy culminates in a remarkably universalistic note—with a recognition of divine providence of "bread for all flesh" (v. 25). The Talmud recognizes the theological profundity of the seemingly mundane point about divine provision of food for all: it is as wondrous as the Exodus event (*n. Pesaḥ.* 118b). More than that, the divine provision of "bread for all flesh" belongs with all the other "great wonders" that together bear witness to the goodness and the enduring steadfast love of God. The recitation of the "great wonders" commences with the creation of the cosmos and reaches its denouement in the divine provision of "bread for all flesh." God the creator, redeemer, and Lord of history, is the giver of our daily bread. Indeed, upon this notice of divine providence in the mundane realm of all who are in need of daily sustenance, the liturgy returns to confess yet again "the God of heaven" (v. 26).

For Those Who Sing Psalm 136

All who sing Psalm 136 participate in a rich history of faithful people who are called to acknowledge the goodness of God in praise and thanksgiving. Jews and Christians alike have read this psalm in their various liturgies. Not surprisingly, there are numerous musical compositions, including Heinrich Schütz's motet, *Confitemini Domino, quoniam ipse bonus* ("Confess the Lord for he is good") published 1625, several hymns entitled *Let us with a gladsome mind* (based on the opening line of John Milton's translation of this psalm in 1645), and more recently, Kirke Mechem's *Give Thanks unto the Lord* (1960). Many composers have found inspiration especially in the invocation (vv. 1–3) and the depiction of the splendor of creation (vv. 4–9), unfortunately missing poignant inclusion of the historical experiences of divine goodness and love in the rest of the psalm. This liturgy implies that divine goodness and love manifest for *us* amid *our* lowliness and adversities (vv. 23–24) and the provision of daily "bread for all flesh" (v. 25) are in some sense on par with the greatest acts of God as creator and redeemer. Indeed, divine attention to our specific daily needs is what impels us to confess, praise, and give thanks.

C. L. Seow

Proclaim the Lord

Psalm 136

Laura Kate Collum

Ruth Ann Somervell

His Love Endures Forever

Psalm 136:1-9

Konstantin Zhigulin
Translation by Mark Shipp

Konstantin Zhigulin

His Love Endures Forever

Psalm 137

Translation

†1 By the waters[a] of Babylon, there we sat. Oh how we wept when we remembered Zion.
*2 On the willows in its midst we hung our lyres,
†3 for there our captors asked us for lyrics of a song, our mockers,[b] for joy: "Sing us a one of the 'Songs of Zion'!"
*4 How shall we sing the LORD's song on foreign soil?

†5 If I forget you, O Jerusalem, let my right hand forget;[c]
*6 let my tongue stick to my palate, if I do not remember you, if I do not bring up Jerusalem above my foremost joy.

†7 Remember, O LORD, as regards the Edomites, the day of Jerusalem, how they said, "Pull it down,[d] pull it down to its very foundation!"
†8 O Miss Babylon,[e] who would be ravaged,[f] how laudable[g] is the one who will repay you the dealing that you have dealt us!
†9 How laudable is one who seizes and smashes your infants against the rock!

[a] The Hebrew word usually means "rivers," though Babylon did not have many "rivers" but did have many canals and marshes.

[b] This apparent root, *tll*, is attested in a different form in Hebrew meaning "to mock." The choice of word may be to play off the word for "hung" (v. 2) and perhaps the root *hll*, "praise," but also "make a mockery."

[c] The LXX and Vulgate read the passive "be forgotten." Some interpreters cite a cognate to suggest the meaning "wither" (see NRSV), but the meaning of that cognate is disputed.

[d] The term has two meanings here—"raze," but also "strip naked."

[e] Literally, "Daughter Babylon."

[f] The original text may be interpreted either as active ("ravager") or passive ("ravaged"). The text as pointed in the medieval period suggests the passive, perhaps expressing a wish for what Babylon will become.

[g] This verb is a synonym of "praise, commend, congratulate," or the like, and its form is similar to Egyptian expressions of admiration.

Structure and Poetry

This psalm is discordant right after "the Great Praise" of Psalm 136. Following the confession of God's goodness, with the twenty-six-fold refrain, "for his steadfast love is enduring," one is baffled to find a poem of a people devastated by grief and desirous of unseemly vengeance.

Yet this psalm is clearly connected to the preceding. The ninefold first person plural—"we," "our," "us" (a single form: *nû* in the Hebrew)—in the first five couplets (vv. 1–4), echoes the fourfold *nû* ("us" and "our") in Psalm 136:23–24. The confessional voice in Psalm 136 affirms God as one who "remembered us in our lowliness" and "redeemed us from our adversaries." Now the "we" in Psalm 137 is abased and needing redemption, thus begging the question if the central claims of "the Great Praise" still hold.

Importantly, the Hebrew verb for "remember" in Psalm 136:23 appears also in Psalm 137:1, 6, 7. Memory is critical in this psalm, for the context is a distant place. Jerusalem has been humiliated, and the exiles are taunted to sing the "Songs of Zion" that celebrate the city as unrivaled in majesty and secure in God's abiding presence (as in Pss. 46, 48, 76, 84). Lamentations 2:15 (NRSV) recounts a similar taunt when passersby sarcastically ask as regards fallen Jerusalem, "Is this the city that was called the perfection of beauty, the joy of all the earth?" So the tormentors in Psalm 137 demanded "joy" (v. 3).

The shift from the plural in verses 1–4 to the singular in verses 5–6 marks a stanzaic turn. The first stanza presents the common sentiment, the collective reaction to disappointment in the failure of a theological tenet. Memory of Jerusalem brought debilitating grief. The poet implies in the first stanza that they do not want to remember, for they cannot sing as before. Yet in the second stanza, the poet speaks not as "we" but as "I," and this "I" is determined to resist the collective impulse not to remember. The lonely "I" vows not to forget. Interpreters have often felt compelled to supply an object for what the right hand forgets, such as "cunning" (KJV) or "skill" (NIV). Yet the ambiguity may be part of the poetry, the object of the forgetting being presently forgotten, as it were.

A change in mood—from the first person in verses 5–6 to an address to God in verse 7—signals the beginning of a third stanza. The psalmist calls upon God to remember, starting with the Edomites who had cheered Jerusalem's demise (see Obad. 10–14; Lam. 4:21–22). Then the poem addresses Babylon, expressing a desire for retribution, not least a morally repugnant wish to have the babies of the enemies smashed against the rocks (vv. 8–9).

Theology and Application

This psalm is full of pathos and honesty. The first stanza in particular has inspired much poetry and music, for it reflects the struggle of a suffering people who find it hard to celebrate as before. They have been humiliated; their beloved city has been destroyed. Yet there is more at stake than sentiments and pride. At issue is a crisis in the theology of the Lord as king that was the central tenet the "songs of Zion" extolled: Zion was inviolable because it represented the abode of the Lord, who was king, the Most High (Pss. 46:4; 48:2). This is why they cannot sing "the

LORD's song" (v. 4), which is what the "songs of Zion" are (v. 3). When reality so blatantly contradicts what faith proclaims, the obvious response may be to hang up the lyre, as it were, and cease singing.

Yet the "I" of the central stanza suggests the risk of accepting silence in the face of the common response. Memory brought the community sorrow and debilitating despair: "there we sat down, yea, we wept, when we remembered Zion" (v. 1 KJV) and so "we hung our harps" (v. 2 NIV) and could not sing. Yet the "I" wills not to forget. In the Bible the verb "forget" is no mere lapse of memory; to forget is to forsake and not care (Jer. 30:14; Ps. 45:10; Job 19:14; 24:20); it is to cease to mention (Gen. 40:23). This forgetting will be consequential: "If I forget . . . let my right hand forget." In Hebrew, as in many other languages, the right hand signifies ability, well-being, and good. The outcome of willful forgetting is that one becomes thus disabled for good. The effect of willful forgetting is inability to speak (v. 6). As often in Hebrew, the verb "remember" may have a nuance of articulation—to remember is not just to bring to mind, but to make mention (see Jer. 20:9; 23:36; 31:20). Failure of memory in this articulate sense will result if one does not "bring up" the subject as a matter of priority even over one's "foremost joy." The expression "bring up" is unusual for speech. It is a common one, however, for presentation of offerings in worship. This prioritization of articulate practice that is tantamount to offerings in worship is this poet's answer to the challenge of "joy" that is difficult to come by amid adversity (v. 3).

Having willed to remember and hence to articulate, the poet calls upon God to also remember (v. 7). This is the third occurrence of the term "remember"—one in each of the stanzas. This divine remembering harks back to the preceding psalm, which confesses that God has remembered people in their lowliness and redeemed them from their adversaries (Ps. 136:23–24). The psalm has moved from the problem of remembering in verse 1 ("we remembered") to the will of one to remember in verse 6, and now it is up to God to remember (v. 7) the lowly who are in need of deliverance. The first remembering (v. 1) brought debilitating despair in the community. The second (v. 6) is born of an individual's fear of losing the ability to articulate. The third (v. 7) comes about because that articulation has indeed not been lost. To be sure, the psalmist, having experienced horrendous cruelty, has some very natural desires for what should happen to those who brought such suffering. Nonetheless, it is clear the redress is now left to God, who has always remembered and redeemed.

For Those Who Sing Psalm 137

The poet who confessed to the difficulty of singing the Lord's song has nonetheless composed one that prompts generations to keep singing. This psalm has inspired poets like John Milton, Emma Lazarus, Christina Rossetti, and composers like Johann Sebastian Bach, Franz Liszt, Antonin Dvorak, Verdi's *Va, Pensiero* ("Chorus of Hebrew Slaves"), and countless others. Yet the beauty of all these must not lead one to forget the truth the poet conveys so honestly: that a life of faith is not all about praises and thanksgiving. On the contrary, there will be many moments of doubt, when our experiences of suffering and the reality of evil will make us want to give up trying to reconcile the realities of life with what faith professes. At such times, those who sing Psalm 137 may be reminded of one whose personal conscience would not permit the response of not caring, but somehow finds a voice to call on God to remember still.

C. L. Seow

We Wept by the Rivers of Babylon

Psalm 137

Glover Shipp (1927–2016) | Michael E. Showalter

through suf - fer - ings that we could hard - ly bear.
My high - est of joys is in you to stand.
O Zi - on, O Zi - on, we long for you.
We cry out to God in our grief.
Be - hold, Lord, this cit - y in dis - re - pair.
De - liv - er us, bring us re - lief.

By the Rivers of Babylon

Psalm 137

Randy Daw (1954–2019)

Randy Daw (1954–2019)
and Michael E. Showalter

PSALM 138

Translation

Of David.

†1 Let me confess you with all my heart; let me make music to you before the gods.

*2 Let me bow toward your holy temple; let me confess your name on account of your steadfast love and on account of your faithfulness, for you have shown yourself to be great above all—your name, your word.[a]

†3 When I called, you answered me; you imbued[b] me with strength within me.

*4 Let all the kings of the earth confess you, O LORD, for they have heard the words of your mouth.

†5 And let them sing about the ways of the LORD, for the glory of the LORD is great.

*6 Although the LORD is exalted, he sees the lowly; though lofty, he knows even from afar.

†7 If I walk amid trouble, he will preserve me despite the anger of my enemies.
You will stretch out your hand, and your right hand will deliver me;

*8 the LORD will acquit me.[c]

* O LORD, your steadfast love is enduring; do not let go of the work of your hand!

[a] I assume a couplet, *ky hgdlty ʿl / kl šmk ʿmrtk*, instead of a prosaic long line.

[b] Literally, "impelled" or "pressed upon."

[c] Verse divisions were not original; they were introduced only in the medieval period. In this case, the first line of what is now verse 8 forms a climactic third and concluding line that began in verse 7.

Structure and Poetry

The superscription—"of David"—identifies this with the fourth and last series of psalms (Pss. 138–145) in the Davidic collection. This superscription signals as well a turn from the painful exilic poem of Psalm 137. That crisis has passed, it seems, and this psalm returns to the language of praise and confession that we find in Psalms 135–136.

The confession is said to be wholehearted (v. 1), echoing Psalms 9:1; 119:2, 10, 34, 28, 69, 145 (cf. Deut. 6:4–5 etc.), thus indicating that faith has remained intact despite the despair that the exile brought. The psalmist, having been delivered and restored, once again makes music and indeed does so "before gods."

Although "the Lord" is not mentioned in the first stanza, there are two references to the divine "name" in verse 2. The term "name" in Hebrew is not just an appellation; one's "name" is one's nature and character. The name is who one is. In this case, the divine nature entails "steadfast love" and "faithfulness," a pair of terms that hark back to the revelation of the Lord's "name" in Exodus 34:6 (also in Pss. 25:10; 26:3; 40:10–11, etc.). This name is also closely linked to the divine "word," the Hebrew term being one that most often refers to divine promise (Pss. 105:19; 119:38, 41, etc.) and "way" (Ps. 18:30). The character of God is further suggested by God's responsiveness to the prayer of one in need (v. 3).

Just as the authorial "I" confesses (vv. 1–3), so "the kings of the earth" will confess (vv. 4–5). Indeed, the "name" explicated in the first stanza is now plainly spelled out as "the Lord," whose name is reiterated in the rest of the psalm. These kings are to confess because "they have heard the words of your mouth" (v. 4), which echoes "your word" in verse 2. The reference to "great glory" (v. 5) echoes the claim that God has shown the divine name and word to be "great" (v. 2). Furthermore, verses 6–8a may be understood as an expansion of the theme of God's care for the needy (v. 3). The stanza ends with confidence that God will "acquit," the Hebrew verb for which also means "to complete" or "to end"—a term that poetically signals closure.

Yet, that is not the end. What follows is a couplet that may be regarded as a postlude, where the "steadfast love" (v. 8b) echoes the same at the beginning of the poem (v. 2), and "hand" (v. 8c) recalls God's saving "hand" and "right hand" at the end (v. 7).

Theology and Application

Midrash Tehillim, a collection of ancient Jewish interpretations on the Psalms, records that interpreters long ago regarded the context of Psalm 138 to be analogous to that of Isaiah 40. The end of exile brought new opportunity to bring the word of God to all the nations of the earth. The poet of Isaiah 40 had a vision of the "glory of the Lord" being revealed universally, so that all will come to know that "the mouth of the Lord has spoken" (Isa. 40:5 NIV). A voice from heaven gives a command to proclaim that "the word of our God endures forever" (Isa. 40:8 NIV; cf. Ps. 138:8b). The poem then portrays Zion-Jerusalem personified as a "bearer of good news," who ascends a lofty mountain to proclaim loudly the good news of God's presence (Isa. 40:9–11). In the chapters that follow, the same poet calls upon the people to "sing to the Lord a new song" (Isa. 42:10 NIV), to be the Lord's witnesses (Isa. 43:10, 12), so that the kings of the earth will acknowledge the Lord (Isa. 49:7). The people have been called by God to serve in this way, and God will hold their hand as they do so (Isa. 42:6).

Following ancient Jewish interpreters, one may take the first stanza of Psalm 138 as the people proclaiming God, which leads to the outcome of the kings of the earth confessing the Lord because "they have heard the words of your mouth" (v. 4), singing about "the ways of the LORD" and recognizing the greatness of the Lord's "glory" (v. 5).

Importantly, while the psalm highlights the universality of God's will and the grand vision of the kings of the earth acknowledging the Lord, the poet never loses sight of the wonder of God's responsiveness to the needs of the individual. The first stanza ends with a note of this divine attentiveness that is evident in the empowering of the individual (v. 3). Even more emphatically, the second stanza reiterates God's responsiveness to the plight of each person, the abundance of divine help poetically conveyed by the metaphor of two hands (v. 7) that will bring about a proper end (v. 8c).

The Hebrew expression for "work of (your) hand" in the postlude is the same one used elsewhere in Psalms of God's "handiwork"—the creation of the universe (Pss. 8:3; 19:2; 106:26) as well as God's marvelous deeds in history (Pss. 92:5; 143:5). Here, the one who has experienced the grace of God's outstretched hand and saving right hand is indeed part of God's "handiwork." As God promises to hold the hand of those who are called (Isa. 42:6), so the poem pleads with God not to let go of the work of that hand.

For Those Who Sing Psalm 138

The psalm holds in tension a wholeheartedness that dares to imagine the universal consequences of a confession of faith together with an acknowledgment of human neediness that can only be met though divine intervention. Faith sings of confidence in God's extended and liberating hand, even as it asks God not to let go of the work of that steady hand.

C. L. Seow

Because of Your Steadfast Love

Psalm 138

Marva L. Hughes | Marva L. Hughes

Because of Your Steadfast Love

Greater than I Understand

Psalm 138

Clyde H. Slimp

Clyde H. Slimp

and I am the work of your hand!
Do not let me go, Lord; help me know
you are great - er than I un - der - stand.
Do not let me go, Lord; help me know
you are great - er than I un - der - stand.

Psalm 139

Translation

Of the leader. Of David, a psalm.

†1 O LORD, you have searched me and you know,

*2 You yourself know when I sit down and when I get up; you have perceived my thoughts from afar.

†3 You have sustained[a] my journeying and my resting; you have seen[b] to all my ways.

*4 For there is no word on my tongue; here, O LORD, you know all of it!

†5 Aft and fore you have encompassed me; you have placed your hand upon me.

*6 Knowledge is too wonderful for me; it is so lofty I cannot attain it.

†7 Where could I go from your spirit; where could I flee from your face?

†8 If I ascend to heaven, there you are; if I bed down in the netherworld, there you are.

†9 If I take wing with the dawn,[c] settle at the end of the sea,

†10 there, too, your hand will lead me; your right hand will take hold of me.

†11 And if I say, "Surely darkness will grip me," and night is the light about me,

†12 even darkness will not be dark from you, and night is radiant as day; darkness and light are alike.

*13 For you yourself have created my reins;[d] you have woven me in my mother's womb.

*14 I confess you, for by awesome deeds[e] I am wonderfully made;[f] wonderful are your acts, which I know full well.

*15 My structure was not hidden from you when I was made in secret,[g] knitted in the recesses of the earth.

*16 Your eye saw my formlessness, yet on your text they were all written. Days were formed before anyone came to be.[h]

*17 As for me, how precious are your thoughts, O God, how numerous are their number.

†18 Should I count them, they would be more than sand; when I awaken,[i] I would still be with you.

†19 If you, O God, would slay the wicked—and the bloodthirsty, turn away from me!—

†[20] those who invoke you maliciously, swearing falsely[j] as those who provoke
you.[k]
†[21] Should I not, O Lord, hate those who hate you, and loathe those who rise
against you?
†[22] With utmost hatred I have hated them; they have become my enemies.

*[23] Search me, O God, and know my heart; examine me and know my
insecurities,[l]
*[24] and see if there is an idolatrous way in me, and lead me in an enduring way.

[a] The verb usually means "to winnow," but as in Aramaic/Syriac and Arabic, it may have developed a secondary meaning "to carry" and hence also "to sustain."

[b] The basic meaning is "to care for" and, in the form here, the verb means "to see to, provide."

[c] An allusion to sunrise in the east, which ties nicely with "the sea," which in Israelite geography also means the west, where the sun sets.

[d] The viscera, one's vitals.

[e] This term is always used of the awesome deeds of God (Deut. 10:21; 2 Sam. 7:23; Isa. 64:2–3; Pss. 45:4; 106:22; 145:6; 1 Chron. 17:21).

[f] The verb in this form always means "to be wonderful," so here, literally, "I am wonderful," but the point is the poet's amazement at being among the wonders of creation.

[g] That is, hidden from human sight.

[h] The Hebrew text is obscure.

[i] Some scholars suggest "come to an end," a meaning the root does not have elsewhere. The root is used several times of awakening from death (Isa. 26:19; Jer. 51:37, 39; Job 14:12; Dan. 12:2). Even if the poet were to count until death, he would still be at it when he awakens.

[j] Reading the form as infinitive absolute, instead of the passive participle in the Hebrew text as it stands. These words together always indicate perjury or slander.

[k] "Your cities" makes no sense. Scholars suggest an Aramaic loanword meaning "enemies," but the root can have the meaning "to protest, agitate, provoke."

[l] The term appears in this precise form in Psalm 94:19, but it is a variant of another form attested in Job 4:13 and 20:2. In all cases, the sense of the term is "disquieting thoughts, restlessness, anxieties," or the like, as suggested as well by its cognate in Arabic.

Structure and Poetry

It is possible that the opening line (v. 1) stands alone as an incipit, that is, a title line for the poem, as is common in ancient Semitic poetry. Yet it may also function as the first line of a triplet (vv. 1–2). The word "know" defines the first stanza (vv. 1–6), occurring three times (vv. 1, 2, 4), each time with God as the subject. Then the stanza ends with the term "knowledge" (or "knowing") in verse 6, a term that may refer to God's knowing of the poet as well as the poet's knowing about this. "Know" would reappear in verse 14 and twice in verse 23—all told, seven times in the poem.

The second stanza (vv. 7–12) revolves around the theme of God's ubiquitous presence wherever the poet imagines going throughout the cosmos—to its height and depth (v. 8), and from the east to the west (v. 9). God's "hand" is a catchword linking the second stanza to the first—the "hand" placed on the poet (v. 5b), a hand leading (v. 10a), and a hand holding (v. 10b). So led and held, one fears not the grip of darkness, for there is light even amid darkness, and darkness does not overcome it (vv. 11–12).

The third stanza (vv. 13–18) focuses on the poet's amazement at having been wonderfully created like all the other wonders of creation. The terms "I am wondrous" and "wonderful" in verse 14 echo the same in verse 6. Human creation is delightfully depicted under the imagery of God's weaving of the human being in a mother's womb (v. 13b) and, at the same time, as a cosmic knitting in the recesses of the earth (v. 15b). This creation is "in secret," yet not hidden from God, who sees even the yet-unformed human as if all were already prescribed on a text.

The poet's wonder is suddenly and inexplicably interrupted by a stanza full of unbridled rage against unnamed enemies (vv. 19–22). Indeed, within this interruption is a disruption (v. 19b). It is not clear what experience prompted this venomous outburst, though verse 24a may suggest that the psalmist has been accused of unfaithfulness. Such is the reality of life, it seems, for even amid one's meditation on divine wonders, life's unpredictable ugliness can intrude and become part of the poetry of one's dialogue with God.

The final stanza (vv. 23–24) returns to the topics introduced at the beginning—God's searching and knowing (v. 1). Whatever intrusion may have caused the disruption of the meditation, the poet remains open to God's examinations and guidance.

Theology and Application

Theologians have long found in this poem nascent notions of divine omniscience and omnipresence, and rightly so. Yet, for all that, the God one encounters in this poem is not a God too far. God's immanence is conveyed by the characterization of God in human terms. We read of God's face (v. 7b), hands (vv. 5b, 10), and eyes (v. 16a). Unlike other psalms that extol the magnificence of God's creation of the cosmos, this poem reflects on the wonder of God weaving an individual in a mother's womb (v. 13b) and knitting that individual in the recesses of the earth (v. 15b). In virtually every verse, the authorial "I" engages the divine "Thou." Thus God is not an abstract concept, an ineffable "It," but an ever-present "Thou" with whom the psalmist converses. When the poet speaks of God's knowledge, it is of God's intimate knowledge of the individual. Indeed, everything God does in the first three stanzas has to do with the individual, even though this is a God whose thoughts are inconceivably numerous (v. 17).

The vitriol in verses 19–22 is shocking, but one must not smooth it over. The psalmist has apparently experienced some terrible injustice and does not hesitate to express his sentiments to God, as one might who truly relates to God and has an I-Thou relationship with God. Life before God is not one where there will be only peace and happiness. There will always be the threat and reality of adversities, all of which may be brought before God, though ultimately left in the hands of God. These verses are descriptive, not prescriptive. They do not offer a model of faithful conduct or of prayer. What we have, rather, is a passionate outcry against injustice and a confession of what is in one's thoughts. Then comes the petition (vv. 23–24). Despite the violent and unseemly outburst, the psalmist remains open to God's searching and knowing. He admits to insecurities, and he petitions to be led still by God.

For Those Who Sing Psalm 139

There is a lot to sing about in this poem: the wonder of a God who is so intimately involved in the existence of each person, the contradiction of a God whose thoughts are infinitely numerous, and yet who knows and acts for each of us, the God whom darkness cannot overwhelm. There are marvelous images and expressions, as well, to reiterate in song: the image of one taking wing with the dawn, God's weaving of a person in a mother's womb, God's knitting in the deepest recesses of the earth, and so forth. These we sing with all the faithful through ages past. We sing with full realization that there will be adversities that set us back and cause us to rage and perhaps even to harbor utmost hate. For we know that in the end we can still petition God to keep being involved with us, with all our insecurities, and lead us still.

C. L. Seow

O Lord, You Have Searched Me and Known Me

Psalm 139

Glover Shipp (1927–2016) & Mark Shipp

Gary Pendergrass

O Lord, You Have Searched Me and Known Me

Search Me, O God

Psalm 139

Greg Straughn

Greg Straughn
Arr.: D. J. Bulls

Psalm 140

Translation

Of the leader. A psalm of David.

†1 Rescue me, O Lord, from evil people; protect me from the violent,
†2 who plot evil things in their mind, constantly instigating[a] wars.
†3 They sharpen their tongues like a serpent; the viper's[b] venom is under[c] their lips. *Selah*

†4 Keep me, O Lord, from the hands of the wicked; protect me from the violent, who plot to trip up my steps.
†5 The arrogant have hidden a trap for me, and with cords they have spread a net; by the side of the road they have laid snares for me. *Selah*

*6 I say to the Lord, "You are my God; hearken, O Lord, to my plea for mercy.
*7 O Lord, my Lord, the strength of my salvation, you have shielded my head on the day of battle.
*8 Do not grant, O Lord, the desires of the wicked; do not let their scheme succeed.[d] *Selah*

†9 When they are arrogant around me, let the mischief of their lips cover them.
†10 Let fiery coals[e] tumble upon them; let them be cast into pits, never to rise.
†11 Let the slanderer not be established in the land; let evil hunt the violent one to his demise.[f]

†12 I know that the Lord will maintain the cause of the afflicted, the right of the needy.
*13 Surely the righteous shall confess your name; the upright shall abide in your presence.

[a] There are several homonyms for this verb. This one may be an alternate form of a verb meaning "to stir up, provoke, instigate."

[b] The Hebrew term is found nowhere else in the Bible. The Aramaic Targum takes it to mean "spider," but the Septuagint, Vulgate, and Syriac assume some kind of snake.

[c] It may be more idiomatic in English to translate the preposition as "on," but the term "under" indicates the deceitful nature of the attack.

[d] The Hebrew text as it stands ends with an isolated verb, "they arise," followed by *selah*. Moreover, the beginning of the next line is also difficult, for it reads, "(a) head around me." It seems likely that *selah* has been incorrectly inserted. We should probably place it immediately after the verb "succeed," and read the last word in the Hebrew text in verse 8 as the beginning of the next line. If so, the Hebrew reads, "they are high (of) head," which, to judge by similar expressions elsewhere, would suggest arrogance or overconfidence.

[e] Literally, "coals with fire."

[f] This term is found nowhere else in Hebrew or its cognate languages, though its root is attested, meaning "to push, drive." The pattern suggests a place. The image is of a hunter chasing his prey into corrals.

Structure and Poetry

Psalm 140 is a petition by an individual for divine intervention in the face of adversities brought by unnamed enemies—a theme that echoes Psalm 139:19–22. The poem consists of 5 stanzas: verses 1–3, 4–5, 6–8, 9–11, and 12–13. The first three stanzas are petitionary, and the end of each of these is marked by the term *selah* (vv. 3, 5, 8). They are followed by a fourth stanza of curses against these enemies (vv. 9–11), and a fifth that expresses confidence in God's justice and acknowledges God's character and beneficent presence (vv. 12–13).

Throughout the poem, the singular "I" of the author is set over against a variety of these pernicious others who are "evil" (vv. 1, 2), "violent" (vv. 1, 4, 11), and "wicked" (vv. 4, 8). The malicious willfulness of the enemies is indicated by the terms "plot" (vv. 2, 4), "desires" (v. 8), "schemes" (v. 8), and their unrelenting instigation of wars (literally, "all day long they instigate wars," v. 2). The enemies are likened to snakes in verse 3, where the metaphor is poetically enhanced in the Hebrew by the repetition of the sibilants *sh* (four times) and *s* (one time) that mimic the hissing of these creatures. The terms "tongue" and "lips" suggest that their animosity consisted of slander, and that is confirmed in verse 9, which refers to the "deceit of their lips" and verse 11's reference to "the slanderer" (Hebrew, literally, "man of tongue"). The "venom" from the lips of the enemies (v. 4) is clarified as "deceit of their lips," which will "cover them"—an ironic turn of phrase, for the verb is one used of concealment (v. 10). The deceitful nature of the attacks, suggested at the outset by the expressions "in their mind" (v. 2) and "under their lips" (v. 3), turns out to conceal inherent danger for the perpetrators. Their acts will bring corresponding consequences upon themselves. The enemies are also described as plotting to catch their victim by laying a variety of traps (vv. 4–5). Against such violent hunters, the poet calls for retribution by way of evil personified as a hunter who would hunt them relentlessly: the hunter will become the hunted (v. 11).

Theology and Application

The declaration in verse 12 makes explicit the theological assumption that is implicit in the rest of the poem: "I know that the Lord will maintain the cause of the afflicted, the right of the needy." The terms here—the verb "maintains" (literally, "does/performs"), together with the word pair "cause" (literally, "judgment") and "right" (the most common word for "justice")—appear together in Psalm 9:4, in affirmation of God as a righteous divine judge and king, who will not let wickedness triumph. Herein lies hope for the poet, who has indeed demonstrated neediness through prayer for God to rescue (v. 1), guard (vv. 1, 4), protect (v. 4), hear the cry for mercy (v. 6), and prevent the success of the wicked (v. 8).

The concluding couplet summarizes what is at stake in the poem—God's "name." The Hebrew term for "name" means not just the appellation of God, but God's character and nature. This is the divine "name" that the righteous will confess, the character of the God before whom the upright will dwell (v. 13). The name of this just deity, whom the poet personalizes as "my God" (v. 6) and "my Lord" (v. 7), is none other than the LORD, whose name is mentioned seven times throughout the poem (vv. 1, 4, 6 [2x], 7, 8, 12).

For Those Who Sing Psalm 140

Those who sing Psalm 140 must do so as people who recognize their need of divine intervention, for even if they are personally powerless against the threats that they face, they can count on God as "the strength of my salvation" (v. 7). They sing, too, in faithful expectation that divine justice will ultimately triumph, even when the evidence in the present may seem less than certain.

The poet's longing for justice leads to curses upon the enemies, not least the tumbling of fiery coals upon their heads (v. 10). This vengeful longing for just retribution runs counter to the counsel of the apostle Paul to treat one's enemies with unilateral kindness, which would metaphorically "heap burning coals upon their heads" (Rom. 12:20–21; Prov. 25:21–22). Yet, in the face of overwhelming evil, the German theologian Dietrich Bonhoeffer once suggested that one must not move too quickly to the New Testament. Indeed, one must passionately contemplate the wrath of God "hanging like grim realities over the head of one's enemies," for only then can one know something of what it means to love and forgive. One must not downplay one's conviction as regards the justice of God in one's proclamation of the mercy and love of God. Here, as elsewhere in biblical poetry, the poet's passion for justice, which is a manifestation of faith in the righteousness of God, results in expressions of ill will toward one's adversaries. These expressions are understandable, for they are human, though they may be surpassed by the "more excellent way" of love toward which we strive. Indeed, Paul quotes verse 10 in Romans 12:20 as part of his argument for the inevitable shortcomings of humanity, which can be overcome only by the sheer grace of God.

C. L. Seow

God Sustains Afflicted Ones

Psalm 140

Mark Shipp

Konstantin Zhigulin

God Sustains Afflicted Ones

Sing 4 times, add a voice each time in order shown

Rescue Me, Lord

Psalm 140

Zach Olson D. J. Bulls

Psalm 141

Translation

A psalm of David.

†[1] O LORD, I call out to you; come quickly to me! Hear me when I cry aloud to you.
*[2] May my prayer be considered incense before you, the raising of my hands like the evening sacrifice.

†[3] Set up a guard for my mouth, O LORD; keep watch over the door of my lips.
†[4] May my heart not be inclined to anything evil, to do wicked deeds with those who cause trouble,
and may I not partake of the tempting treats they offer.[a]
†[5] When a righteous person strikes me, it is an act of kindness. When such a person rebukes me, it is oil on my head—my head will not refuse it, for I continue to pray against the works of the evildoers.
†[6] When their leaders[b] experience God's judgment,[c] those who remain will be able to hear how pleasant are my words.
†[7] As one plows and breaks up the ground, so now our bones are scattered at the opening of *Sheol*.

*[8] But to you, O LORD, my Lord, I direct my eyes; in you I take refuge; do not expose my life to danger.
*[9] Protect me from the nets they have set for me, from the snares of those who do evil.
*[10] May the wicked be caught together in their own nets, while I pass safely by.

[a] Or, "eat their delicacies."
[b] Or, "judges."
[c] Literally, "are cast into the hands of the rocks."

Structure and Poetry

Psalm 141 consists of an opening cry for God's help (vv. 1–2), followed by a request for protection from sin in the midst of the crisis (vv. 3–7), and a final expression of confidence in God's ability to deliver (vv. 8–10).

The opening general petition for help in verses 1–2 clearly marks Psalm 141 as an individual lament. This short psalm contains abundant and diverse imagery (comparing prayer to incense and the smoke of the evening sacrifice, the mouth to a door that needs guarding, righteous rebuke to anointing oil, and the plots of the wicked to nets and snares).

Theology and Application

God at times tests his servants directly, but the life of faith in a fallen world inevitably does so on a regular basis. Biblical laments present us with the struggles of believers who live in the tension between the prosperous periods of those who practice evil and the time when they fall.

Many laments portray attacks against the righteous at the hands of the wicked. In Psalm 141, the danger derives more from the temptation of being drawn to the current success of the wicked. The acrostic Psalm 37 addresses such unwise responses in greater detail.

The emphasis on the heart and the lips in Psalm 141 reflects the close relationship between the affections of our hearts and the speech that comes from our mouths (Prov. 4:23; Luke 6:45). Both our hearts and our mouths need to be guarded.

The faith community provides one critical safeguard when we experience temptations. Like the "faithful wounds" of a friend (Prov. 27:6), even painful discipline reflects the kindness (*ḥesed*, covenant love, loyalty) of God. In the end it is soothing and refreshing, like oil on the head (see Ps. 23:5). Psalm 141:6 anticipates a time when God vindicates his servant. The faithful servant's words prove to be "pleasant" in the end. The Hebrew root for "pleasant" also lies behind the "tempting treats" in the last line of verse 4. This parallel points to an important contrast between short-term temptations and ultimate blessing, a difficult message for humans who frequently prefer short-term solutions.

The closing expression of confidence in verses 8–10 affirms the trustworthy nature of God and provides another basis for resisting the temptation to align with the wicked when their ways seem to prosper. This psalm adds to the great common reservoir of testimonies that believers share, filled with all the ways God has delivered his people. These powerful acts also reveal God's sovereignty. In the same way Haman's murderous intent toward Mordecai in the book of Esther was turned back on him, so God allows the wicked in general to fall by their own devices.

For Those Who Sing Psalm 141

Worship realigns us to the truth about God as we live in a world that seeks to allure our hearts through tempting counterfeits. In Psalm 141 we find an honest confession of the attractiveness of these alternatives (see Gen. 3:6). Like the psalmist, we should pray for God's protection of our hearts in light of the many traps that lie before us. We also gain strength by regularly expressing our confidence in God's power to save, as well as God's commitment to overthrow the wicked.

Terry Briley

To You, O Lord, I Raise My Eyes

Psalm 141

Joel Holt

James W. Tackett

Lord, I Call upon You

Psalm 141

Mark Shipp | Rachel McInturff

Psalm 142

Translation

A maskil of David. When he was in the cave. A prayer.

†1 I cry out to the Lord; I appeal to the Lord for mercy.

†2 I pour out my complaint before him; I proclaim my distress before him.

*3 When my spirit grows weak, you are the one who knows my way. In the path I walk others have hidden a trap for me.

†4 Look to the right and see, there is no one who notices me. My refuge has vanished; no one seeks my well-being.[a]

*5 I cry out to you, Lord; I say, "You are the one who shelters me, you are my portion in the land of the living."

†6 Give attention to my cry for help, for I have been brought very low; deliver me from those who persecute me, for they are more powerful than I.

*7 Bring me out of my prison, that I may praise your name, that the righteous might gather around me because of the way you have dealt with me.

[a]Literally, "my life."

Structure and Poetry

Psalm 142, an individual lament, begins with a general cry to God for help (vv. 1–2). The psalmist next confesses God as his sole source of help since, on a human level, everyone has either abandoned him or opposes him (vv. 3–5). The closing section of the psalm anticipates God's deliverance, which will reunite the psalmist with the righteous in praising God (vv. 6–7).

The heading of the psalm connects it to David's experience in the cave as he fled from Saul. Perhaps the experience of being in a "prison" (or "dungeon," v. 7) while seeking true refuge suggests this association. Psalm 57 contains a similar heading and shares some of the language of this psalm.

Theology and Application

As with many laments, Psalm 142 roots its dilemma in the contrast between God's past demonstration of faithfulness and a current experience that seems to call God's faithfulness into question (see Ps. 22:1–10). He acknowledges God as his shelter (v. 5). In addition, he realizes that God "knows" his way (v. 3). This "knowledge" by God represents not simply an awareness, but also sustaining power. In Psalm 1:6, God "watches over" (literally, "knows") the way of the righteous; but, by contrast, the way of the wicked "will perish."

The psalmist's crisis has to do with powerful persecutors on the one hand (who also know his path and set a trap for him in it), and a lack of support from the expected human advocates on the other. Such advocates would typically stand to the right of the person in need (see Pss. 16:8; 109:31; 121:5 with reference to God). Perhaps these people were "missing in action" because they feared to come forward or because they believed in the psalmist's guilt.

David faced a similar situation toward the end of his time fleeing from Saul. A band of men and their families had joined David, but while the men were away, their camp was raided and everyone's family, including David's, was taken captive. At this point, perhaps the lowest of David's time on the run, he felt completely alone because his men spoke of stoning him. David prevailed only because he "strengthened himself in the LORD his God" (1 Sam. 30:6 NRSV).

We find a similar moment in this psalm with the words, "You are my portion in the land of the living" (v. 5; see Pss. 16:5; 73:26). The "portion" refers to the allotment God gave to the Israelite tribes and clans to support them. The Levites, however, did not receive such an allotment and depended on God as their "portion." Ultimately, especially during times of hardship, God is the portion of all Israel. The most striking statement of this principle appears in the beautiful words of Lamentations 3:24 (NIV), confessing, "The LORD is my portion," even in the midst of defeat and exile. As a result, the author says, "I will wait for him."

Psalm 142 expresses a similar confidence in God, anticipating the time when God's direct advocacy will allow the psalmist to reunite with the righteous, a time when together they can once again freely praise God for his goodness to his servants.

For Those Who Sing Psalm 142

We are relational beings, and God desires to work in and through us. Human relationships, however, fall prey to human frailties. Others may attack us, with or without just cause. Even those on whom we depend most will often fail us, preferring not to get involved with our troubles out of fear or self-preoccupation. In such times our faith in God may be sorely tested, but these times can also drive us closer to God as our ultimate refuge.

Terry Briley

For Help and Mercy I Will Cry

Psalm 142

M. W. Bassford | Konstantin Zhigulin

O Lord, I Cry Out for Help

Psalm 142

Mel Witcher

Mel Witcher

Psalm 143

Translation

A psalm of David.

†1 O LORD, hear my prayer; give ear to my appeal for mercy in your faithfulness; answer me in your righteousness.

†2 Do not enter into judgment with your servant, for no one alive is righteous before you.

†3 For the enemy has pursued me, he has crushed me into the ground; he makes me live in darkness like those who died long ago.

†4 Therefore my spirit is weak; my heart is desolate within me.

†5 I remember earlier times; I meditate on all your works and reflect on what your hands have done.

†6 I reach out my hands to you; my life is before you like parched ground. *Selah.*

*7 Answer me soon, LORD; I feel the end coming.[a] Do not hide your face from me lest I become like those who descend into the pit.

*8 Let me hear of your covenant faithfulness in the morning, for I have put my trust in you. Let me know the way I should go, for I offer up my life to you.

*9 Deliver me from my enemies, LORD, for unto you I have fled.[b]

*10 Teach me to do what you desire, for you are my God; your good spirit guides me onto level ground.

*11 For the sake of your reputation,[c] LORD, preserve my life; in your righteousness, bring me out of trouble.

*12 In your covenant faithfulness, bring an end to my enemies; destroy all who have attacked me, for I am your servant.

[a] Literally, "my spirit has come to an end."

[b] The verb here is literally, "I have covered," but that makes no sense in the context. The translation above reflects the ancient Greek version.

[c] Literally, "your name."

Structure and Poetry

Psalm 143 has traditionally been included in a group of penitential psalms (along with Pss. 6, 32, 38, 51, 102, and 130). By content, however, it should be identified as an individual lament.

The psalm divides into two six-verse segments, with verse 7 roughly paralleling the general opening appeal in verses 1–2. No one knows the precise meaning of the Hebrew term *Selah* at the end of verse six, but it likely provides an additional indication of a break at this point. While specific details differ between the two halves, they share several broad elements in common.

Theology and Application

In the psalmist's distress, the nature of the covenant relationship takes center stage. Scholars understand God's covenant with Israel to be largely modeled after ancient Near Eastern covenants between a greater and a lesser power. God, the greater power, is characterized by mercy, faithfulness, justice, and righteousness, as well as the capacity to deliver from enemies. In addition, God's reputation is bound up with his covenant partners.

In Psalm 143, the psalmist represents Israel, God's covenant partner. Apart from God, he is characterized by weakness and an inability to live up to God's standards of righteousness. Enemies have thus besieged and crushed him, so that he resides at the edge of the pit (i.e., *Sheol*/the grave).

What can the psalmist do under such circumstances? The actions of the three main verbs in verse 5—remember, meditate, reflect—provide a start. The latter two verbs are the typical words in Psalms for "meditate." By paralleling them with "remember," the psalmist highlights what it means to "remember" in the Bible. We do not simply offer an occasional reminder of God's nature and works; we mull them over, we reflect deeply on them, we celebrate them, and as a result, we anticipate their continuation.

As a result of this process, especially in difficult times like those reflected in this psalm, we express our trust in God and pray for God to deliver as has been his custom. We know that God's servants have suffered in the past, so such an experience for the psalmist or for us today is not strange. Yet knowing how God has delivered in the past leads us to desire God's very presence ("face," v. 7) to strengthen us and rescue us as well. In the meantime, we also seek God's guidance for the path we should walk in order to please him (vv. 8, 10).

For Those Who Sing Psalm 143

It is often rightly noted that Old Testament sufferers appeal for deliverance quickly and in this life because they possess no certainty about life to come. Yet even Christians share this longing for things to be made right in the present, not some distant future. The frequent Old Testament cry, "How long?" finds its echo on the lips of the Christian martyrs in Revelation 6:10.

The goal is not solely our vindication or rescue, but ultimately the vindication of God, whose reputation in the eyes of others is connected to our condition.

Psalm 141 represents the best of human prayer as it reflects back to God what God has already revealed and promised. We meditate on what Scripture teaches us about God and call for God to remain true to that nature. We pray, ultimately, for that which pleases God and reflects well on the name (character/reputation) of God. At the same time, as we recognize our limitations in knowing God and God's ways, we seek guidance as well as deliverance.

Terry Briley

O Lord, Accept My Ardent Prayer

Psalm 143

Jack R. Reese | James W. Tackett

O Lord, in Your Faithfulness

Psalm 143

Marva L. Hughes — Marva L. Hughes

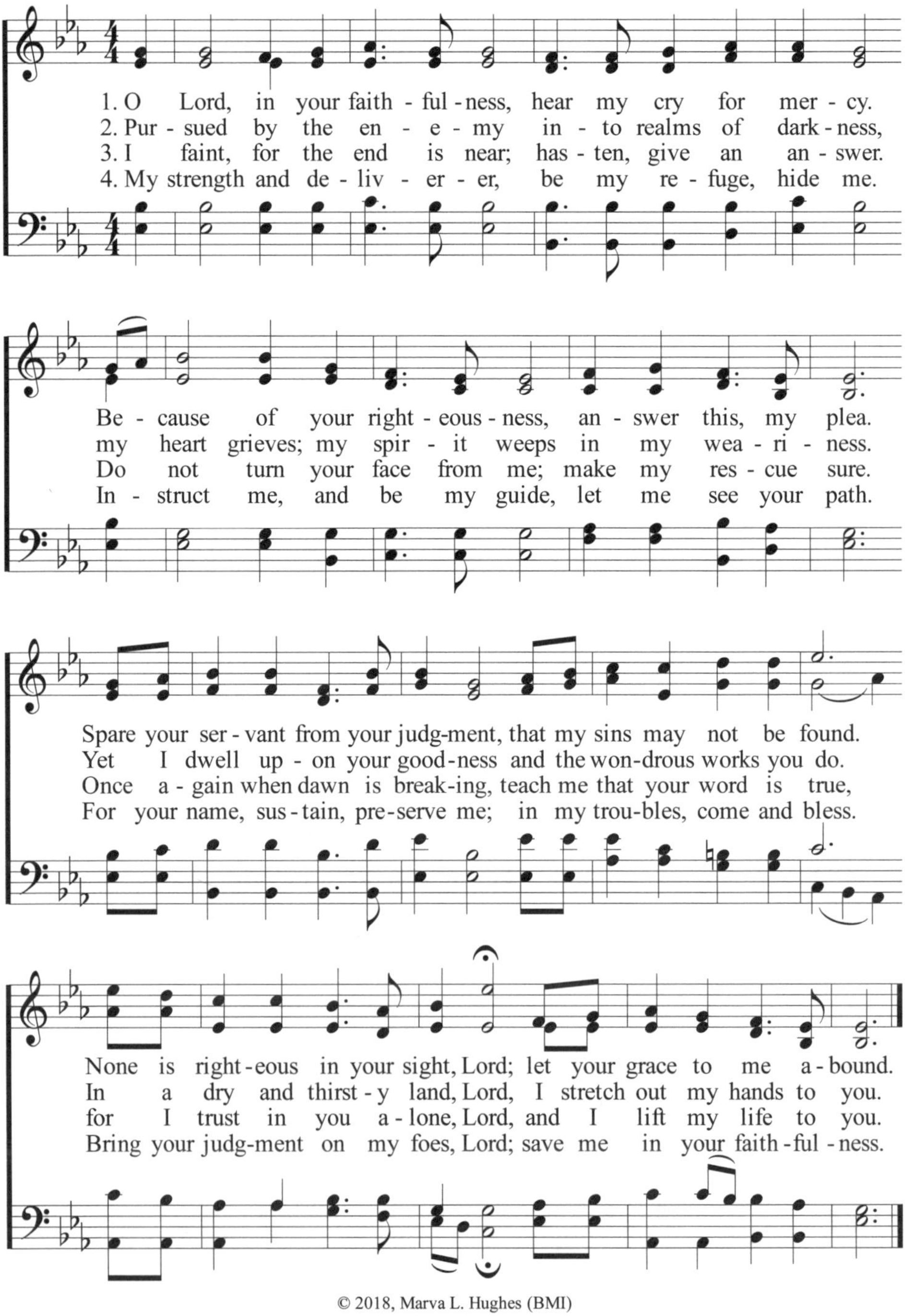

Psalm 144

Translation

Of David.

†1 May the Lord, my rock, be praised, the one who equips my hands for battle, my fingers for warfare.
*2 He is the one on whom I can rely, my fortress, my refuge and my deliverer, my shield and the one in whom I take shelter, the one who subjects nations[a] to[b] me.

†3 O Lord, what are human beings that you take note of them, mortals, that you consider them?
*4 Humans are like a fleeting breath, their days like a passing shadow.

†5 O Lord, extend your heavens and come down; touch the mountains and let their smoke billow.
†6 Let lightning flash and scatter them;[c] unleash your arrows and confuse them.
†7 Reach out your hand from the heights; snatch me away and deliver me from the raging waters, from the hands of foreigners,
†8 whose mouths speak lies, whose right hands convey falsehood.
†9 O God, let me sing a new song to you; with the ten-stringed lyre let me praise you,
†10 who gives victory to kings, who snatches away his servant David from the treacherous sword.
†11 Snatch me away and deliver me from the hands of foreigners whose mouths are full of lies, whose right hands convey falsehood.

*12 Then our sons in their youth will be like thriving plants and our daughters like engraved pillars of a palace.
*13 Our storehouses will be full of all kinds of produce; our sheep will increase by thousands, by tens of thousands in our fields.
*14 Our livestock will be loaded down with produce, with no one to break in and take it away[d] or cause a cry of alarm in our streets.
*15 Blessed is the nation that experiences such a life; blessed is the nation whose God is the Lord.

[a] Hebrew, "my nation," but some versions read "nations," which makes more sense in context.

[b] Literally, "under."

[c] i.e., "those who oppose God/the psalmist."

[d] Some translations understand this phrase to refer to a time when the livestock will not fail to bear their young.

Structure and Poetry

Psalm 144 appears from one perspective to be a royal psalm (especially vv. 1–2, 10), but it also reflects elements of a lament (vv. 6–8, 11). It could thus be called a royal lament. One of the most interesting aspects of this psalm is its adaptation of language and themes from other psalms (Ps. 18 in particular, but also others, such as Pss. 8 and 33).

The psalm begins with the king's praise for God's protection and deliverance from enemies (vv. 1–2). The king then expresses wonder that God would shower attention on such transient creatures (vv. 3–4). As a result of this grace, he cries out to God for fresh deliverance (vv. 5–8) and promises to compose a new song in anticipation of this deliverance (vv. 9–11). The psalm closes with a vision of a prosperous future for God's covenant people and a blessing upon all who enjoy such favor from God (vv. 12–15).

Theology and Application

Lament psalms arise out of a tension between familiar, promised ways God acts on behalf of his servants, individually and collectively, and times when this positive relationship does not appear to be the case. One result of this tension in lament psalms is the appearance of praise for God's past faithfulness and a longing for fresh manifestations of this faithfulness that will allow for a "new song" of praise (v. 9).

The royal dimension of Psalm 144 brings an additional element into the function of a lament. Along with priests and prophets, kings play a mediating role between God and Israel. As mediator, the king not only stands between God and Israel, he also serves as the representative Israelite.

In this light, the king in Psalm 144 can reflect on the ways God has trained and strengthened him, protected and delivered him, and subjugated nations to him, even though many other Israelites were also involved in the process. Despite his exalted position, in verses 3–4 (as in Ps. 8), the king appropriately marvels at and is humbled by God's attention to frail humans. This awareness enables him, in the current distress, to appeal to God to enter human affairs as he has in the past (see Ps. 18:9; Isa. 64:1) and deliver the king from his (and Israel's) enemies. The reference to David in verse 10 also invokes God's past covenant promises.

The first-person singular language of verses 1–11 highlights the king's representative role, but the shift to the plural in verses 12–15 clarifies the broader implications of God's faithfulness to the king. The positive future on the other side of the present trouble resolves the tension of the lament and enables the world to witness the blessedness of "the nation whose God is the Lord."

Psalm 144, like all laments, helps later generations respond properly to their own tensions of faith and trust in God's ultimate faithfulness. In addition, it reminds all leaders of God's people of the importance of their role and relationship with God as mediators on behalf of their respective communities. The way this later psalm draws upon earlier portions of the collection also highlights the way we can incorporate these precious texts in our worship and prayers.

For Those Who Sing Psalm 144

Psalm 144 encourages us to consider the lives of our leaders today. How rooted are they in the biblical witness to God's faithfulness, as well as God's faithfulness in their own lives? How sensitive are they to their impact on those they are called to lead? How clearly do they envision the way their communities should reflect God's blessings to the surrounding world?

We find encouragement in Psalm 144 to draw on the rich storehouse of testimony the Psalms and the Bible as a whole contain for the benefit of each succeeding generation. We need to remember that Israel's king does not simply lead the people, but also represents the people before God. He should also mediate God to the people. For this reason, the king is a messianic foreshadowing whose imperfections are fulfilled in Jesus. We as God's covenant people also possess a royal status (Exod. 19:6; 1 Pet. 2:5, 9), allowing psalms such as this one to speak to us meaningfully. How extensively and thoughtfully have we taken advantage of this resource for enhancing our worship and strengthening our faith? How can we absorb the language and experiences of those who have gone before us so that they inevitably shape our own speech and actions?

Terry Briley

May God, My Rock, Be Praised

Psalm 144

Jerry Shipp

Konstantin Zhigulin
arr. Ruth Ann Somervell

May God, My Rock, Be Praised

May the Lord, My Rock, Be Praised

Psalm 144

Tim Berman

James W. Tackett

Psalm 145

Translation

A psalm of praise. Of David.

†1 (א, *aleph*) I exalt you, my God and king; I bless your name forever and ever.
†2 (ב, *bet*) Every day I bless you and praise your name forever and ever.
*3 (ג, *gimel*) Great is the Lord and exceedingly praiseworthy; his greatness is incomprehensible.
†4 (ד, *dalet*) Generation after generation will praise your works; they will declare your mighty deeds.
†5 (ה, *he*) I meditate on the splendor of your glorious majesty, on the accounts of your wondrous acts.
*6 (ו, *waw*) They talk about your powerful, awe-inspiring works, and I recount your great deeds.
†7 (ז, *zayin*) They overflow with many recollections of your goodness and sing in celebration of your righteousness.
†8 (ח, *het*) The Lord is gracious and compassionate, slow to anger and great in covenant loyalty.
*9 (ט, *tet*) The Lord is good to all; he shows compassion to all he has made.
†10 (י, *yod*) All your works testify to you, Lord; your faithful ones bless you.
†11 (כ, *kaph*) They declare the glory of your kingdom and speak of your power,
*12 (ל, *lamed*) so that humanity might realize your[a] power and the glorious splendor of your[a] kingdom.
†13 (מ, *mem*) Your kingdom is a kingdom for all time, and your reign continues for all generations. The Lord is trustworthy in all his words and faithful in all his deeds.[b]
†14 (ס, *samek*) The Lord supports all who are falling and raises up all who are bowed down.
*15 (ע, *ayin*) The eyes of all look to you for hope, for you are the one who gives them their food in its season,
†16 (פ, *pe*) opening your hand and satiating the desire of every living thing.
†17 (צ, *tsade*) The Lord is righteous in all his ways, loyal in all his works.
*18 (ק, *qoph*) The Lord is near to all who call on him, to all who call on him sincerely.
†19 (ר, *resh*) He fulfills the desire of those who fear him; he hears their cry and saves them.
†20 (שׁ, *shin*) The Lord protects all who love him, but all the wicked he will destroy.
*21 (ת, *taw*) My mouth will proclaim the praise of the Lord; may all humanity bless his holy name forever.

[a] Hebrew says "his."

[b] The second line of verse 13, which keeps the acrostic intact with the letter *nun*, is not in most Hebrew manuscripts (see more details below under "Theology and Application").

Structure and Poetry

Psalm 145 possesses several distinctives within the larger collection. It is the last of the "Psalms of David." It is also the last of the acrostics, those psalms in which the first word of the first verse begins with the first letter of the Hebrew alphabet, the second verse begins with the second letter, and so on. As a praise psalm, it sets the tone for the final five psalms, although it does not begin with the phrase, "Praise the LORD," like Psalms 146–150.

Acrostic psalms typically reflect a theme. Psalm 37, for example, addresses the dilemma of the prosperity of the wicked, and the most famous acrostic, Psalm 119, celebrates the gift of God's law. The acrostic structure tends to limit the psalmist's capacity to convey a smooth development of thought, resulting more in a succession of loosely connected statements on the theme. Psalm 145, however, maintains both an acrostic structure and a meaningful flow of ideas.

Perhaps the relative simplicity of a praise psalm's structure makes this flow possible. The two primary elements of a praise psalm are exhortations to praise God and elaborations of why God deserves this praise. Psalm 145 contains an inclusion, a bracketing device. It begins with the mention of "praise" in the heading, along with the psalmist's example in verses 1–2. It concludes in verse 21 with a second use of the word "praise," along with the call for "all flesh" to bless God's name.

The acrostic format suggests a comprehensive treatment of its theme. As we might say it, the subject was covered "from A to Z." Such an approach mines deeply the relevant vocabulary on the issue at hand, as demonstrated in Psalm 145 with the multiple calls to praise, along with the praiseworthy attributes of God. To further establish this notion of comprehensiveness, the word "all" or "every" appears throughout the psalm, along with references to "forever and ever" (vv. 1–2, 21) and "generations" (vv. 4, 13).

Theology and Application

In light of the acrostic form, the words chosen to represent the succeeding letters of the Hebrew alphabet play an important role in conveying the message of the psalm. Since these words do not necessarily appear at the beginning of a verse in English translation, and English translations of Hebrew words vary, the following list indicates the opening Hebrew word of each verse in the translation above:

> "exalt" (v. 1); "(in) every day" (v. 2); "great" (v. 3); "generation" (v. 4); "splendor" (v. 5); "(and) powerful" (v. 6); "recollections" (v. 7); "gracious" (v. 8); "good" (v. 9); "testify" (v. 10); "glory" (v. 11); "so that . . . realize [literally, 'to make known']" (v. 12); "your kingdom" (v. 13); "trustworthy" (v. 13b); "supports" (v. 14); "eyes"

(v. 15); "opening" (v. 16); "righteous" (v. 17); "near" (v. 18); "desire" (v. 19); "protects" (v. 20); "praise" (v. 21). [Verse 13b, "The LORD is trustworthy . . .", does not appear in most Hebrew manuscripts, but is found in one Psalms manuscript in the Dead Sea Scrolls and the Greek translation of the Old Testament (the Septuagint). Without it the Hebrew letter *nun* is missing from the acrostic, but other acrostic psalms are missing a letter or two (Pss. 34 and 37, for example).]

Psalm 145 begins its praise of God in terms of kingship (v. 1), returning explicitly to that theme in verses 12–13. Within that overarching rubric, God's praise falls under the categories of greatness and goodness. The challenge of combining both of these qualities in one being recalls a famous dialogue between Susan and Mr. Beaver (about meeting Aslan) in C. S. Lewis's classic, *The Lion, the Witch and the Wardrobe*. Susan, nervous about encountering a lion, asks, "Is he—quite safe?" Mr. Beaver replies, "Who said anything about safe? 'Course he isn't safe. But he's good. He's the King, I tell you."[21]

If Psalm 145 reflects, as many believe, a later period in the Old Testament, the nation had experienced by this time numerous human kings who were great (powerful) but not good. Even more kings were neither great nor good. Israel's one constant was the reign of a great and good God. The same applies to the church.

For Those Who Sing Psalm 145

Those who would sing Psalm 145 will find in it a veritable guidebook for praising God. While not literally all-encompassing, this acrostic psalm helps the worshiper deeply understand why God deserves to be praised. Like several other praise psalms, it recognizes the critical role God's covenant people play in helping all humanity recognize God's goodness and greatness so that they will join in the chorus of praise.

Not only does God deserve praise from all creation all the time, but all of humanity also needs to praise God. Such worship properly orients humanity to life within God's creation. Only when we are properly oriented to God can we model God's reign within the creation, while also reflecting God's goodness rather than becoming tyrants. Verses 8 and 9 reflect one of the most prominent passages in the Old Testament: God's self-revelation to Moses of compassion and patience as the essence of the divine nature (Exod. 34:6–7). Only when we recognize the truth about God can we "become what we worship" in the best sense.

Terry Briley

[21] C. S. Lewis, *The Lion, the Witch and the Wardrobe*, The Chronicles of Narnia, book 2 (New York: Harper Trophy, 1950), 79–80.

Come Sing in Celebration

Psalm 145

Clyde H. Slimp

Clyde H. Slimp
arr. Randy Daw

1. The Lord is full of grace; our God is slow to ang - er.
2. How faith-ful is the Lord! His words are all trust - wor - thy;
Great is he and good to all. De-clare his might-y deeds, his
eve - ry need he sat - is - fies. The Lord draws near to all who
last time D.C. al Fine
glo - ry and his splen - dor. Bless his name; his works re - call.
call on him sin - cere - ly, res - cues them, and hears their cries!

Lord, I Exalt You

Psalm 145

Marva L. Hughes | Marva L. Hughes

Great is the Lord! Great is the Lord! Great is the Lord, my
Lord my God and
king! Great is the Lord! Great is the Lord! All peo-ple praise and
king! praise the Lord and
sing, "Great is the Lord!" Great is the
sing, "Great is the Lord!"
1, 2, 3, 4
Lord! Great is the Lord! Lord! Great is the Lord!
Great is the Lord! Great is the Lord!
5
rit.

Psalm 146

Translation

†1 Praise the LORD!

† Let my whole being praise the LORD!
*2 I will praise the LORD with my life! I will sing a psalm to my God as long as I exist.

†3 Do not put your trust in royalty, nor in any human being; in them there is no salvation.
*4 Their life breath departs; they return to the ground. On that day their policies perish.

†5 Happy are those whose help is the God of Jacob, those who look expectantly to the LORD their God,
*6 who made heaven and earth, the sea and everything in them, who is always watching over *them* faithfully,
†7 who establishes justice for the oppressed, who gives food to the hungry. The LORD sets prisoners free.
*8 The LORD opens the eyes of the blind. The LORD lifts up those who have been kept down. The LORD loves the righteous.
†9 The LORD watches over the immigrants; orphan and widow he restores, but the way of the wicked he subverts.

*10 The LORD reigns forever; your God, O Zion, generation after generation.

* Praise the LORD!

Structure and Poetry

Very appropriately, Psalm 146 begins a collection of songs of praise (Pss. 146–150) that concludes the book of Psalms, which in Hebrew is entitled simply "Praises." Each of Psalms 146–150 begins and ends with *hallelu-yah*, "Praise the LORD!" And the sweeping movement of the collection is from an individual's praise in Psalm 146:1–2 to the praise of "everything that has breath" in Psalm 150:6.

The psalmist's commitment to praise in verses 1–2 is followed in verses 3–4 with some advice or instruction that makes it clear that praise is ultimately a matter of trust, properly directed not to human individuals or systems, but to

God alone. God's character and characteristic activity are the focus of verses 5–9, and verse 10 offers a concluding proclamation/promise before the final *hallelu-yah*.

Not surprisingly, given its placement, Psalm 146 recalls Psalm 1 in several ways. To be truly "Happy" (v. 5; this word is often translated "blessed") is to live a fundamentally God-centered life (see Ps. 1:1–2). Such a life does not involve a comfortable and carefree existence—indeed, "Many are the afflictions of the righteous" (Ps. 34:19 NRSV)—but the affirmation that God "knows the way of the righteous" in Psalm 1:6 (NASB) is matched in Psalm 146:8 by the assurance that "The LORD loves the righteous." Conversely, in both Psalms 1 and 146, "the way of the wicked" (1:6; 146:9) is what God opposes (see "perish" in 1:6; 146:4).

Theology and Application

As verses 1–2 make clear, praise is a matter of both *liturgy* and *lifestyle*. The psalmist's commitment is not only to "sing a psalm," but also to praise God with "my whole being" and "with my life." Liturgy and lifestyle go together. In short, worship is not finished on Sunday morning when we leave the church building. Indeed, it is just beginning, as we entrust our whole selves and lives to God (vv. 3–5), and as we join in God's work in the world that God created (v. 6) and claims as God's own (v. 10; see Isa. 1:10–20; Amos 5:21–24, where worship is deemed unacceptable and even offensive to God when it is not accompanied by doing what God wants done).

In other words, Psalm 146 calls us, as Jesus calls us, to enter and live in the sphere of God's reign (see Mark 1:14–15). Notice that the language is political—"reigns" (v. 10) and "royalty" (v. 3; the underlying Hebrew word is translated by the NRSV as "princes" in Pss. 47:9; 113:8; 118:9). The realm or kingdom of God is to be our highest political allegiance. Our ways are to be patterned after God's ways.

And what is God up to in the world? Verses 7–9 make it very clear. In a word, God "establishes *justice*" (v. 7). And unlike justice in most or all human systems (see vv. 3–4), God's justice is not about giving people what they deserve, but rather about giving people what they need—food (v. 7), liberation from enslaving conditions and circumstances (v. 7), advocacy that empowers and uplifts (v. 8; "blind" here can be understood figuratively as well as literally). No wonder that verse 9 locates God's characteristic activity specifically among society's and the world's most vulnerable people, then and now—immigrants, orphans, and widows (see Exod. 22:21–22; Lev. 19:33–34; Deut. 10:18; 14:28–29; Ps. 94:4–7). The "way of the wicked," or we could say "the way of the world," tells us that God helps those who help themselves. But the Psalms, including Psalm 146, and the prophets, and the gospels tell us that God helps those who *cannot help themselves*!

For Those Who Sing Psalm 146

It is fitting that Psalm 146 articulates the psalmist's commitment to "sing a psalm to my God" (v. 2), and it is fitting that we are still singing psalms to our God these thousands of years later. As Psalm 146 demonstrates, faithful singing is a powerful activity. Indeed, it is nothing short of world-changing! And this is especially so for those whom the world often deems insignificant, even expendable. In a world like ours, in which injustice, hunger, and oppression abound, our singing praise to God is the promise of good news—the same good news that Jesus proclaimed and embodied (see Luke 4:16–21; Matt. 25:31–46). This good news is the reason that the next psalm, Psalm 147, begins with these words: "How good it is to sing a psalm to our God!"

J. Clinton McCann Jr.

Let My Soul Praise the Lord

Based on Psalm 146

Zach Olson

Debbie Dorman

Praise to the Lord

Psalm 146

Marva L. Hughes — Marva L. Hughes

Psalm 147

Translation

†1 Praise the Lord!

† How good it is to sing a psalm to our God! How delightful and appropriate is a song of praise!
*2 The Lord builds Jerusalem; he gathers Israel's exiles.
†3 He heals the brokenhearted and bandages their injuries.
*4 He counts the stars; he assigns each of them a name.
†5 Great is our Lord and superior in strength! There is no limit to his understanding!
*6 The Lord restores the afflicted; he brings down the wicked to the earth.

†7 Sing to the Lord with thanks; sing a psalm to our God with a lyre!
*8 He covers the sky with clouds; he provides rain for the earth; he makes grass sprout on the hillsides.
†9 He gives each animal its food, even to the baby ravens when they cry.
†10 He does not delight in a horse's strength; the legs of a runner[a] do not please him.
*11 What is pleasing to the Lord are those who honor him, those who hope in his loyal love.

†12 Worship the Lord, O Jerusalem! Praise your God, O Zion!
*13 For he strengthens the bars of your gates; he blesses the children in your midst.
†14 He establishes peace within your borders, and he satisfies you with the best wheat.
*15 He sends out his command to the earth; his word runs fast.
†16 He gives snow like wool; he scatters frost like ashes.
†17 He throws down hail like tiny crumbs. Who can stand in the face of his cold?
†18 He sends his word, and it melts them; he causes his wind to blow and waters flow.
†19 He proclaims his word to Jacob, his statutes and rules for justice[b] to Israel.
*20 He has not done this for any other nation; the rules for justice[b] they do not know.

* Praise the Lord!

[a] Hebrew says, "the legs of a human."

[b] This Hebrew word is usually translated "ordinances" and often appears together with "statutes" (as in v. 19) and "commandments." But the word is from the Hebrew root that means "judge" or "establish justice." The translation above suggests that the intent of God's teaching is to move God's people and the world toward the justice that God wills (see Pss. 146:7; 149:9).

Structure and Poetry

Psalm 147 is the second psalm in the collection of songs of praise that concludes the book of Psalms (Pss. 146–150; see comments on Ps. 146). Psalm 146 begins with the psalmist's promise to "sing a psalm to my God as long as I exist" (v. 2). Psalm 147 opens by reinforcing this promise, and in effect, it continues the song: "How good it is to sing a psalm to our God!" As was the case with Psalm 146 (and with the songs of praise in general), Psalm 147 provides reasons for praise in each of its three sections, all of which begin with an invitation to praise.

The first section is verses 1–6. After the initial invitation to praise and commendation of praise in verses 1–2, the reasons for praise are given in verses 3–6. Like Psalm 146 again, these reasons involve both God's creative activity (vv. 4–5; see Ps. 146:6) and God's characteristic work of compassionately meeting the needs of the vulnerable and victimized (vv. 2–3, 6; see Ps. 146:7–9). Psalm 147:6b clearly echoes Psalm 146:9c; that is, God opposes "the wicked," those who create victims and prey upon the vulnerable (see also Ps. 1:6; 1 Sam. 2:4–7; Luke 1:51–53).

The invitations to praise in verse 7 open the second section, verses 7–11. Again, God is to be praised for God's work in both creation and providence; and in this case, God's provision includes even food for hungry animals (v. 9; see Pss. 36:6; 104:27–28)!

After the invitation to praise in verse 12, the final section (vv. 12–20) describes once again not only God's actions to meet needs in the human community—providing security, food, and guidance (vv. 13–14, 19–20)—but also God's activity in the created order (vv. 15–18).

Theology and Application

Psalm 147's consistent portrayal of God's activity both in creation and in the meeting of needs in the human (and animal) community has profound theological significance. It is most clearly in view in verses 15–20, where the three occurrences of "word" (vv. 15, 18, 19) sharpen the theological point. In the first instance, God's "word" is the active force behind the weather (vv. 15–18). This should not be understood to mean that God orchestrates every particular blizzard or hailstorm for some unknown purpose. Rather, God's power stands behind the forces that drive a life-sustaining creation that depends quintessentially on water (vv. 8, 18). But in the second instance, God's "word" is addressed specifically "to

Jacob" (v. 19); and this word is aimed at teaching God's people how to enact justice (vv. 19–20), which is the essence of God's will (see Ps. 146:7). In other words, the striking and crucial biblical claim is that the power that drives the universe (vv. 4, 8, 15–18) is the same power that works toward "healing the brokenhearted" (v. 3) and "restoring the afflicted" (v. 6). In short, the power behind the universe is ultimately God's "loyal love" (v. 11); this good news is the ground of our hope, and indeed, the hope of the world (v. 11; see Ps. 146:5).

That Jacob/Israel is singled out among the nations to receive God's "word" (vv. 19–20) should be understood not so much as a privilege, but rather as a responsibility. Knowing God's "rules for justice," the people of God are called to share that knowledge by modeling God's justice (see Ps. 146:7–9)—"building" (v. 2), "healing" (v. 3), "restoring" (v. 6), feeding (vv. 9, 14), and "establishing peace" (v. 14). After all, such has been Israel's mission from the beginning of its story with Abraham—that is, the call not only to receive and enjoy GodIs

[AU: please correct] blessing, but also to share it with nothing short of "all the families of the earth" (Gen. 12:3 NRSV). For the psalmists, this expansive mission underlies their vision of the world-encompassing congregation that is invited to praise God as Psalms 146–150 bring the Psalter to a close: "Let everything that has breath praise the LORD!" (Ps. 150:6).

For Those Who Sing Psalm 147

Like Psalm 146, Psalm 147 is a reminder of why it is so "good . . . to sing a psalm to our God!" (v. 1), and why we continue to sing the Psalms. In short, we sing gratefully because God is so good. We sing because God has created and is sustaining a universe that supports the miracle of life—our human lives and the lives of all creatures. We sing because God has spoken a word to us, God's people, inviting us not only to receive and enjoy the blessings of creation, but also to share them with all the world. In the words of our psalm, "How delightful and appropriate is a song of praise!" (v. 1).

J. Clinton McCann Jr.

Jehovah Is Building His City

Psalm 147

Mark Shipp

Michael E. Showalter and Ruth Ann Somervell

num - bers them one by one. The Lord will re - store the af -
run - ner brings no de - light. He fa - vors the peo - ple who
word, and the wa - ters flow. His sta - tutes he gives to his
flict - ed, but by him the wick - ed will be un - done.
fear him and wait for his mer - cy by day and night.
peo - ple; his pre - cepts his en - e - mies do not know.
Come wor - ship the Lord, all his peo - ple! Come sing to the Lord a
psalm of praise! How fit - ting to sing to Je - ho - vah, give thanks to him
all of our days.
CODA sing after last verse
rit.
Give thanks to him all of our days.

How Good It Is to Praise the Lord

Psalm 147

Joel Holt | Randy Daw (1954–2019)

Psalm 148

Translation

†1 Praise the LORD!

† Praise the LORD from the heavens! Praise him in the highest places!
*2 Praise him, all his messengers! Praise him, all his attendants![a]
†3 Praise him, sun and moon! Praise him, all stars of light!
*4 Praise him, highest heavens, and waters above the heavens!
*5 Let them praise the name of the LORD, for he gave the command and they were created.
*6 He has set them in place forever; a decree he gave, that none may cancel.

†7 Praise the LORD from the earth, sea monsters and all depths,
*8 fire and hail, snow and storm clouds, stormy wind that obeys his word,
†9 mountains and all hills, fruit trees and all cedars,
*10 wild animals and all cattle, things that crawl and birds that fly,
†11 kings of the earth and all peoples, princes and everyone on earth entrusted with doing justice,
*12 young men along with young women, the old and the young!
*13 Let them praise the name of the LORD, for his name alone is exalted, his majesty above earth and heaven.
*14 He has raised a horn for his people, praise for all his faithful, for the children of Israel, a people close to him.

* Praise the LORD!

[a] Heb. "hosts."

Structure and Poetry

Psalm 148 is the third psalm in a collection of songs of praise that concludes the book of Psalms (Pss. 146–150; see comments on Psalm 146). Its two main sections begin in a similar manner. Praise is first invited "from the heavens" and occupants of the heavens (vv. 1–6). Then praise is invited "from the earth" and its occupants (vv. 7–14). Both sections also move toward a conclusion with an identical formulation, "Let them praise the name of the LORD" (vv. 5a, 13a), followed in each case by reasons for praise (vv. 5b–6, 13b–14).

Despite the similarities, the two sections are also rather different. Verses 1–6 contain nine occurrences of the word "praise," including seven that are identical in grammatical form. This may not be coincidental, since the number seven often communicates totality or completeness, that is, Psalm 148 calls for total praise, including praise from all sectors of the universe!

The seven-times-repeated form of "praise" in verses 1–6 occurs only once in verses 7–14, and it is the first word in this section. It is the invitation to praise; although it occurs only once, it is addressed to *twenty-three* different parties—animals of various kinds (vv. 7, 10), plants (v. 9), weather phenomena (v. 8), inanimate features of creation (vv. 7, 9), and finally, people of various kinds (vv. 11–12)! The intent to be inclusive is unmistakable. Everybody and everything, living and nonliving, is invited to praise God! Psalm 148 is actually more inclusive than the climactic, concluding verse of the Psalter that invites "everything that has breath" to praise God (Ps. 150:6). Here, *everything that is* is invited to praise God. Since Psalm 148 is the centerpiece of the collection, Psalms 146–150, perhaps the poets wanted it to be the pinnacle of expansiveness and inclusivity, in terms of the invitation to praise God.

Theology and Application

Psalm 148 clearly continues and extends the creation themes found in Psalms 146 and 147 (see Pss. 146:6; 147:4–5, 8–10, 15–18) by way of its claim that everything in the heavens and on earth derives from God (see especially v. 5) and thus belongs to God's worshiping community. In short, God is the Lord of all!

This profound theological conclusion has far-reaching implications. If "all peoples" (v. 11) really belong to God—powerful and ordinary, men and women, young and old—then every single human being is to be viewed as and treated as a child of God! What a challenge! What an opportunity!

Similarly, if all creatures and all features of creation really belong to God, then they too are to be treated with dignity and respect. The ecological implications are staggering! What a challenge! What an opportunity! To be sure, a bird or a tree or a snowflake will not praise God the same way that we humans praise God. Perhaps our unique place and role is to enable the whole creation to thrive, not just so that we and our children will have a livable future, but also so that God can enjoy the majestic universe that God has created (see Pss. 8 and 104).

This role seems to be what is in view in verse 14, the specificity of which is a noticeable contrast to the expansiveness and inclusivity of verses 1–13. Why is Israel singled out (see also Ps. 147:19–20)? For what is Israel strengthened (which seems to be the meaning of "raised a horn for his people"; see Ps. 89:17, 24)? What is Israel's "praise"? In the context of the remarkable expansiveness of verses 1–13, the answer to these questions seems to be that the people of God are chosen and equipped—that is, honored and praised—to facilitate the praise of the entire human community, and indeed, of the entire creational community. How does this happen? It seems that it happens when the people of God share God's apparent delight in the created order and as the people of God enact and embody what God wills for the world (see above on Pss. 146 and 147).

For Those Who Sing Psalm 148

Those who sing Psalm 148 are invited to picture themselves as part of not just a world-encompassing community but also a universe-encompassing community of praise. St. Francis of Assisi had it right when in his famous *Canticle of the Sun* he addressed sun, wind, fire, moon, waters, and earth as brother and sister. Psalm 148 invites us to contemplate not only how the earth can serve us but also how we can serve the earth. As servants of our sovereign creator and of the creation that derives from and belongs to God, we become the praise that God intends us to be.

J. Clinton McCann Jr.

From the Heavens Praise the Lord

Psalm 148

Glover Shipp (1927–2016) Aaron Shotts

Praise the Lord, All His Creation

Psalm 148

Marva L. Hughes
Marva L. Hughes

Praise the Lord from the Heavens

Psalms 148

Glover Shipp (1927–2016) | Randy Daw (1954–2019)

Psalm 149

Translation

†[1] Praise the LORD!

† Sing to the LORD a new song, a praise song for him in the congregation of the faithful!
†[2] Let Israel be glad because of its maker; let the children of Zion rejoice in their king.
†[3] Let them praise his name with dancing; with tambourine and lyre, let them sing a psalm to him.
†[4] For the LORD takes pleasure in his people; he crowns the afflicted with salvation.

*[5] Let the faithful celebrate with glory; let them shout joyfully on their beds.
*[6] Let the highest praise of God be in their mouths, and a two-edged sword in their hands,
*[7] to seek redress[a] among the nations, correction[a] among the peoples,
*[8] to bind their kings with restraints, and their important people with iron chains,
*[9] to establish justice among them, as it is written. This is honor for all the faithful.

* Praise the LORD!

[a] The Hebrew words underlying the translations "redress" and "correction" are usually translated "vengeance" and "punishment." These translations suggest that God is essentially vindictive rather than gracious, merciful, and loving (see Ps. 145:8; Exod. 34:6). The above translation suggests that God's ultimate intent is to set right what is wrong, which is what God's "justice" is about (v. 9).

Structure and Poetry

Psalm 149 is the fourth psalm in a collection of songs of praise that concludes the Book of Psalms (Pss. 146–150; see comments on Ps. 146). The first four verses demonstrate the typical structure of a song of praise, with invitations to praise (vv. 1–3) followed by reasons for praise (v. 4). Verses 5–6a function as another invitation to praise (the mention of "beds" in v. 5 may suggest constant praise, even throughout the night); but verses 6b–9 proceed with something like a job description for "the faithful" that are mentioned in verses 1, 5, and 9. The problem with this unexpected turn is compounded by the violent imagery employed—"sword" (v. 6b), "restraints" (v. 8a), and "iron chains" (v. 8b).

The unusual character of Psalm 149 may be explained by its placement in the Psalter. It is likely that it is meant to be understood in relation to Psalm 2—that is, the second and the second-from-the-last psalm should be heard together. Not only does their placement correspond, but so also does their content in at least one important way. In Psalm 2, the earthly king is responsible for turning the nations in the direction of serving God (see 2:11–12), whereas in Psalm 149, "the faithful" have apparently inherited the responsibility of dealing with the nations so that they will do what God wills—in a word, "justice" (v. 9; see Pss. 146:7; 147:19–20).

The mode of operation for turning the nations and their leaders to God's way seems disturbingly violent in both Psalms 2 and 149 (compare 2:8–9 with 149:6b–8). This problematic dimension of Psalms 2 and 149 should not be too easily dismissed, because Psalm 149 has been used historically by Christians to justify the use of armed force against alleged enemies (who, as it often turned out, were other groups of Christians!). The danger of misusing and abusing Psalm 149 is diminished when the *goal* of the work of "the faithful" is given priority—that is, "justice" (v. 9), which the preceding psalms have described quite clearly as compassionately meeting human need (see Pss. 146:7–9; 147:2–3, 6, 13–14) and leading others to do the same (see Pss. 147:19–20; 148:14). Furthermore, the actions of "the faithful" are depicted as fundamentally defensive rather than offensive—that is, they are to restrain the powerful and important people of the earth from creating more victims (note that v. 4 suggests that God's people are or have been afflicted in some way).

Theology and Application

In a real sense, Psalm 149 is an elaboration upon the implications of Psalms 146:1–2, 7–9; 147:19–20; and 148:14—that is, the people of God are chosen and equipped to praise God by doing in the world the justice that God wants done. This role or function was at one time the special responsibility of the earthly king (see Ps. 72), but the monarchy disappeared in 587 BCE at the beginning of the Babylonian exile. So in the postexilic era, it was logical that the responsibility for establishing God's justice in the world would have fallen to "all the faithful" (v. 9). To serve God in such a way would indeed have been an "honor" (v. 9), something worthy of praise (see Ps. 148:14).

In any case, service to God is clearly what is implied by addressing God as "king" (v. 2; see Ps. 146:10, and Pss. 93, 95–99). Not surprisingly, the mission of enacting God's will in the world is associated elsewhere with singing "a new song" (v. 1). For instance, the commission to be "a light to the nations, to open the eyes that are blind, to bring out the prisoners from the dungeon, from the prison those who sit in darkness" (Isa. 42:6–7 NRSV) is followed in short order by the invitation to "sing to the LORD a new song" (Isa. 42:10 NRSV). Isaiah 42 originated in the early postexilic era, and one of the "new things" (Isa. 42:9 NRSV) that God was doing was positioning the whole people of God to take over the responsibility that had been lodged formerly in the now nonexistent monarchy. A new mission would have logically invited the singing of a new song.

Not surprising, either, is that the servant-mission described in Isaiah 42 is a ministry aimed at world-encompassing justice (see Isa. 42:1, 3, 4), as is also the case in Psalm 149. In other contexts as well, when the goal is world-encompassing justice, there are invitations to sing a new song. For instance, Psalms 96 and 98 move toward a conclusion by portraying God coming into the world "to establish justice on the earth!" (Pss. 96:13; 98:9 CEB). Both Psalms 96 and 98 begin with this invitation, "Sing to the LORD a new song" (Pss. 96:1; 98:1 CEB). Many interpreters consider Psalms 96 and 98 to be part of a collection (Pss. 93, 95–99, all of which proclaim God's kingship) that is the theological center of the book of Psalms. If this is correct, then Psalm 149 is moving the Psalter to a conclusion by echoing the Psalter's central affirmation of God's kingship and inviting an appropriate response—that is, the singing of a new song (v. 1) and participation in the enactment of God's justice in the world (vv. 6–9).

For Those Who Sing Psalm 149

Those who sing Psalm 149 will be reminded that insofar as we address God as "king" (v. 2), we thereby position ourselves as servants, who honor God not only with our liturgical activities—singing "a new song" (v. 1) or "a psalm" (v. 3)—but also by joining God at God's work of establishing world-encompassing justice (vv. 6–9). Indeed, what greater honor could there be? The best possible response from "all the faithful" is simply, "Praise the LORD!"

J. Clinton McCann Jr.

Let Children Dance

Psalm 149

Randy Daw (1954–2019)

Aaron Shotts

Let Children Dance

Sing a New Song to the Lord

Psalm 149

M. W. Bassford

Michael E. Showalter

Psalm 150

Translation

†1 Praise the LORD!

† Praise God in his holy place! Praise him in the firmament of his strength!
*2 Praise him for his mighty acts! Praise him for his exceeding greatness!

†3 Praise him with trumpet blast! Praise him with harp and lyre!
*4 Praise him with tambourine and dance! Praise him with strings and flute!
†5 Praise him with clashing cymbals! Praise him with joyful-sounding cymbals!

*6 Let everything that has breath praise the LORD!

* Praise the LORD!

Structure and Poetry

Psalm 150 is the fifth and final psalm in a collection of songs of praise that concludes the book of Psalms (Pss. 146–150; see comments on Ps. 146). Given its position, it is appropriate that Psalm 150 departs noticeably from the typical structure of a song of praise—that is, it consists exclusively of invitations to praise, although reasons for praise are discernible amid the invitations in verses 1–2. As such, Psalm 150 serves as a very appropriate concluding doxology for Book Five of the Psalter (Pss. 107–150; see the doxologies that conclude Books One through Four in Pss. 41:13; 72:18–19; 89:52; and 106:48), as well as for the collection of songs of praise in Psalms 146–150. The concluding verse of Psalm 150 recalls the final verse of Psalm 145. Both verses envision a world-encompassing community of praise, thus framing the concluding collection of the Psalter with a cosmic perspective. This cosmic perspective, culminating in Psalm 150:6, also means that Psalm 150 provides an appropriate concluding crescendo of praise for the entire book of Psalms, which in Hebrew is entitled "Praises."

The invitations to praise in verses 1–2 are similar in that both suggest reasons for praise. The invitations to praise in verses 3–5 cohere in that they all mention musical instruments. The invitation to praise in verse 6 employs a different grammatical form, thus setting it apart as a climactic conclusion to the psalm, to the current collection (Pss. 146–150), to Book Five (Pss. 107–150), and to the entire Psalter.

Theology and Application

Psalm 149 addresses God as "king" (v. 2), recalling the theological center of the book of Psalms (Pss. 93, 95–99) as well as echoing Psalms 145:1, 11–13 and 146:10. While Psalm 150 does not explicitly call God "king," the vocabulary of verses 1–2 reinforces the affirmation of God's royal reign. For instance, God's "holy place" (often translated "sanctuary") can be thought of as God's throne room; and in Psalm 68:24, God is addressed as "my king" as he enters this location. The paralleling of "holy place" with "firmament of his strength" suggests that God is not only the king of Israel (Ps. 149:2), but also the Lord of all. The Hebrew words underlying "strength" in verse 1 and "mighty" in verse 2 occur together in Psalm 24:8, where God is called "the king of glory." Psalm 24 begins with the affirmation that "the earth is the LORD's and all that is in it" (v. 1 NRSV). The language of Psalm 150 reinforces this affirmation of God's cosmic kingship. This perspective, of course, explains why all people and all creatures are invited to praise God (v. 6; see also Ps. 148, where *everything that is* is invited to praise God).

The entire temple orchestra is in view in verses 3–5. Given the language in verses 1–2 that affirms God's sovereignty, it is worthy of note that a "trumpet blast" (v. 3) elsewhere accompanies the proclamation of God's kingship (see Pss. 47:5–7 and 98:6). Several of the musical instruments in verses 3–5 are mentioned in the ceremony described in 2 Samuel 6. Here the ark—that is, the representation of the earthly throne of God—is brought to Jerusalem. God's enthronement is celebrated with music and dance, as in Psalm 150 (2 Sam. 6:5; see also the mention of musical instruments in 1 Chron. 15:28; 2 Chron. 5:13; Neh. 12:27; Pss. 33:2–3; 43:4; 68:24–25; 71:22; 98:5; 147:7; 149:3). Cymbals are the final instruments mentioned (twice in v. 5), apparently marking a climactic moment, just as cymbals often still do in musical performances.

Verse 6 suggests that the ultimate climactic moment in praising God, however, comes from a combined choir composed of "everything that has breath" (see also Pss. 66:1–3; 100:1; 103:22; 145:21; 148:1–13). The word "breath" recalls Genesis 2:7 where it represents the origin of human life. Thus, the final verse of the Psalter suggests that human life—indeed, the life of all creation—finds its proper goal in grateful submission to God and God's will. In short, we live to praise! As the Westminster Shorter Catechism famously puts it, our "chief end is to glorify God."

For Those Who Sing Psalm 150

For those who sing Psalm 150, it will inevitably be the case that they are part of a much larger congregation than they are able to see—in short, they are part of the congregation of "everything that has breath." That praise in the Psalms is regularly sung (see Pss. 146:2; 147:1; 149:3) is significant, because music has the power to enable us to transcend ourselves. In other words, music can facilitate the experience of being "lost in wonder, love, and praise" (see "Love Divine, All Loves Excelling"). This sort of self-abandonment is precisely what praise is all about—the offering of the whole self to God in liturgy and life (see above on Ps. 146). The good news is that this sort of self-abandonment makes for the abundant life that God intends, because it puts us in harmony with God and in community with each other and with creation. Like the psalmists in this final collection, we move from praising God with our individual lives (Ps. 146:1–2) to praising God in the congregation of "everything that has breath" (Ps. 150:6). Praise the Lord!

J. Clinton McCann Jr.

Praise the Lord, Our God in Heaven

Psalm 150

Jack R. Reese | Jack R. Reese

Un-der-neath his right-eous ban - ner praise our God, the Lord of peace!
6. Praise the Lord; all crea-tures praise him, eve-ry breath his name a - dored.
All cre - a - tion stands be - fore him. Hal - le - lu - jah! Praise the Lord!
All cre - a - tion stands be - fore him. Hal-le - lu - jah! Hal-le - lu - jah!
Hal - le - lu - jah! Praise the Lord!

Praise the Lord!

Psalm 150

Michael E. Showalter

Michael E. Showalter

Alphabetical Index of Composers and Arrangers

ALPHABETICAL INDEX OF LYRIC CONTRIBUTORS

Index of Commentators

Index of Song Titles

Metrical Index

CM = Common Meter, 8.6.8.6
LM = Long Meter, 8.8.8.8
SM = Short Meter, 6.6.8.6

D = Doubled
T = Tripled

Index of Song Difficulty

Psalm 107	Give Thanks to Jehovah for He Is Good
Psalm 108	Let Your Glory Be over the Earth, O Lord
Psalm 112	The Upright One
Psalm 114	Steeped in Mercy
Psalm 114	When Israel Departed from Egypt
Psalm 116	Thank Offering
Psalm 117	O Praise the Lord Our God
Psalm 119:1–16	Blessed
Psalm 119:17–32	I Am a Stranger on the Earth
Psalm 119:49–64	Hold to Your Promise, Lord
Psalm 119:81–96	My Soul Cries Out for My Release
Psalm 119:145–160	Give Me Life
Psalm 121	He Watches Over You
Psalm 121	I Lift Up My Eyes to the Hills
Psalm 122	May There Be Peace
Psalm 123	To You I Lift Up My Eyes
Psalm 130	My Soul Waits
Psalm 134	Come and Bless the Lord Forever
Psalm 134	O Come to Bless the Lord
Psalm 135	O Praise God's Name Together
Psalm 135	The Lord Is Great
Psalm 136:1–9	His Love Endures Forever
Psalm 136	Proclaim the Lord
Psalm 137	We Wept by the Rivers of Babylon
Psalm 140	Rescue Me, Lord
Psalm 142	For Help and Mercy I Will Cry
Psalm 144	May God, My Rock, Be Praised

Psalm 100	Make a Joyful Noise
Psalm 105	God Has Kept His Covenant
Psalm 107:2–15	They Cried Out to the Lord
Psalm 109	For Your Sake
Psalm 110	Sit at My Right Hand
Psalm 122	I Was Glad When They Said unto Me
Psalm 140	God Sustains Afflicted Ones
Psalm 150	Praise the Lord, Our God in Heaven

BIOGRAPHICAL INDEX OF COMPOSERS, LYRICISTS, ARRANGERS, COMMENTATORS, AND *TIMELESS* COMMITTEE MEMBERS

CYNTHIA AGNELL, *Round Rock, Texas.* Cynthia holds a Master of Arts in Theological Studies from Austin Graduate School of Theology. She met Dr. Shipp and became involved with *Timeless* while a student at Austin Grad.

RODNEY ASHLOCK, *Abilene, Texas.* Dr. Ashlock holds a PhD from Baylor University and is on the faculty at Abilene Christian University.

MATTHEW W. BASSFORD, *Spring, Texas.* Matthew is a graduate of the University of Texas School of Law, a minister, and the author of a number of hymns.

SARAH BERMAN, *Granbury, Texas.* Sarah is a graduate of Harding University and a certified public accountant.

TIMOTHY L. BERMAN, *Granbury, Texas.* Timothy is a software product manager, user experience practitioner, and hymnist. He is an editor for the *Sing to the Lord!* hymn publication and teaches hymn writing at the *R. J. Stevens Singing School.*

TERRY BRILEY, *Nashville, Tennessee.* Dr. Briley holds a PhD from Hebrew Union College and currently is a Professor of Bible at Lipscomb University. His books include two volumes on Isaiah and *Delighting in the Lord: The Story of Israel and Christian Faith.*

MICHELE BROADWAY, *Austin, Texas.* Michele holds a Bachelor of Music Education from Abilene Christian University. She has taught band and secondary math in Texas public schools and now teaches mathematics at Brentwood Christian School in Austin, Texas.

JULIANNE GRACE BROWN, *Austin, Texas.* Julianne studied music at the University of Nebraska–Lincoln and Texas State University. She has fifteen years of experience teaching Fine Arts subjects in public school, and piano and voice privately. She is a member of Sigma Alpha Iota.

D. J. BULLS, *Tyler, Texas.* D. J. is a church musician, composer, arranger, and hymnologist. Dr. Bulls has served in worship ministry for over twenty years. Most importantly, he's Meghan's husband and Mackenzie's dad.

KELLY CAVENDER, *Austin, Texas.* Kelly is an award-winning musician with broad experience in performance and composition as well as a researcher, lecturer, and teacher of New Testament studies. He currently manages DC strategy for a Fortune 200 fintech.

BRAD EVERETT CAWYER, *Dallas, Texas.* Brad holds a graduate diploma from the Saint Petersburg Conservatory in Russia and is pursuing a doctoral degree as a musical conductor. He is a composer of hymns in Russian and English and sings with the spiritual music ensemble Psalom.

Wanda Childress, *Austin, Texas.* Wanda is a musician and composer and lives in Austin, Texas.

Laura Kate Collum, *Bear, Delaware.* Kate is a Texas native who studied piano and voice as a child and is now an attorney at a global investment bank.

Charlotte E. Couchman, *Aurora, Colorado.* Charlotte is an author and composer of a cappella hymns and an editor of the hymnal, *Psalms, Hymns, and Spiritual Songs*, published in 2012. She serves as a member of the board of directors for Sumphonia, a nonprofit foundation whose purpose is to compose, publish, and promote hymns for congregational worship.

M. L. Daniels, *Austin, Texas.* Dr. Daniels, retired Abilene Christian University music professor, has won numerous composition contests and published more than one hundred compositions for various ensembles. He is currently Composer in Residence with the Williamson County Symphony.

Randy Daw, (1954–2019), *Greenville, Texas.* Randy earned a degree in music education from West Texas State University and was senior pulpit minister at the Creekside Church of Christ in Greenville. He was also the Associate Editor of *Timeless.*

Nancy L. deClaissé-Walford, *Wadesville, Indiana.* Dr. deClassé-Walford has written several books, including *Reading from the Beginning: The Shaping of the Hebrew Psalter*; *The Book of Psalms: New International Commentary on the Old Testament*; and *Psalms: Books 4–5, Wisdom Commentary Series.*

Debbie Dorman, *Austin, Texas.* Debbie is the retired director of worship ministries at Hope Chapel in Austin, Texas, and is the composer of many published hymns.

Jack K. Dorman Jr., *Austin, Texas.* Jack learned music by participating in the Wink school system band. He went on to sing in church choirs. In 1978, Jack and his wife began forty years as musical worship pastors for Hope Chapel.

Tammy L. Driskell, *Austin, Texas.* Tammy is a graduate of Abilene Christian University, where she was a clarinetist with the Big Purple for four years. She served as a missionary in Austria and Germany and recently retired from the Austin Independent School District after thirty-one years as a Special Education Teacher.

N. Lincoln Hanks, *Malibu, California.* A professor of music at Pepperdine University, Lincoln holds a doctorate in composition and remains active as a professional composer and early music singer.

Christopher Heard, *Moorpark, California.* Dr. Heard earned his MA in Old Testament from Abilene Christian University and his PhD in Religious

Studies from Southern Methodist University. He focuses on the book of Genesis and on biblical reception in popular culture.

JOEL P. HOLT, *San Juan, Puerto Rico.* Raised in Tennessee, Joel has preached for fifteen years in Alabama and Puerto Rico. He has studied in and taught hymn lyric writing courses and is an administrator and contributor to the Church of Christ Hymn Writers Facebook group.

MARVA L. HUGHES, *Weatherford, Texas.* Marva has a BS degree from Abilene Christian University. She is an ASCP certified Medical Technologist, and a composer of hymns.

KARL N. JACOBSON, *Minneapolis, Minnesota.* Dr. Jacobson is senior pastor of Lutheran Church of the Good Shepherd in Minneapolis. His books include *Invitation to the Psalms: A Reader's Guide for Discovery and Engagement, Crazy Talk: A Not-So-Stuffy Dictionary of Theological Terms,* and *Crazy Book: A Not-So-Stuffy Dictionary of Biblical Terms.*

ROLF A. JACOBSON, *Saint Paul, Minnesota.* A Professor of Old Testament and the Alvin N. Rogness Chair of Scripture, Theology, and Ministry at Luther Seminary, Dr. Jacobson's books include *The Book of Psalms* (NICOT) and *Invitation to the Psalms.* He also cohosts two popular podcasts, *Sermon Brainwave* and *The Narrative Lectionary.*

KEITH LANCASTER, *Goodlettsville, Tennessee.* Keith and his wife Sharon travel the world conducting congregational singing weekends as "musicianaries" and also serve the Cullman, AL, Church of Christ. Keith is the president and chief composer for Acappella Ministries and director of the Worship Leader Institute.

BARBARA JANE LITTLE, *Dallas, Texas.* Barbara has worked as a bookkeeper and secretary/stenographer and has taught children's Bible classes, K through 8th grades. Her poems are frequently published in a Greenville, Texas, newsletter.

JESSE C. LONG JR., *Lubbock, Texas.* Dr. Long is a Professor of Old Testament and Biblical Archaeology at Lubbock Christian University. He serves as Codirector of the Archaeological Expedition to Khirbat Iskandar, Jordan and his publications include *1 & 2 Kings* (College Press, 2002).

TREMPER LONGMAN III, *Alexandria, Virginia.* Dr. Longman is the Distinguished Scholar and Professor Emeritus of Biblical Studies at Westmont College. He is the author or coauthor of over thirty books, including a commentary on the Psalms.

JOSEPH M. MARTIN, *Austin, Texas.* Joseph earned his master's degree in piano performance at the University of Texas at Austin. He is Director of Sacred Publications for Hal Leonard/Shawnee Press and Artist in Residence at Concordia University, Austin. Joseph has over 2,000 compositions currently in print.

J. CLINTON MCCANN JR., *Webster Groves, Missouri.* Dr. McCann is the Evangelical Professor of Biblical Interpretation at Eden Seminary. He is the author of the Psalms commentary in *The New Interpreter's Bible*, as well as several other books and numerous essays on the Psalms.

Ray McClendon, *Belmont, California*. Ray is semiretired after thirty years of ministry and service as a law enforcement chaplain. He is a poet and the author of the Angels Whisper series of children's books.

Rachel McInturff, *Austin, Texas*. Dr. McInturff serves as the Director of Finance and Administration for the Armstrong Community Music School and is a freelance composer, arranger, and recording engineer.

Brad Merrell, *Austin, Texas*. Brad has performed in or directed several Gilbert & Sullivan operettas and is a past president of the Gilbert & Sullivan Society of Austin. He has also sung with the Chamber Ensemble and the Symphonic Choir of Chorus Austin.

Dan Merrell, *Austin, Texas*. Dan, an artist specializing in watercolors, serves as the director of the Brentwood Oaks Church of Christ chorus.

Laura Merrell, *Austin, Texas*. Laura works as an IT Manager for Financial Applications. She enjoys singing with the Sweet Expressions and the Brentwood Oaks Church chorus.

Michael Morgan (1948–2022), *Atlanta, Georgia*. Michael was the Organist Emeritus at Central Presbyterian Church in Atlanta and served for twenty years as a musician at Columbia Theological Seminary. He played for a variety of events in the United States and Europe and assembled one of the most comprehensive private collections of English Bibles and Psalters in the country.

John A. Ogren, *Dallas, Texas*. John Ogren lives in Dallas, Texas, where he is leading Open Table Oak Cliff, an open and affirming congregation of Churches of Christ. He has been writing songs, poems, and hymns for forty years.

Zach Olson, *San Antonio*, Texas. Dr. Olson is a radiation effects engineer who has written hymns for the last eighteen years. He specializes in lyrics and dabbles in composition.

Gary Pendergrass, *Greenville, Texas*. An engineering director, Gary wrote songs for and sang in the a cappella gospel quartet Family Reunion with his father and two brothers for over twenty-five years.

Christiana Worley Peterson, *Ohio*. Dr. Peterson grew up in Texas, received a PhD in Creative Writing from St. Andrews University in Scotland, and currently lives with her husband and four children in Ohio. In addition to music, she writes nonfiction books, poetry, and essays.

Matthew K. Porter, *Hewitt, Texas*. Matthew studied music at Stephen F. Austin State University and earned his MA in Theological Studies at Austin Graduate School of Theology and an MS in Library Science at the University of North Texas. Matthew also plays trombone for the Waco Jazz Orchestra.

Jack R. Reese, *San Antonio, Texas.* Dr. Reese was trained as a pianist and has composed and performed music much of his life. He is the author of *At the Blue Hole: Elegy for a Church on the Edge* (Eerdmans, 2021) and is the Executive Minister of the Northside Church of Christ in San Antonio.

Byron Rogers, *Lubbock, Texas.* With a PhD in Chemistry and a Master in Music Composition, Byron is a thirty-six year veteran of the Lubbock Christian University classroom and has written and arranged for vocal and instrumental groups on and off the LCU campus for more than forty years.

Mike Rogers, *Abilene, Texas.* Mike is an Associate Professor in the Department of Music at Abilene Christian University, where he serves as Director of Jazz Studies and Coordinator of Music Theory.

C. L. Seow, *Nashville, Tennessee.* Dr. Seow is the Vanderbilt, Buffington, Cupples Chair in Divinity and Distinguished Professor of Hebrew Bible at Vanderbilt Divinity School, Vanderbilt University. He is the author of numerous books on the Old Testament and the ancient Near East.

Glover H. Shipp (1927–2016), *Austin, Texas.* Dr. Shipp was a member of the *Timeless* Lyrics Committee and taught at the Austin Graduate School of Theology. He was an artist, writer, editor, poet, and composer of more than 150 hymns. He served for eighteen years in Brazil as a missionary, an editor, and a publisher.

Jerry Shipp, *Round Rock, Texas.* Jerry has been a licensed marriage and family therapist for over thirty-eight years. He is the author of *Marriage Minutes: Building a Healthy Marriage One Minute at a Time*, co-composer of *Hinds' Feet on High Places*, and is a contributor and associate editor of *Timeless*.

R. Mark Shipp, *Austin, Texas.* Dr. Shipp is an independent Old Testament scholar and composer. He is the general editor of *Timeless: Ancient Psalms for the Church Today* and co-composer of *Hinds' Feet on High Places.*

Rachel Shipp, *New York City, New York.* Rachel is a Senior Marketing Manager with WearSafe Corporation. She is also a lyricist.

Sarah Shipp, *Garland, Texas.* Sarah is a freelance theatre technician in Dallas. She has an MFA from the University of Alabama.

Aaron Shotts, *Fate, Texas.* While working full-time as an airline pilot, Aaron also serves as an instructor for the Texas Normal Singing School and has recorded over seventeen a cappella Praise & Harmony albums.

Michael E. Showalter, *Austin, Texas.* Michael is a full-time composer and songwriter of church music published by Hal Leonard Corporation/ Shawnee Press.

Clyde H. Slimp, *Cleburne, Texas.* Clyde is the preaching minister for the Westhill Church of Christ and is a member of the American Society of Composers, Authors, and Publishers (ASCAP). He has an MA from Harding

School of Theology with a concentration in the Old Testament. He is nearing completion of his DMin degree from Abilene Christian University.

MARK R. SNEED, *Lubbock, Texas.* Dr. Sneed is a Professor of Bible at Lubbock Christian University, Texas, and author of *Taming the Beast: A Reception History of Behemoth and Leviathan*, *The Social World of the Sages: An Introduction to Israelite and Jewish Wisdom Literature*, and *The Politics of Pessimism in Ecclesiastes: A Social-Science Perspective.*

RUTH ANN SOMERVELL, *Beaverton, Oregon.* Ruth Ann is a music editor and composer. She holds a Bachelor of Music degree in Choral Music from the University of Texas at Austin.

BECKY STEWART, *Austin, Texas.* Becky is a retired middle school teacher with many years of experience singing in college, community, and church choral groups.

CHRIS STIVERS, *Agoura Hills, California.* Dr. Stivers received his MBA and EdD from Pepperdine University where he is Assistant Professor of Communication Emeritus. He has decades of music experience as a composer, arranger, and musical director. He serves as an elder and worship leader at Conejo Valley Church of Christ.

JAMES TACKETT, *Austin, Texas.* James retired from NCR Corp as a computer technician. He teaches at the ACU Singing School and owns The Paperless Hymnal and Austin Christian Acappella Music.

W. DENNIS TUCKER JR., *Waco, Texas.* Dr. Tucker is Professor of Christian Scriptures at Baylor University's George W. Truett Theological Seminary. His publications include *Psalms, Volume 2*, coauthored with Jamie Grant; *Jonah: A Handbook on the Hebrew Text*; Baylor Handbook on the Hebrew Bible; and *Constructing and Deconstructing Power in Psalms 107–150* (Society of Biblical Literature Press, 2014).

MARY ELISABETH (LIBBY) WEED, *Austin, Texas.* Dr. Weed is an Educational Consultant and Principal Emerita at Brentwood Christian School, where she has taught music classes and directed a chorus.

JUDY WITCHER, *Austin, Texas.* Judy sings with The Sweet Expressions, a Christian vocal group.

MEL WITCHER, *Austin, Texas.* Mel is a former band director who has both a BA and MA in music education. He currently teaches at Brentwood Christian School.

MELINDA WORLEY, *Austin, Texas.* Melinda has a BS in education from Abilene Christian University and an MAR from Yale Divinity School, where she sang with the chapel choir. She has produced musicals and taught high school choir at Brentwood Christian School.

Kevin J. Youngblood, *Searcy, Arkansas.* Dr. Youngblood is Professor of Biblical Studies at Harding University and author of the Jonah volume in the *Zondervan Exegetical Commentary on the Old Testament.*

Konstantin Zhigulin, *Saint Petersburg, Russia.* Konstantin's ministry in the church is in congregational worship development: composing new hymns, leading singing, and teaching worship leadership. He is director of the vocal ensemble Psalom.